THE SUBJECT
OF CHILDHOOD

Rethinking Childhood

Joe L. Kincheloe and Gaile Cannella
General Editors

Vol. 38

PETER LANG
New York • Washington, D.C./Baltimore • Bern
Frankfurt am Main • Berlin • Brussels • Vienna • Oxford

MICHAEL O'LOUGHLIN

THE SUBJECT OF CHILDHOOD

PETER LANG
New York • Washington, D.C./Baltimore • Bern
Frankfurt am Main • Berlin • Brussels • Vienna • Oxford

Library of Congress Cataloging-in-Publication Data

O'Loughlin, Michael.
The subject of childhood / Michael O'Loughlin.
p. cm. — (Rethinking childhood; v. 38)
Includes bibliographical references and index.
1. Child psychology. 2. Educational psychology. 3. Child development.
4. Child rearing. I. Title.
BF721.O56   155.4–dc22   2008014444
ISBN 978-1-4331-0347-6 (hardcover)
ISBN 978-1-4331-0120-5 (paperback)
ISSN 1086-7155

Bibliographic information published by **Die Deutsche Bibliothek.**
Die Deutsche Bibliothek lists this publication in the "Deutsche
Nationalbibliografie"; detailed bibliographic data is available
on the Internet at http://dnb.ddb.de/.

Cover photo courtesy of the author:
Michael, P.J., and Frances O'Loughlin, Ireland, 1959

The paper in this book meets the guidelines for permanence and durability
of the Committee on Production Guidelines for Book Longevity
of the Council of Library Resources.

© 2009 Peter Lang Publishing, Inc., New York
29 Broadway, 18th floor, New York, NY 10006
www.peterlang.com

Printed in the United States of America

This book is dedicated to my mother, Anne O'Loughlin, and to the memory of my father, Patrick O'Loughlin

TABLE OF CONTENTS

PREFACE

This book makes a usual request: readers are asked to examine their preconceptions of two fields of thought, education and psychoanalysis, by way of their dreams of childhood and the child who dreams. And, we are asked to ponder the difference between these experiences—the dream of childhood and the child who dreams—through the ways in which each is negated under the name of education, which, in this book, means analyzing any story of progress that expels our capacity to doubt and our right to self expression. Indeed, there are small negations to attend to: the adult's urge to make childhood better, more resilient, less chaotic, and less fragile in the hope that the child will be more focused, workmanlike, and objective. Or, we may be urged to recollect times when our fear of the chaos of the emotional world foreclosed our capacity for creativity and sublimation, leaving us in the wake of our anxiety.

Reading this book invites our interest in what is most personal, most idiomatic, most condensed, and then, most displaced. This is, I think, what Michael O'Loughlin means by autobiography; and, he will find in the individual so much that matters: group psychology, lost history, family romances, screen memories, and unconscious messages. We are invited into a mind-world that understands the personal as pertinent to the capacity to think and be with others, provided that the personal can become a narrative. In imagining the emotional world of childhood—our own and those of others—we are requested to tolerate what is not yet understood and give consideration to our ignorance about this unknown thought. We are requested to play in what Winnicott called a potential space of culture.

Let us note, as O'Loughlin notes, that straying dreams thoughts hold no currency in daily classroom life. They are too enigmatic, too inarticulate, too sexual, and, too much about sleep. Their images that trade transmission with transgression make us laugh. Dreams, Freud wrote, are not made for the purpose of being understood. They propose what is most preposterous about considerations of representation and what is most inventive about the dream work. They give us access to our unconscious life world and each night while we sleep, present what cannot be understood but is nonetheless felt: our wishes, our fears, our comic missteps, our enigmas, and lost history. Dreams urge us to play in our inattentiveness, absurdity, non-sense. They are our most enigmatic resource and carry neither directions nor rules. And, like the time of childhood, dreams are fleeting, hard to remember, concealed by forgetfulness, difficult to pin down, and, more often than not, confuse our conscious mind with their refusal of reason, of time, and of negation. Both dreams and childhood leave us with questions: are they scenes where we think whatever we want? Do they signify that thinking and wishing are never so far apart? As for the adult, can dreams become a model for the teacher's and the analyst's education?

If we can dream of childhood and the child who dreams, O'Loughlin, suggests, we may enter the strange portal of the subject, and find what is enigmatic about its promises, proposals, quirks, signatures, accidents, yearnings, and disappointments. Whatever we can find and create, O'Loughlin proposes, will be subject to analysis: to free association, or to the saying of what is furthest from the mind, then rearranged again through the arts and crafts of interpretation, and then, freed again with narratives Freud called "working through," Klein called "reparation or gratitude," and Lacan called "the desire to desire." Readers will meet these analysts in the pages that follow along with a contemporary psychoanalysis and its new theories of both the subject and its own transference adventures. What seems constant, however, is that work of becoming a subject involves the capacity to mourn our losses *and* the desire to refind, in the world of others, something new in our lives. Where education and psychoanalysis meet, then, is their faith that putting these unspeakable things into words matter to how one lives.

The request is startling, for just as we try to imagine something like the subject of childhood, we suddenly find ourselves unable to approach the actual child who is present. We learn in this book that childhood happens: that its accidents will suffer the burden of meaning, that it cannot be prepared for or even protected, that its events cannot follow the smooth developmental schemas our manuals promise, that the traumas of history and of having history feel repetitive and insurmountable, and, that all of these adult anxieties pro-jected onto the screen of the subject of childhood signify a fun house mirror, distortions that have already happened to us in our own childhood. All of this marches into our autobiography and that means that we narrative a crowded world. This world, however, can be endless deferred if all that is on offer is the *as if* model adult and child demonstrating a puppet show of life. Indeed, one of the bravest observations O'Loughlin makes is that when he faces the child in his clinical practice, he finds the notion of the child elusive. And child-hood, from whatever side, must propose a profound obstacle to and even a revolt against education, itself on the side of preparation, anticipation, and, as O'Loughlin writes, has the potential to contain a capacity to open itself to its own "predicament of marginality," ironically made from a crowded world. To revolt, it seems, is to enliven our narratives.

So readers will meet a cast of characters and learn what happens as they try to express their mental pain, their blank depression, their hatred of school, their shame in the writer's block, their inhibitions, and their excitement and hopes. There will be anxious adults who fail the child as they worry over the failed child. Some will insist loudly that school is hell while others will barely make any noise at all. There will be parents who cannot tell their child the truth and teachers caught in the prison-house of their own passion for ignorance, or their tiny measures of readiness. In the midst of all of this will be the reading unconscious, itself a movement of lost objects, eruptions, and a storehouse made from who knows what. Evidence will be as fragile as we are and will lean upon the mythic, the archaic, and even what never happened at all but still exist in wishes and dreams.

O'Loughlin is a consummate teacher and a psychoanalyst, a combination of stances, thoughts, desires, fears, and style of being that finds their way into his writerly world and creates his investments and growing sense that thinking imagination begins only when we open the gates of both education and psycho-analysis to the chaos of the actual world. His commitment is to present himself and his subject as becoming, and he knows full well there is no such thing as a teacher or analyst without others. Radical relationality is the heart of the book. If these positions are to be creative, we learn, each encounter must be invented as a way to honor what is most unrepresentable about presenting the subject who calls us to its side. This psycho-education may also be meant to address what can only be thought of as the two solitudes: Psychoanalysis and Education. There is a history of transference migraines, fights, misunderstandings, wrong-headed assumptions, and miles of ignorance that keep each field narcissistically enclosed in its own regard. But O'Loughlin has the wherewithal to introduce to educators the clinical style of the analyst's thinking, and share with the analytic community, the pedagogical thinking of the teacher. To write clinically and creatively about one's practices, then, is to begin with the question of how one is affected by working with others who themselves are affected. To write clinically is to write the autobiography of the childhood of one's profession and the difficulties of growing up.

The result, then, is what O'Loughlin terms "depth pedagogy." I hope this name grabs hold of our imagination, for "depth pedagogy" draws sustenance and resilience from the well of being. It takes pleasure in narrating the accidents of life, the mishaps of having language, the necessary losses that are the subject of childhood, the poetics of the self when facing the other, and the sleepy, inchoate, world of dreams. Depth pedagogy is ironic; it plays between the lines of reality and phantasy to permit the work of constructions and the revitalization of doubts about what really happens. We can then become curious about why screen memories wipe this complexity away. And in Michael O'Loughlin's clinic, depth pedagogy wants to listen to the dreams of a child who dreams, and to interpret the dreams of fields of thought and theory that also propose our urge to write our human condition.

Deborah P. Britzman
Toronto, Ontario

ACKNOWLEDGMENTS

This work has been so long in the making that my intellectual debts are incalculable. My thanks goes particularly to those colleagues, who, throughout the years, gently inquired when a book of my writings might be available, and who continued to offer gentle but insistent encouragement when no book was published. Many of those colleagues belong to one of my imagined communities, Reconceptualizing Research in Early Childhood Education. I tried out many of these ideas for the first time before that group. A second imagined community of great importance to me has been the Adelphi Postdoctoral program in Psychoanalysis and Psychotherapy. The training, supervision, and analysis that I experienced under the auspices of that program shifted my life and opened doors I never imagined. I have been especially privileged to present at three Joint International Psychoanalytic Conferences in Dublin, Cape Town, and Vancouver, with this group where I took the risk of trying out autobiographical narratives to receptive audiences. I would also like to thank my colleagues at Unitec, Institute of Technology, Auckland, Aotearoa/New Zealand, where I was privileged to teach in summer 2008, and at the University of Hawai'i at Manoa, where I taught for four summers. Those experiences were formative in my engagement with difference, and particular with developing an understanding of issues in indigenous education.

XIV ACKNOWLEDGMENTS

On both a personal and intellectual level, in addition to members of the groups mentioned above, I am indebted to the late Patrick Buckheister of Eastern Michigan University my first friend and first mentor in the U.S.; John Broughton and the late Jeanette Fleischner of Teachers College; Rick Meyer of the University of New Mexico; Joe Tobin of Arizona State University; Gail Boldt of Penn State University; Jonathan Silin of Bank Street College; Donna Grace and Hanna Tavares of the University of Hawai'i; Jenny Ritchie and Yo Heta-Lensen of Unitec, Auckland; Alison Jones and Nola Harvey of Auckland University; Sailau Sualii of the University of Otago; Conrad Pritscher and the late Malcolm Campbell, mentors in my first academic position at Bowling Green Sate University; Rob Koegel; and Esther Kogan of Adelphi University. My deepest thanks go to Deborah Britzman of York University who wrote the Preface, and Rich Johnson, currently a colleague at Adelphi University, who wrote the Introduction. Both have served as sources of inspiration and admiration.

I wish also to acknowledge receipt of a sabbatical leave from Adelphi University to assist in completion of this work, and to acknowledge Amir Azam Ali, Marta Blyth, Erin Donohue, and Sara Lettiere for assistance with research and copyediting. I acknowledge the invaluable contributions of my earlier graduate assistants, Brennen Bierwiler and Marta Serra, in Chapter 11. My greatest debt is to the many children with whom I have worked and continue to work, in my clinical practice and in schools. They have been wonderful teachers.

From Peter Lang my great thanks to Shirley Steinberg, who supported this project from its inception, to my editor, Chris Myers, and to Sophie Appel who shepherded the work through production.

While, in acknowledgements like this it is customary to read of the toll book writing took on the author's family. I think the writing was greeted with relief in my family, where my sometime absence of productivity exacted a greater price. Thanks to Margaret Healy, my wife, and to our children Brian and Jennifer O'Loughlin who often asked what I was working on but learned never to ask when it might be finished! A special thanks to Mark Speaker, M.D., Ph.D., an ophthalmic surgeon at New York Eye and Ear Infirmary, whose deft surgery restored my sight through a corneal transplant and enabled me to continue my life's work with ease.

INTRODUCTION

The Setting

The diverse nature of the contents of this collective is a tribute to many years of work with children, teachers and teacher educators in a multitude of different contexts, experiences that continue for the author today. As well, this book reveals an exhibition and further detailed explorations of a wealth of highly personalized experiential and experimental theoretical work on childhood education. Moving within and beyond that firsthand experiential and theoretical work, in this collection Michael O'Loughlin illustrates his uncanny desires to (re)shape historical and current meaning as he (re)theorizes *The Subject of Childhood.*

To assist in positioning the structure and thematic content of the coming chapters, I'm going to follow Michael's lead and break a bit with the typical structural layout of an *Introduction* whereby I briefly name the content in each of the upcoming Chapters. Instead, I will attempt to highlight what I believe are some of the key issues attended to in differing degree(s) and detail and woven throughout this book, hopefully providing the reader a sense of what to expect in reading the book.

Movement

Michael's initial and continuous referral to issues of movement is a critical stance that undermines so much of what we have seen in so many disciplines, especially education, whereby the normative notion of the static has tended to dominate theorizing. Throughout this work he highlights how "human subjectivity [is] constantly in the process of becoming." This is a powerful way of perceiving how our own individual and collective work can be visualized and enacted as always "becoming"—moving, shifting, repositioning, always in motion and well clear of static tradition(s). This work reverberates with other critical theoretical perspectives, echoing Sharon Todd in *Learning Desire*, where she notes that, "In insisting upon the nature of the subject as simultaneously contingent, multiply determined, and constantly shifting, post-structuralism has occasioned awareness of the place of indeterminacy in thinking" (1997, p. 3).

The highly personalized contents of this extensive narrative represents Michael's direct and indirect movement(s) within education. This movement beckons one, just as Michael has, to consider at an honest, deep level one's journey(s) into subjectivity as an indirect movement "into subjectivity [but] also a wrenching journey away from subjectivity." This journey involves personalizing or naming your respective responsibilities as they relate to your identity. For example, in this work Michael speaks openly and honestly to white people about claiming ownership of historical inequalities and oppression around notions of privilege. These multiple, active identifications entail "enormous challenges' for one's subjectivity as one considers their historic movement and future directions from potentially critical perspectives. The multiple references to "border crossing" in the book provide an effective way for naming this potential movement and the personal gains and losses people experience in this deliberate, engaging action of naming.

In the active, participatory way in which this narrative pursues the *known and the unknown*, Michael attempts to more dynamically call into question things that once seemed stable, that appeared to be readily fixed, and that looked as if they were normal and typical, but upon further consideration and theorizing are presented as strangely unfixed and unfamiliar. In his pursuit of the unknown, critical theoretical perspectives are highly assistive in the work presented here, especially given Michael's interest in countering so-called truth(s) and his ability to identify these in the format of theoretically recognizable "autonomous site[s] of contestation" (Cohen, 1998, p. 7).

In Search of the Lost Language of Childhood

After a critique of conventional early childhood education, the book then shifts attention to a *"search for the lost language of childhood"* which, for Michael, and those of us whose views resonate with his, is an ongoing search. Building off of issues brought up in the opening, his argument begins with a structured critique of the "myth of childhood innocence" and questions authoritative "official" notions of childhood historically and in the present. The focus on "being a child" within these paradigmatic normative structures is readily accessible and transferable for me as I consider our very own "being" as educators and special- ists struggling within a theoretical and practical world "where adults have very particular scripted notions of childhood as being a certain way." Here, and across other chapters, Michael explicitly illustrates the "increasingly burdened notions of normativity" practitioners encounter as we address our sense of subjectivity on an ongoing basis. Later in this chapter he then addresses how we as teachers need to actively seek out "freeing spaces" in our "coming to know." I found this quite useful in envisioning further our active stances as we too embolden our individual and collective actions, consistently taking action in our "search for the lost" in our respective theoretical and practical work.

The Curious Subject of the Child

The address of child(hood) subjectivity woven throughout this book is profound as Michael shares highly personalized narratives of his own childhood and current accounts of working as a therapist with children, as he locates the "curious subject of the child." I especially admired how this book addresses schools and schooling practices as they continue to "shut down subjective possibilities for children" and engage in the political imperative of silenc- ing children and teachers. His work here echoes other scholars who have poignantly portrayed urban school life, such as when he cites Polakow's work (1993) that vividly illustrates the ongoing "pervasive ethos of containment and regulation—drilling children to produce the correct response, regulating their imagination…" (p. 150). The critical address of childhood subjectivity through multiple lenses "opens up expansive possibilities" and provides personalized notions of where we might go with this knowledge as we seek change. I was especially pleased with his localized notions of how we might incorporate this work into our day-to-day lives with real-life practical examples of teaching and schooling practices offered throughout this work.

For instance, when this critical work addresses *The development of subjectivity in young children*, Michael reveals how schools might be (re)envisioned and (re)thought of as "reparative communities—places in which teachers and caregivers work with students to diminish persecutory anxieties, and to create with students opportunities to engage in nonthreatening ways with the Other of their worlds…" For someone like me, a teacher educator who has worked closely with pre- and in-service teachers in school settings for 20 years, this is a powerful notion which needs to be enacted in our future collaborations with teachers, principals, and larger communities. Like much of what this book considers, Michael's continuous referral to the notion of "human subjectivity constantly in the process of becoming" speaks to how we can actively name, problematize, reconfigure and rethink emerging, diverse, and creative movements which can assist us in moving within and beyond deeply rooted normative structures. These are intelligent, hopeful, and highly practical considerations honestly spoken and creatively offered in an ongoing time of normative theoretical dread in education.

On Knowing and Desiring Children

Given that I have worked with children for the better part of my teacher education career and I have addressed *desire* within my own work on "no touch" issues in education and associated notions of risk and risk awareness, the focus on "*knowing and desiring children*" is quite profound. I believe focusing on children's desire is critical for all current and future teachers, beginning with the notion of designing and co-constructing curriculum that "supports children in identifying the things that they desire to know and be in the world."

Michael's work also targets the idea of 'acting as advocates for students' as he speaks to a multitude of different ways that teachers can "humanize schooling and help them negotiate its power structures" as they pursue the craft of teaching in an interactive, "make a difference" activist manner. In this pursuit he also actively addresses critical issues around why we do what we do and our subjective sense of problematizing both the known and unknown as we seek to make sense involved in our identity work (Sarup, 1996). In this regard his work further engages and problematizes our colonial relation to a host of Others as he advocates the processes of deconstructing (Stoler, 1995; Sualii, 2000), disentangling (Pieterse & Parekh, 1995; Smith, 1999), and decentering (Narayan & Harding, 2000) as we reflect on our involvement in actively "civilizing Others." The focus here—on how teachers and caregivers could be more "liberatory" as they pursue pedagogical practices centered on "healing and possibility"—have profound implications for both pre- and in-service teacher education.

I especially appreciated Michael's proposal of addressing the above issues with the articulation of an "evocative pedagogy for children" that addresses the "unconscious, the soul, and the spirit, [and that] has the capacity to unhook particular, culturally located children from the anomie of an amnesiac, universalist, globalized consumer society to begin to reconnect with their latent historical subjectivities." His referral here to a "troubling decolonizing pedagogy" coupled with his description of historical accounts of residential schooling and government movements supporting assimilationist schooling for indigenous communities, proves quite helpful in supporting his various activist stances against this historically and currently as he urges us to collectively come to question this history on an ongoing basis (e.g., through studies of trauma and indigineity). When he asks, "Is it possible for teachers to find gaps in the received curriculum that might enable children to do the kind of critical memorial exhumation that I have in mind?" I envision and psychically feel the relevance of this critically engaging work. Other relevant examples he incorporates into this work include focusing on "Recreating the social link between children and their histories." Here Michael provokes us to "engage children in narrative possibilities that allow for the construction of new lore" just as Michael continually does throughout this narrative, as we, educators, attempt to move forward with a firm grounding in the past.

The work shared in this volume reveals a highly critical, conscientious author who is willing to openly share and critically analyze the story of his own childhood and coming to be as well as accounts of the struggles of the children he sees for psychotherapy. Michael's upbringing and his background as an educator and therapist contribute boldly to his notions of what could and should happen in our daily interactions with children as teachers, caregivers, providers and community workers. By recognizing that we need to work against the long-held beliefs that we must "know ahead of time what a particular child needs," his beliefs guide us toward realizing our "unthought knowns." Like the children he serves in therapy, we too have the potential of actively "symbolizing [our] unconscious knowledge and releasing [our] imaginations." This heartfelt provocation, is typical of so many other related examples in his rich narrative.

This highly conscientious and personalized, liberating work pushes us to consider, all the time, our continuous movement toward expertise in "coming to know, rather than [serving as] containers and dispensers of received knowledge." Michael spent a year engaging in literacy activities with children in a poor urban community. At the conclusion of that year he states, "I am haunted by the children's voices. I hear the beauty, the potential, the yearning for affirmation and connection. I warm to the beauty of their expressions of love. I marvel at the imaginativeness of their boundary crossings." These thoughts propel us to look inside our collective selves and consider our further action(s) as theorists and practitioners. As a teacher, my work with and for children and students is illustrated here as a profound vocation and Michael speaks to this notion from a deeply grounded, personal perspective. The honesty and integrity of this inspirational work is profound.

Fig. 1. Rich Johnson and Michael O'Loughlin at Highlander Center, TN, March 2007

Having known and worked closely with Michael for close to twenty years now, I am fully aware that his creative crafting of this thoughtful, provocative narrative, *The Subject of Childhood*, will assist others, as it has thoughtfully assisted me in "opening up expansive possibilities." This book did that for me at so many different junctures and across so many different levels as it opened up and presented a far-reaching venue of alternative trajectories and creative paths for me to travel down (Fig. 1), if I so chose. This choosing was not difficult given Michael's various prompts that pushed me along the collective path. I'll leave off here one last written and visual reference to Michael's referral in the third chapter to Barthe's (1981) conjecturing how photographs contain a *punctum*. Michael refers to this as "a detail from which it is possible to re-view events from an angle that opens up expansive possibilities." just as the path below allowed Michael and I to participate in, as the two of us "re-viewed events" from a particular angle as we continue our journey in life.

References

Cohen, J. (1996). *Monster theory: Reading culture*. Minneapolis: University of Minnesota Press.

Narayan, U. & Harding, S. (Eds.). (2000). *Decentering the center: Philosophy for a multicultural, postcolonial, and feminist world*. Indianapolis: Indiana University Press.

Pieterse, J. N. & Parekh, B. (Eds.). (1995). *The decolonization of imagination: Culture, knowledge and power*. London: ZED Books.

Sarup, M. (1996). *Identity, culture and the postmodern world*. Athens: The University of Georgia Press.

Smith, L.T. (1999). *Decolonizing methodologies: Research and indigenous peoples*. London: ZED Books.

Stoler, A.L. (1995). *Race and the education of desire: Foucault's history of sexuality and the colonial order of things*. Durham: Duke University Press.

Suaalii, T. M. (2000). Deconstructing the "exotic" female beauty of the Pacific Islands. In A. Jones, P. Herda, & T. Suaalii (Eds.), *Bitter sweet: Indigenous women in the Pacific*, pp. 93–108. Dunedin: University of Otago Press.

Todd, S. (1997). *Learning desire: Perspectives on pedagogy, culture, and the unsaid*. New York: Routledge.

· 1 ·

TROUBLING CHILDHOOD

It is now almost a quarter century since the publication of the seminal book *Changing the subject: Psychology, social regulation and subjectivity* (1984) by Julian Henriques and colleagues. Combining theoretical strands from left French intellectuals, notably Louis Althusser, Michel Foucault, and Jacques Lacan with the work of Raymond Williams and colleagues from the Center for Contemporary Cultural Studies in Birmingham, the authors asked searching questions about the effects of the psychological gaze. Challenging essentialist understandings of self, they offered an interrogation of subjectivity, and, in particular, they explored the deeply vested interests that lie beneath what appear to be common-sense understandings of childhood and child pedagogy. They argued that there is no *natural* childhood, and that all notions of childhood are, to use the words of Wendy and Rex Stainton-Rogers (1992), "manufactured." Of course the principal manufacturing agent is early childhood pedagogy, and Henriques et al. (see especially Walkerdine's discussion in that volume) argued that the alliance between theories of child growth and development and early childhood pedagogical practices is especially nefarious in sedimenting practices of education that naturalize certain forms of subjectivity as desirable, and preordained.

Widening the lens a little further, Henriques et al. argued that the naturalized notions of childhood and pedagogy that were advanced were part of a much larger attempt to install bourgeois consumer capitalist ways of being as the natural order of things worldwide.

Their critique has been remarkably prescient. With the collapse of the Soviet Union, the ascent of China as a protocapitalist society, and the globalization of trade, the last twenty five years have witnessed a remarkable expansion of western ideological influence. Viewing video of preschool centers in the United States, Europe, China and Japan made by early childhood researcher Joe Tobin (2009), and from my own observations in preschools in Aotearoa/New Zealand, in Europe, and in the United States, I am struck by what appears to be the profound sameness of the experience. Every detail, including the architecture of the space, the design of the child-friendly furniture, the specific range of developmentally appropriate toys, and the carefully sequenced and packaged curriculum, all seem designed to elicit certain dispositions and ways of being from children. It is as if we already *know* what children need to become and we have structured specific pedagogical experiences in carefully engineered environments to ensure that the subjectivities of all children are shaped and normalized accordingly. My chagrin at the startlingly universalist assumption behind these practices is exceeded only by my even greater fear that perhaps we are engineering children to be a certain way because that is what the demands of a stratified, global capitalist society demands. Is it possible that we are commodifying childhood so that children may grow up to take their place as acquisitive and acquiescent consumers in a global society built around consumption and conformity?

Recently, as I was touring the new multi-million dollar Early Learning Center on my campus, a staff member proudly gestured through a picture window at an expanse of newly laid turf for what is to be a grassy play area for the children. "They put this big window here," she told me, "because, you know, in the Reggio Emilia philosophy, children need to be connected to nature and the outdoors." "Reggio," as it is affectionately known, has been commodified, such that this pastoral notion and many others—can be readily transplanted from a bucolic Italian village setting, and brought to life as part of a corporately manufactured grassy space engineered to give young children on Long Island *the same experience*. Huh?

Visiting an early childhood center I stopped to chat with a teacher from a kindergarten room, a woman I know. "It's going to be a difficult start to the year", she said, "they just added another child to my room and he is two months under the cut-off for kindergarten. They want to move him up to make room for a new child." I asked what her concern was. "I don't know how

I am supposed to program curriculum for him," she replied, "because he is too young for this class." This kindergarten teacher's concern about the developmental readiness of a child, by no means an atypical concern, makes me wonder where she acquired such a *normative and essentialized* notion of childhood. Where do the singular norms of early childhood education come from? Whose interests do they serve? How have they become so deeply entrenched as common-sense ways of thinking about child-rearing and pedagogical best practices? How have we arrived at the point that age norms are so precise that two months is presumed to make such a difference in a child's capacities? One could quibble, perhaps, that this particular teacher has an overly reified understanding of developmental stages, and perhaps she does. However, there is no arguing that, in principle, her thinking is highly consistent with notions of developmental readiness, and with what the National Association for the Education of Young Children [NAEYC] in the U.S. describes as Developmentally Appropriate Practice (NAEYC, 1997).

Although aspects of the critique discussed here have been developed and expanded by a number of writers (e.g., Bradley, 1989; Burman, 1994; Donzelot, 1979; James & Prout, 1997; Kehily, 2004; Morss, 1995; Richards, 1984; Stainton-Rogers & Stainton-Rogers, 1992; Walkerdine, 1984, 1987, 2002, 2004) it has not penetrated mainstream discourses about children and their lives since acceptance of this critique would require a fundamental rethinking of the formation of childhood subjectivity and of the forms of pedagogy that are implied. As the most recent revisions to the statement on Developmentally Appropriate Practice (NAEYC, 1997) reveal, disciplining institutions such as NAEYC incorporate only changes that permit them to maintain prevailing ideological systems and practices. Thus, discourses of bilingualism and of exceptionality, and rhetorics of family and community involvement, for example, are included in the 1997 revision of the statement on Developmentally Appropriate Practice in a manner that allows them to be absorbed as enhancements to an unchanging core belief system. Questioning the very origins of childhood subjectivity, and thereby challenging the ideological underpinnings of the pedagogical prescriptions and assessment tools that have grown up around Developmentally Appropriate Practice, however, would endanger the entire ideological structure, and is therefore avoided.

The Subject of Childhood

British psychoanalyst D.W. Winnicott (1958, 1989) conceptualized the beginning of the development of self in the child as transition from a state of

"Me" to a state of "Not-me." His idea was that the child in utero is in a state of symbiosis with the biological mother, and he described early infancy as a period of gradual disillusion for the child in which increasing awareness of maternal limitations in providing unconditionally available nurturance causes the child to begin to adjust to a world outside of self. Apart from issues feminists have raised with notions of unconditional and unlimited feminine nurturance as a basis for successful parenting (cf. Burman, 1994; Henriques et al., 1984), Winnicott's account raises the thorny issue of the assumption of an essential self. His assumption—and this assumption is a cornerstone of the edifice of developmental psychology, and hence of early childhood education—is that there is indeed a primordial or essential self that is pre-given. The self then enters the world and grows through experience. This begs the question where the original "I" comes from, and how it develops an awareness of its own existence.

An alternate, as Barry Richards notes in *Capitalism and infancy* (1984; cf. also Molino, 2004) is to avoid the binary that much of psychology and psychoanalysis poses between the interior subject and the material environment, and look instead at ways in which a human being, through immersion in material culture, becomes the ongoing person that they are. As I explore in Chapter 7, Lacan's work has been key to this conceptualization in that he enumerates the construction of subjectivity through the process of entering symbolic systems, most notably language. There is no self therefore, only a subjectivity constantly in process through interaction with particular linguistic and discursive contexts.

Essentialized notions of selfhood regard the agency of the individual as non-problematic. Underlying the ideology of developmental psychology and early childhood education, as I will discuss below, is the ideal of the rational, autonomous decision-maker who is increasingly free to think logically and act independently. The issue of agency is greatly complicated if the individual is viewed as developing subjectivity through a process of becoming a participant in particular linguistic and discursive communities. As Judith Butler notes in *The psychic life of power* (1997), becoming a subject means, in some respects, becoming *subject to* particular discursive regimes of truth. While Henriques et al. argue that there are ways around the determinism of the original Marxist and Althusserian formulation, this is a critical issue for educators of young children. If we choose to expose children only to unitary or monological discursive formations, or only to discursive formations alien, for example, to their pre-existing class, gender, and ethnic identifications, we are severely limiting the possibilities of such children constructing expansive and emancipatory subject positions for themselves. My discussion of the problematics of imposing mainstream discursive rubrics on indigenous children in Chapter 9 illustrates this issue, as indeed, does the discussion of the pedagogy of poverty in Chapter 11. While NAEYC officials may opt for the high road and argue that Developmentally Appropriate Practice is built around principles of respect, valuing, and care, which is undoubtedly true, nevertheless this discourse too must be recognized for what it is: a particular disciplinary regime of truth that is singular and directed by a very particular ideological turn. It is only when such educational and pedagogical discursive practices subject themselves to the kind of critical self-reflexivity that Henriques et al. exemplify, that we can have confidence that they are working in the interests of diverse children in diverse sociopolitical and socioeconomic contexts.

The Normal Child and the Sanitary Cordon

In *The policing of families*, Jacques Donzelot (1979) offers a Foucaultian analysis of how westernized child-rearing practices came to be. Contrary to romantic notions of child-centered pedagogy and child-centered family practices as progressive public policy, Donzelot illustrates how technologies of pedagogy and child-rearing were invented to constrain the body of the child and the space in which the child might move. As Donzelot bluntly notes, a pedagogy of control and surveillance was needed to maintain a *sanitary cordon* around bourgeois children, and to limit the impulses of working class children:

> What of childhood? In the first instance, the solicitude of which it was the object took the form of a *protected liberation*, a freeing of children from vulgar fears and constraints. The bourgeois family drew a sanitary cordon around the child which delimited his sphere of development: inside the perimeter the growth of his body and mind would be encouraged by listing all the contributions of psychopedagogy in its service, and controlled by means of a discreet observation. In the second instance, it would be more exact to define the pedagogical model as that of *supervised freedom*. The problem in regard to the working-class child was not so much the weight of obsolescent constraints as excessive freedom—being left to the street—and the techniques employed consisted in limiting this freedom, in shepherding the child back to spaces where he could be more closely watched: the school or the family dwelling. (p. 47)

Donzelot's analysis serves as a salutary reminder, as indeed does Foucault's work (e.g., 1988, 1995) that there are no neutral discourses. All institutional discourses arise from social and political purposes, are grounded in power relations, and are designed to discipline and limit our subjective capacities. Nowhere is this more true than in the case of pedagogical and psychiatric discourses whose very existence depends on defining normality and remediating any deviations from that normality (see Chapter 4 below). The sanitary cordon, which depends on technologies of assessment, evaluation, and surveillance, is essentially a carefully disguised policing function that sanctions modes of child-rearing and forms of schooling that produce what societal institutions deem normal. Inevitably, such systems are accompanied by technologies of pathologization that label as deficient those who either are not yet "ready," or those who fail to achieve at predetermined levels. These technologies, in turn, beget further regimes of surveillance, remediation, incarceration, and still more testing, surveillance and regulation for those who continue to deviate from the predetermined normal path (Stainton-Rogers & Stainton-Rogers, 1992).[1] Edifices such as special education and child psychiatry are built around the institutionalization of these technologies.

In visiting schools, child care centers, toy stores etc. the issue, therefore, is not the nature of the ostensible invitation extended to the child through play experiences, curriculum experiences, grassy playgrounds and so on. Rather, the pressing question is what kind of discursive regimes are operative beneath the surface of the glittering toys, the neatly packaged curriculum, even the inviting picture window. The question is not "What is being asked of this child?," but rather "What is *really* being asked of this child?" The latter gets to the issue of the demands and limitations the total discursive situation places on the child's capacity to become a subject. Erving Goffman's (1961) discussion in *Asylums* of the powerful shaping role "total institutions," such as psychiatric hospitals, have in structuring the subjectivity of psychiatric patients and other inmates names a similar ideological mechanism.

Imagine for a moment that instead of thinking in terms of normalization, individual achievement, and totalizing forms of pedagogy that seek to shape all children inexorably in predetermined ways, we entertain a notion of child growth that acknowledges that children grow up in contexts. Instead of plucking children from the bosom of their families and communities at a tender age, imagine that we honor the apprenticeship that is entailed in acquiring membership in the sort of collective subjectivity Jonathan Lear describes as so critical to human purposefulness in *Radical hope* (Lear, 2006; see also O'Loughlin, 2008). Barbara Rogoff (1991, 2003) and Jean Lave (1988; Lave & Wenger, 1991) have described just such a process in the socio-cognitive domain, and of course dialectical thinkers such as Klaus Riegel (1978, 1979), Lev Vygotsky (1978), and

Mikhail Bakhtin (1981, 1986) have always located humans in dynamic social and cultural contexts. In Chapter 9, addressing the lives of indigenous children, I offer another imagining, one based on recuperation of ancestral memory, acknowledgment of indigenous ways of knowing, and a valuing of how the creation of a vibrant collective culture, rooted in a group's history, spirituality, and ways of knowing, can lead to powerful capacities for the construction of affirming subjectivities and hopeful futures for indigenous children.

Now, if you will, consider the contrast between these embedded notions of being and what is valorized in developmental psychology and supposedly progressive child-centered early childhood pedagogy. Wendy and Rex Stainton-Rogers, for example, remind us that "to be able to see a 'child' requires that we already know what (for our purposes) a child is" (1992, p. 17). They go on to point out that current conceptions of child development are profoundly biased in favor of sociobiological explanation. They take issue with Lloyd de Mause's (1974) teleological account, in *The history of childhood*, in which he portrays modern enlightened child-rearing as "a civilizing journey from infanticide, cruelty and neglect, to a time of love, care, and attention." (Stainton-Rogers & Stainton-Rogers, 1992, p. 66). Grand redemptive narratives such as deMause offers, embodying universalist assumptions about the sameness of all children's experience and the benevolence of contemporary adult society, are oblivious to the infanticide, famine, disease, poverty, neglect, child prostitution, child labor, child slavery, displacements, and use of child soldiers that continue to be endemic in our world. What developmental rubric, for example, would encompass the experience of Abdul, a young man I had the privilege of meeting recently?

I interviewed Abdul[2] as part of volunteer work that I do for a human rights clinic in New York. Abdul, who is currently fifteen, is seeking permanent immigration status in the United States based on persecution in his country of origin. He grew up in an African nation, and, when he was three and a half years old, his village was attacked by rebels. The people of his village were lined up and sprayed with machine gun fire. He witnessed his entire family and most of his neighbors being massacred. Then the rebels kidnapped him and some other surviving children and took them on a forced march. By age four Abdul was versed in the use of an AK-47, and six months later he was put in charge of a group of child soldiers and ordered to shoot to kill any child that failed to follow orders. He did as he was told, and shot his fellow children when they failed to meet his expectations. For the next four years, often fortified by alcohol and cocaine, he witnessed and participated in unspeakable atrocities, including amputations, gruesome murders, and the shooting of babies and older people. At age eight and a half Abdul managed to escape, and he then spent four tumultuous years moving from one transitional living space to another. Today, while awaiting his judicial hearing, Abdul lives with a middle-class family in the United States. He is an A student in high school with ambitions to become a human rights lawyer. Abdul's story serves to remind me of the perils of universality in thinking about children. Is there a way to speak of Abdul's childhood within the rubric of our theories of childhood, or are Abdul's childhood experiences merely awkward facts that are best ignored?

In *Visions of infancy*, Ben Bradley (1989) offers additional critique of developmental psychology as a basis for conceptualizing the lives of children. Bradley takes up a point of view now well established in the sociology of science by Bruno Latour and others that all scientific activity is profoundly interpretive (e.g., Knorr-Cetina, 1999; Latour et al., 1986). As Bradley notes, "There can be no 'empirical' observation of babies that does not imply an evaluative vision of infancy" (1989, p. 180). Matters such as the idealization of infancy, the naturalization of processes of development, and notions of normality and deviance are necessarily socially constructed, and child researchers who do not take the trouble to understand the social circumstances that are conditioning and commodifying the knowledge they produce, or who fail to come clean about such matters, are continuing to perpetuate forms of scientism that give the field an aura of authoritativeness that is quite preposterous.

Norm(a)(l) goes to School!

Valerie Walkerdine (1984) wonders if the idea of a child-centered pedagogy that supposedly sets children free is actually a pipe dream. As she notes, the very concept of "the developing child" locates certain specific capacities within the child. As Claudia Castañeda notes, "The condition of childhood therefore finds its value in potentiality. At the same time, the form that the child's potentiality takes is consistently framed as a normative one, in relation to which failure is always possible." (2002, p. 4). Castañeda correctly notes the inherently teleogical nature of all developmental schemes—schemes that specify an optimal linear path and, by default, label those who fail to meet appropriate normative expectations as deficient, just as surely as a child who fails to make it into the normal range in the growth chart at the pediatrician's office is labeled as having stunted growth (2002, p. 4). Since the apparatus of schooling is constructed to advance certain teleological goals as universally desirable, then, by definition, any child who fails to become a certain way, is, as Castañeda notes, "a flawed child, an incomplete adult" (p. 4).

The problem of normativity, therefore, which specifies desired outcomes, is what forces our attention onto the hegemonic assumptions behind the social engineering, the school architecture, the curriculum, the accreditation mandates, and the daily practices of early education. The term "appropriate," so prominently displayed in the title "Developmentally Appropriate Practice," betrays the inherently normative and teleological intent of the writers. The description of "practice" as singular, as opposed to plural, further underlines that there is one exclusive path to goodness and success. Throughout her work Valerie Walkerdine (1984, 1987, 2002, 2004) has consistently raised the question as to who is privileged by such a stance. To state the issue in more starkly political terms, what forms of hegemony are embodied in technologies of education such as Developmentally Appropriate Practice and other purportedly progressive and child-centered approaches? What kind of child do we want Norm(a)(l) to be and at what cost to the epistemologies, cultures, values, belief systems, and potential of children who will end up labeled stunted and flawed because of either resistance to becoming Norm(a)(l) or because of their inability to meet the standards that being Norm(a)(l) demands?

The analysis in Walkerdine's work, and in *Changing the subject*, suggests that what is being explicitly produced by the discursive practices of early education is a bourgeois subject who will function compliantly in a global consumer capitalist world. As Sarah Kay notes, quoting from Žižek's *Mapping ideology* (1994), the material practices into which we are inserted exert powerful ideological influence over our subjectivity: "Thus, instead of our acts reflecting our beliefs, it is rather our beliefs that are born of our acts: repeating the act of praying will instill in us the belief in the reality of prayer. That is why, for Althusser, the practices imposed by various social apparatuses are the means whereby ideology is perpetuated...the 'external' ritual performatively generates its own ideological foundation" (2003, p. 106). Becoming a subject, therefore, is inherently performative, and the nature of the space schools provide for this performance are, therefore, of critical importance.

Since capitalism is founded on notions of inequality and stratification, meaning that for every captain of industry a large low-wage proletarian workforce is required, bourgeois pedagogy can only accomplish its goals by sustaining inherent inequality. Thus, the vast majority of children in the world are destined to fail at being or becoming Norm(a)(l) and our educational systems must develop rationales and procedures then for dealing with the many children who are "failures" and ultimately for dealing with the "dysfunctional" responses such failure produces in so many children. Such children will be encouraged to aspire to be Norm(a)(l), but, as Jay MacLeod (1995) discovered in the field work described in *Ain't no makin' it*, oftentimes there ain't no makin' it (for further discussion see Chapter 8 below). Nods to multiculturalism, class inclusion, and inclusion of children with learning exceptionalities, however well-intentioned, are exercises in self-delusion if the pedagogy being promulgated is fundamentally designed to support, legitimate, and even extend the hegemony of the status quo.

Appropriate for Whom?

In the early 1990s a critical zeitgeist appeared to be emerging in early childhood education in the U.S. At that time I wrote a series of papers, some of which were presented at the Reconceptualizing Early Childhood Education conferences (O'Loughlin, 1991, 1992c, 1995a), where I advanced a series of propositions concerning children and their worlds that were designed to encourage questioning of the hegemonic epistemological assumptions of conventional early educational and child development discourses, and thereby produce critical new possibilities.[3] The response of NAEYC to the upsurge of critique at that time was to make cosmetic changes in their policy statements, as noted earlier. No substantive changes, however, were made, and the critical chorus faded to a distant echo in subsequent years. Following is a series of assertions that have arisen from my work in this area, as well as brief commentary on each.

Assertion #1: Child development and early childhood education are filled with limiting assumptions and orthodoxies that need to be examined and challenged.

Perhaps the most limiting assumption of all is the notion of "child" as generic. It is as if we can speak of all children as *having* the same experiences, or as *needing* the same experiences in the process of becoming adults. This, coupled with assumptions of linearity, invariable sequencing, readiness, and normativity, shoehorns children into narrow notions of being, and by definition, pathologizes children who are unready or unwilling to be thus limited. The notion of "childhood" is also unexamined. As the critical authors cited earlier note, the norm seems to be a Rousseauesque image of childhood innocence and goodness coupled with a notion of child as blank slate. There is no intimation of a childhood unconscious (see below), of the child as product of history, nor of the child as inserted into what Castañeda (2002) calls "circuits of exchange" such as, wars, genocides, economic and labor transactions, and so on. Neither is there a notion of becoming a subject as a dynamic process.

What has puzzled me most about child development as a field is not only the positivist empiricist orientation of the field, but the apparent reduction of a large component of what develops to cognitive and mental processes. This no doubt has its origins in Piaget's influential work and in Kohlberg's appropriation of the cognitive-developmental model to moral development. That form of reductionism is disconcerting enough, but to find the same linear, invariant, stage-wise, and yes, even cognitive, assumptions deployed to describe modes of attachment and emotionality is quite bizarre. I cannot but help recall Bradley's (1989) comment that developmental models of childhood tell us more about the mental models of the theorists than they tell us about the minds of the children they purport to describe. Looking at the discourses of child development in a larger sociohistorical context, as Henriques et al. (1984) have done, the cognitive-developmental outlook is consistent with the worldview that underlies western science. This view privileges enlightenment and Cartesian notions of objectivity, rationality, and empiricism at the expense of narrative, culture, history, and plural notions of epistemology. Recall that the Piagetian ideal of thinking, the hypothetico-deductive method, is premised on an image of the child as budding rational scientist as its central trope.

Assertion #2: There is no "child" independent of race, ethnicity, social class, gender, religious beliefs, cultural and subcultural membership, and history: All children are ancestrally and sociohistorically located.

Key to understanding the ideology underlying early education and child development is the notion of individuality. Inherently in western ideology, and particularly in a U.S. epistemology grounded in vaunted frontier individualism and the Horatio Alger myth of self-sufficiency, is the notion of the individual as agent of her or his own success (cf. Kessen, 1979). This emphasis on individualism precludes introspection about history and ancestral memory, and precludes consideration of the significance of participation in a particular group on the subject formation of individual members. Jonathan Lear's (2006) *Radical hope*, for example, details the profound devastation experienced by the Crow nation in the U.S. when their collective culture as a warrior nation was obliterated. Documentation of the destructiveness of the residential schools operated in Australia, Canada, and the U.S. for indigenous children offers further evidence that failure to conceptualize the importance of collective cultural identification, and systematic attempts to destroy social linkages between children and their communities are profoundly damaging to children's emerging subjectivities, and that, indeed, this damage has catastrophic intergenerational consequences (O'Loughlin, 2008; see also Chapter 9 below). Children's emerging subjectivities are not only located within sociohistorical and ancestral epistemological and narrative traditions, but they are also bound up with generational legacies of imagined communities (cf. Anderson, 2006). These imagined communities include notions of national identity, class, race, ethnicity, gender, religion, attitudes to disease and exceptionality, and other forms of social relations that profoundly shape the being and becoming of particular children.

If our ways of thinking about children's experience preclude discussion of the multiple sources of subject formation, or if the effect of our models of child development and early education is to replace children's emerging subjectivities with an insistence that all children be a certain way or become a certain way—a way that valorizes rationality, bourgeois aspirations, whiteness, heterosexuality, and Christianity, for example—this is potentially as damaging to particular children as the disastrous attempts western societies made to assimilate indigenous peoples in North America and Australia through their abduction and placement in culturally annihilating boarding schools. Basil Bernstein's (1990, 2000) work on *invisible pedagogy* makes it abundantly clear that schools create privileging systems that clearly benefit middle-class, dominant culture children. These systems facilitate the subject formation of that group of children, and confirm their capacity to maintain their privileges and pursue their dreams. Despite a wealth of literature on the deleterious effects of such privileging systems on children who do not fit the bourgeois norm (e.g., Cummins, 2001; Delpit, 2006; Erickson, 2004; Fine & Weis, 2003; Gee, 1996, 2004; Heath, 2006; Katz, 1990; Lemke, 1990; Lipka et al., 1998; MacLeod, 1995) it is dispiriting to find that, at best, "cultural difference" gets token acknowledgment in mainstream discourses of child development and early education.

Assertion #3: The child has an unconscious life and theories of childhood and approaches to child pedagogy are too often silent on this presence.

The patient in my psychotherapy office is a middle-aged business woman. We have worked together for some time now, but both of us have reached the point where we can acknowledge to each other that the therapy appears superficial. My patient expressed the feeling this way: "I could sit here and talk with you all night. But then again I can do that with my friends." "I am paying you, you know," she added pointedly. She left, and I had a week to ponder the situation. The following week, after some desultory chat she got to the point: "Well, what do you recommend that I do?" she prodded. I actually had held an opinion for some time as to what this patient needed, but I had postponed making a suggestion as I felt that my take on the situation was somewhat critical of her. Readers will appreciate that psychotherapists do not love the self-help industry of feel-good manuals, gurus, self-help workshops and so on. We have legitimate concerns that they are ineffective (except in making money for their purveyors), but they also represent glitzy competition and provoke our envy. This patient was an avid consumer of every self-help fad she could lay her hands on and she spent considerable money on traveling to and participating in workshops. I felt that she was seeking solutions from the outside to avoid turning inward. However, I had avoided expressing this very judgmental thought. Now, however, confronted with her demand, I simply said "I think it might be very helpful if you lay on the couch and just stayed with your own thoughts and we'll see what happens."

She complied, and began to offer the kinds of free-floating thoughts that psychoanalysts refer to as free association. She began ruminating about her relationship with both her mother and her sister as a child. As she spoke she began to experience stomach cramps. "I don't know why these thoughts are bothering me," she said, "but my stomach is hurting." Soon, a picture emerged of a profoundly lonely child standing on the periphery of her family waving frantically, desperately trying to gain the attention of her parents.

The story of my patient and her stomach cramps offers a timely reminder that human beings are motivated powerfully by unconscious forces and hidden knowledges. Despite important contributions to our understanding of children by child analysts, including Sigmund Freud, Anna Freud, Melanie Klein, Allesandra Piontelli, Catherine Mathelin, D. W. Winnicott, and others, and important work on the effects of intergenerational trauma transmission by Selma Fraiberg, Louise Kaplan, Marilyn Charles, and others,[4] mainstream discourses about children and early education are conducted almost entirely at the level of rational discourse. This leaves the field impoverished from a psychic perspective, and I hope my discussion in Chapters 2 through 7 and in Chapter 9 of this book helps redress the balance. It is only since I began studying psychoanalysis that I have begun to understand the importance of narrative and autobiographical work as a foundation for a depth pedagogy (see Chapters 3, 7 & 9).

Lacanian psychoanalysis has also alerted me to the importance of desire and the relative ease with which children can be shifted from desire to the assuaging of adult demand (see esp. Chapters 2, 3, 5 & 7). In addition, combining discursive and historical analysis through combinations of the writing of discourse theorists, Lacanian psychoanalysts, and theorists who have explored the mechanisms by which trauma is transmitted intergenerationally has given me an understanding of how subjectivity is actively constructed at the vortex of ancestral memory, sociohistorical circumstance, local discursive practices, and the mediating influences of language, schooling and other official regulatory processes. I believe that awareness of this complex of forces gives us the possibility to conceptualize child growth and child pedagogy in ways in which the possibility of any child developing an expansive and affirming subjectivity is enhanced (see esp. Chapter 9). Critical narrative is a particularly useful rubric for conceptualizing this process.

Assertion #4: Constructivist notions of learning, e.g., "discovery learning," are inherently teleological and grounded in bourgeois epistemological assumptions.

To claim that learning is an active process of construction is both charming and intuitively plausible. All of us have experienced such learning in some form, and it certainly appeals to the liberal ideal of early education as child-centered and freeing, as Valerie Walkerdine has discussed throughout her writings. The intuitive plausibility of the claim, and the apparent neutrality with which it is enunciated make it, like many of the home truths of child development and early education, difficult to refute. In a binary world in which progressive approaches to pedagogy are invariably contrasted with the evils of didactic pedagogy, it is very hard to argue against such a transparently child-centered approach. Appearances, however, can be deceptive.

First, in the wake of the intellectual revolution by post-structural and critical theorists that challenged the hegemony of positivism as the basis for knowing, there is considerable support for the notion that all knowledge is partial and positional, that knowledge is constructed interpretively, and that knowing is therefore an interpretive process. Thus, we cannot detach author from text, knower from known, because understanding is inherently interpretive. As opposed to positivist knowing, where knowledge is authoritative, objective, and absolute, and where the relationship between author and text is concealed, in constructed (or deconstructed) knowing, the relationship between author and text is a key object of inquiry. Thus, an emphasis on constructed knowing ought to be welcomed in child pedagogy.

While there is some truth to the idea that children learn through actively speaking, reading, and writing (cf. Barnes, 1992), critical knowing only occurs when the learning situation allows opportunities for critical interaction between the emerging subjectivity of learners and the power relations inherent in the production of the knowledges to which the child is exposed, whether this be via talk, printed text, visual media, auditory media or whatever. A key test, then, in assessing the viability of constructivist or active learning in early education is whether it permits this kind of critical inquiry on the part of children. What if, in a typical active learning situation, the knowledge is already fully known to the teacher? What if there actually is a *right answer* that the child is meant to derive from interaction with cleverly designed curriculum materials? What is the point of active learning unless the purpose is to engage the child in the critical construction of new knowledges? Is it possible that much of what has been dressed up as active learning is just a clever bourgeois trick to keep parents and teachers happy with the fantasy of child-centeredness when, in actuality, the truths the child will "discover" through "active learning" have been predetermined and built into the putative "discovery" process?

Second, there is a concern, arising particularly from the work of Basil Bernstein (1990, 2000) on pedagogic codes and from work such as Shirley Brice Heath's (2006) on the different language registers of culturally different children and children from different social classes that what supposedly child-centered pedagogy mainly accomplishes is to privilege the indirect ways of knowing and speaking that are the norm in middle-class communities (cf. also Delpit, 2006, and discussion in Chapter 2 below). This, again, is a compelling example of the pitfalls of proclaiming a universal or generic mode of pedagogy as a solution to the educational needs of all children. More fundamentally it once again exposes the fundamental hegemonic intent of pedagogies that masquerade as child-centered but that are fundamentally privileging of the children who are destined to inherit the power structures of societies. How differently would early pedagogy be conceptualized if the intent were to offer all children opportunities to develop critical subjectivities that took advantage of their ancestral knowledges, that privileged multiple ways of knowing, and that viewed schooling as a venue in which all children could expand the identificatory opportunities available to them and thereby add an expansive repertoire to their possible ways of being. This is counterintuitive to mainstream education, a system that privileges the status quo; a system that makes little room for ancestral or local ways of knowing and being; and most particularly a system that provides structured, pre-packaged curriculum because teachers cannot be trusted to create relevant, empowering curriculum for and with the children and communities whom they ostensibly serve.

Assertion #5: "Mind" as an independent entity does not exist. All thought is dialectical and socioculturally situated.

It follows from the foregoing discussion that rational disembedded modes of thinking, such as those valued in western forms of education, whether didactic or supposedly "child-centered," are cultural constructions that only have the status of being natural because we live in societies which naturalize such modes of thought. Thus, to westerners, the concept of "mind" as an abstract, thought processing entity is obvious. Indeed, in the 1950s and 1960s information-processing theorists did not hesitate to develop computer models of the mind, where the computer served as a literal analogy for mental processes (e.g., Miller et al., 1967; Newell & Simon, 1972). Contemporary cognitive science is built on this foundation. Sociocultural theorists, however, view the individual as shaped by culture, and as acting on culture using meditational means, particularly language. Thus, the inherently social and socio-historical nature of thought processes is inherent in conceptualizations of language (e.g., Bakhtin, 1981, 1986; Vygotsky, 1978, 1986), activity (Wertsch, 1998, 2006) and even the unconscious (Lacan, 1968). In this way of thinking, instead of an autonomous mind that develops capacity for abstraction through a series of stages, as Piaget suggests, ultimately arriving at the holy grail of formal operations, what is posited is that children become subjects who learn to think and act symbolically through entry into the language and symbolic systems of particular societies. The title of Vygotsky's (1978) collection, *Mind in society*, accurately captures this idea.

In terms of pedagogy, instead of an autonomous child advancing through a series of progressively difficult mental challenges to develop the capacity for objective, dispassionate thought, what emerges is a dialectical notion of the relation between the child and the world. The thinking and feeling child is recognized as coming out of history and viewing the world through particular sociohistorical lenses. The child's growth is conceptualized as an apprenticeship in culture, one in which mediational means such as language and other symbol systems (e.g., cultural rituals, religious symbols) are utilized to gain meaning and enter the collective identity of particular cultures. Likewise, the pedagogical setting is recognized as an ideological context, one that is situated in larger societal contexts, and that, too, possesses its own mediational means and symbol systems. For school to provide emancipatory possibilities, therefore, multivocality and dialogicality (cf. Bakhtin, 1981, 1986; Wertsch, 1998, 2006) are privileged so that the child can see him or herself in the experience. The child can find multiple identificatory possibilites that offer a plurality of ways for conceptualizing his or her being and becoming in the world. Any single authoritative mode of pedagogy, curricular system, or text is inherently hegemonic, and inevitably privileges *one* way of knowing and one mode of being. Any univocal pedagogy that privileges a particular mode of speech or way of knowing, therefore, is necessarily a means of indoctrination, however carefully it may be embedded in rhetorics of progressive, child-centered, or democratic education.

Assertion #6: Exploring Après Coup & the problem with linear time

We know that children grow up. In some respect there is a qualitative difference between the experience of being a child and the experience of being an adult. One way to characterize the changes from childhood to adulthood, as I have discussed above, is through a notion of development as linear, progressive, and cumulative. In such a conceptualization time moves forward. What then am I to make of the experiences of the patient who experienced stomach cramps while lying on the couch in my office reaching for her early memories? Is she still an adult at that moment? Is she literally recalling events from her childhood, or is she now imposing new meanings for the first time on previously experienced events? What if this were a patient recovering for the first time a memory of a trauma with which she had unconsciously lived for her entire life? What if she actually acted out a childhood experience and re-experienced it in my presence, as Ellen did in her sexual trauma therapy with Annie Rogers (2006)? Psychologists never lack for an explanation and concepts such as regression have been invented to cover some of these situations. But is it regression if a patient returns, *now as an adult* to revisit a childhood event? Is it not rather the case that the adult is visiting a previously encoded—or perhaps never encoded—event, and is thereby doing something old and new simultaneously? She might well be visiting an old event from her childhood, yet also doing it for the first time. This kind of playing with the directionality of time is evident in the autobiographical vignettes from my life that appear in many chapters of this book.

This way of thinking, which twists our notions of time, order, and linearity was first described by Freud under the term *Nachträglichkeit*, and glossed by Lacan as *après* coup (see Kay, 2003, pp. 18–19). As Dana Birksted-Breen (2003) notes, one particular meaning of après coup is that "something is perceived but only takes its meaning retrospectively" (p. 1501). Thus, there is no definite cleavage between present and past because what is taking place in the present influences the past, and the past reinterpreted, thereby influences the present. This, after all, is one of the indicators of a successful psychoanalysis: the reconfiguration of past experience in the present. A well-lived life, in this way of thinking, would not be one of linear, forward motion. Instead, success would be conceptualized as a recursive process in which past, including by all accounts ancestral and spirit pasts, present ways of being, and possible futures come into dynamic integration in the service of articulating present subjectivity.

This then calls for a much more dialectical and fluid relationship between present and past beings. The child becomes the adult. Yet the adult recreates childhood. This recreated childhood directs the course of adult being, which in turn leads to recreation of childhood being. This is a process in which both are constantly in a dialectical relation of being and becoming. This has some correlates with chaos theory (e.g., Prigogine, 1981, 1997) and concepts of development as patchy and ecosocial (cf. Lemke, 1990).

Whither the Question Child/Adult?

I think what bothers me most about the grand narratives of childhood that are so endemic to conventional wisdom about children and pedagogy is the determinism of the child's life path. Where is there room for questions? How is the child to ever develop imaginative possibilities and experience desire if all of life is hemmed in with the ever-increasing demand of teachers, parents, pediatricians, pastors and others? If we, the adults who conceptualize childhood and schooling, cannot enter into dialogue with our own child selves, and if we cannot break out of the narrow pathways of our own experience, what hope is there for emancipatory, opportunistic, or imaginative dreaming among the children of our future?

· 2 ·

IN SEARCH OF THE
LOST LANGUAGE OF CHILDHOOD

As a child therapist, I meet with children in my consulting office every week to address their struggles in being children. Yet I still find the notion of childhood quite elusive. My child patients have taught me that being a child is often a serious and very fraught enterprise. In *Strange dislocations* (1995) Carolyn Steedman refers to the "emotional tawdriness" of romantic notions of childhood innocence. To keep the complexity in childhood, Steedman prefers to refer to "littleness" to capture the highly complex nature of children's emotional experiences. Jacqueline Rose's study, *The case of Peter Pan* (1992), offers a useful window into understanding how western societies have constructed a myth of childhood innocence. Her study shows how the story, written by James Barrie (1902), has been transmuted from its original purpose as an adult tale crafted to seduce a boy, into a magical story into which are projected fantasies of childhood innocence and sweetness. "*Peter Pan,*" Rose notes, "is a front—a cover not as concealer but a vehicle—for what is most unsettling and uncertain about the relationship between adult and child. It shows innocence not as a property of childhood, but as a portion of adult desire." (1992, p. xii). Rose challenges some of our favorite shibboleths about childhood, including the cult of childhood innocence; the belief that social realism should take precedence over fantasy in children's fiction; and inevitably, the ventriloquation of adult desires and expectations through the language of child psychology, child care and pedagogy, as discussed in Chapter 1. She argues that psychoanalysis challenges the normative discourse of childhood "in that it undermines the idea that psychic life is continuous, that language can give us mastery, or that past and future can be cohered into a straightforward sequence, and controlled" (1992, p. 134).

Each year I teach courses on children's emotional lives, on child therapy and on child development. Students invariably react with surprise when they learn that children experience just as complex a range of pleasures, anxieties, and losses as what they themselves experience as adults. Could it be that in ascribing "cuteness" and "innocence" to children we are trying to ward off the possibility that little people can experience anger, rage, desire, loss, worry, terror and so on? It is as if we do not wish to be reminded of the abyss of our own childhoods.

Children often serve as containers into which adults project their fantasies of childhood to ward off the potential for stirring up the buried emotions of their own childhoods. Little Josh, aged five, was in my office one day with his mom and, without warning, he went to the doll house and began snapping the heads off all of the female dolls and throwing them violently against the wall. His mom, panicked, asked me what he was doing, though it was clear from her expression that she knew all too well the depths of his emotional anguish. Understandably she could not bear it.

Although a considerable amount of this book is devoted to autobiographical explorations of my own childhood history, these memories are necessarily reconstructions. My childhood is irretrievably gone. Freud (1899/1960), in his discussion of our earliest memories, which he called screen memories, noted that early memories are reconstructions or fantasies. We see the child in front of us through fantasies which are remnants of our own lost childhoods. These fantasies represent our unconscious efforts to rehabilitate, rescue, or seek vengeance for the separations and losses that have become signature aspects of our character as adults.

Psychiatrist Dori Laub (1992; see also 1995) recounts the story of Menachem, a Holocaust survivor. When Menachem was five he was placed with his parents in the Plashow labor camp near Krakow. His parents managed to have Menachem smuggled out of the camp, wrapped in a shawl, and clutching a photograph of his mother. He was often reduced to living on the streets of a local town and he sought constantly to evade capture by the Nazis. After the war he was reunited with his parents. They had become emaciated, toothless, traumatized caricatures of their former selves. Menachem had immense difficulty bonding with them since the beatific image of the mother in the photograph that had sustained him for so long was so discordant from the actual mother that stood before him. Difficult though it was, life resumed, and Menachem became a colonel in the Israeli Army and ultimately a physician. He got married and when his wife returned from the hospital with their newborn daughter she was astonished to find that Menachem had built an elaborate model train set that took up an entire room of their house. At the time Menachem could offer no explanation except that he wanted his daughter to have something to play with. Later, after analysis, Menachem tearfully admitted that the train set was not constructed for his daughter. Instead, he was unconsciously seeking to restore to himself the childhood that had been so cruelly wrested from him at age five.[1]

In many ways, being a child represents a struggle *to be* in a world where adults have very particular scripted notions of childhood as *being a certain way* based on their fantasied remembrances of the pleasures and lacunae of their own childhood experiences. A child typically shows up in my consulting room with a symptom, e.g., anger, anxiety, depression, resistance to schooling, fear of failure. These symptoms often emerge because the child is having a particular difficulty with or resistance to the implicit or explicit expectations that have been placed on him or her. A child whose path to *being* is stifled will develop symptoms and the task of the child analyst is to decode the communication inherent in these symptoms to understand how the child might regain a sense of the possibilities of his or her existence. To use the language of Lacan here, the therapist's task is to help understand the pressures of external *demand* placed on the child and to seek to replace those pressures with the idea that the child may begin to experience the possibilities inherent in her or his own *desires*. To be sure, as Maud Mannoni (1970) notes, this psychoanalytic approach to children is the exception. Behavioral and cognitive-behavioral therapies, as well as some psychoanalytic approaches, can be considered mere adjustment therapies in that they seek to enable the child to adjust to society, school and family as is. The psychoanalytic approach I value and attempt to practice privileges freedom and creativity wherever possible as vehicles for the child's expression, motivated by my belief that the presenting symptoms had their origin in inhibition of the child's desire.

The process of recovering a sense of *being* for a child is greatly complicated by the degree to which parents seek to employ the therapist as an instrument to bolster their own authority in seeking to coerce their child into being a certain way. In *The broken piano* Catherine Mathelin (1999) deftly illustrates how prevalent this tendency is among parents. Much of my own rumination about my childhood is, I believe, motivated by a sense of regret that, faced with implicit parental demand, I developed a sense of dutifulness that caused me to suppress my own desire to be, substituting for it an impetus to be dutiful in order to earn the love of my parents and to hold our family together. Ironically, an earnest sense of duty in a child, so often admired by parents and teachers alike—"a pleasure to have in class"—can be a troubling symptom of the child's suppression of desire.

Official Childhood

Patrick Chamoiseau's (1997) delightful memoir *School days* tells the story of a little boy who envied his older brothers and sisters whom he witnessed making a mysterious odyssey to school each day. The little boy developed a powerful desire for learning, one that got him into lots of trouble as he pestered his parents and siblings with questions and plastered the hallways of their apartment building in Martinique with ambitious scribbles. And then he went to school—to a school reminiscent of the one I attended (see Chapter 3)—a blunt instrument that mercilessly attempted to beat and slap its hapless victims into submission at the bottom of that society's social order. While such schools still exist and visit profound psychic harm on children we should not be misled that it is only the most inhumane and custodial schools that are problematic.[2]

As I noted in Chapter 1, there is a long tradition of child-centered educational practices in early childhood education. Early childhood educators typically value play, exploration, hands-on learning, and emotional safety. Educators in early childhood centers spend a large portion of their day teaching children interpersonal skills and notions of reciprocity and mutual respect. Yet, as the first significant point of contact between an individual child and society, early childhood centers and kindergartens have as one of their primary obligations to teach young children the norms and mores of society. These two conflicting goals produce tensions that have become exacerbated in recent years in the U.S. and elsewhere.

Much school time during the early years is spent on mastering routines and rituals and considerable pressure is placed on children who resist conformity. A number of the young children that are referred to me each year are brought by parents at the behest of teachers who tell them that their children are impulsive or inattentive. Often teachers suggest the ultimate adjustment therapy, a prescription of Ritalin or Adderall for attention deficit hyperactivity disorder (ADHD), and they dispatch parents to the pediatrician for a readily available prescription. Some of these parents bring their children for therapy because of their recognition that ADHD medications are a retrogressive solution, while some also wisely recognize that the "problem" imputed to their child may in fact be a result of the inappropriate expectations of particular school environments.[3]

Unfortunately, early childhood education has become increasingly burdened by notions of normativity in recent years. Normativity is inherent in developmental checklists and evaluations, in behavioral expectations, in the notions of kindergarten readiness, and, as I illustrated in Chapter 1, in the core assumptions of developmental psychology. The increasing academicization of kindergarten in the United States and elsewhere, with the pressure of high-stakes testing putting increasing pressure on teachers of ever younger age children, has led to increasingly normative, cognitive, and academic notions of early childhood education. In her recent book *A child's work* (2004a), Vivian Paley indicates that as early education has increasingly shifted toward high-stakes testing and early skills instruction the emphasis on play and creativity has diminished markedly. Indeed the very notion of early childhood education as a place of freedom and discovery is rapidly facing obsolescence. A preschool director, interviewed by Paley, expressed it this way:

> I'm not inclined to encourage fantasy play any more if my teachers can't handle it…If the teachers are worried about what's coming out, especially with the fours and fives, everyone is better off if we stick to lesson plans and projects.
>
> "Has the play changed that much?" I asked.
>
> The teachers think so. Maybe it's the increased tension since 9/11. Children do seem less prepared, more at risk. We're on safer ground with a somewhat academic curriculum. It's more dependable. (2004a, p. 7)

It is striking that while some of the most seminal work on children's emotions has been done by psychoanalysts including Sigmund Freud himself (1909/1960); Anna Freud (1935/1979), Donald Winnicott (1958, 1965, 2002) and Melanie Klein (1984a, b) in Britain; French Lacanian child analysts including Didier Anzieu (1990), Françoise Dolto (1999), Laurent Danon-Boileau (2001), Maude Mannoni (1970, 1999), and Catherine Mathelin

(1999); and Italian psychoanalyst Alessandro Piontelli (1992), this canon of work is virtually unknown in the curriculum of child development and early childhood teacher preparation. In addition, there is the seminal work of the therapists at the Tavistock clinic in London where infant observation was pioneered and where therapists have worked therapeutically with a wide variety of exceptional children including touch-sensitive, psychotic and autistic children and adolescents for generations.[4] While the work of John Bowlby (1988) and colleagues in attachment theory is typically acknowledged, and the value of play as an educational medium is typically taught, the psychoanalytic underpinning of these approaches is neither named nor explored and so they become instrumental rubrics rather than powerful conceptual approaches to working with children.

What accounts for this appalling omission? On the one hand there may be a deep resistance among early childhood teachers and school administrators as well as teacher educators to acknowledging the workings of the unconscious in the child. As I noted above, acknowledgment of deep primal emotions in children appears to stir up primal anxieties in adults, anxieties that we typically suppress by postulating the child as innocent and pure. After the World Trade Center collapse in New York City on September 11, 2001, many communities in my area of Long Island suffered catastrophic losses, with literally dozens of families in some towns and villages losing family members to the disaster. The typical response of many public school districts, inexplicably, was to ban discussion of the event. As the event unfolded and news filtered through to children from scattered cell phone calls, glimpses of television news coverage etc. many school administrators responded by instructing teachers to say nothing. In subsequent days, as the extent of the losses became apparent, many schools maintained the ban on conversation, depriving teachers and children of a shared opportunity to grieve and to experience each other's humanity. Stories began to appear in newspapers of early childhood centers banning children from incorporating any reenactment of the World Trade Center attack in their play. What were children expected to do with the overload of terrifying emotions many of them undoubtedly experienced? What of those children who had no safe space in their homes to give voice to either their fears or their losses? In confronting the child, we must acknowledge the tattered remnants of our own childhood losses and primal fears. Apparently, for some people, it is easier to just close the door on such feelings, thereby producing another generation of children who defensively need to close down emotional possibilities for future generations of children with whom they will interact.

Writing in 1955, psychoanalyst Arthur Jersild discussed this issue and it is indeed striking how little has changed in the more than half a century since in how many teachers respond to children's emotional needs:

> We contribute to the growing child's isolation and loneliness whenever we, in effect, tell him that we do not wish to know how he feels. Yet there is much in the school life of both boys and girls that would make the sturdiest child express intense emotion if the pressure against it were not so strong. In some schools, it is true, there is much gaiety and laughter, but painful emotions are often squelched. At the elementary school level, for example, millions of children feel the sting of failure, the lash of sarcasm, and the pain of rejection. There are thousands, who, week after week, know the torture of helpless rage. If all these children, and others who encounter countless hurts—some deliberately and maliciously imposed, some that arise in the natural course of life's struggle—if all of these were free to cry, as well they might, there would be a flood of tears at school. But such signs of distress would be unseemly. It is better, for the sake of decency and order, to keep up a pretense that all is well. And by a strange irony, which persists in our culture from a more primitive time, it is more appropriate in our culture, if one is deeply moved, to show it through signs of anger (sarcastic laughter for example) than through grief and affection. An outpouring of feeling would be frightening to teachers who have rigidly schooled themselves never to let the hurts and tender emotions of their own lives show in public. We ask that the child hold back his tears and swallow the lumps in his throat, swallow his rage and his fear and his pride. We ask compassionate teachers to do the same. To do this is like swallowing a sword. It can be done, but it is not easy; it takes long practice, and it leaves scars. (1955, pp. 68–69)

In the U.S., and increasingly elsewhere, the definition of education in terms of norms of accountability, definable in terms of academic and cognitive outcomes has been highly effective in shifting education to an instrumental and objectivist stance. As teachers know all too well, what matters is what is measured, and what is measured is invariably reduced to observable cognitive and academic achievements. The creation of behavioral and moral norms that label as deviant or pathological any behavior that does not fit within certain definable criteria has led to a mentality of classification of children rather than a mindset that seeks understanding of the meaning of an individual child's behavior. As early childhood becomes increasingly academicized we can expect the incidence of symptomatic or "problem" behaviors among young children to increase. Teachers deserve the least blame in this process since they are inserted into technocratic discursive practices and are deprived of instruction in decoding the emotional underpinnings of children's behavioral symptoms.[5]

Teacher educators, however, are instrumental in creating the worldviews used by accreditation bodies to discipline and shape the field. They create the curriculum and textbooks and serve as academic gatekeepers for what constitutes the received view of the field. Why the institutional leaders of the field have allowed early childhood education to be thus defined was the subject of Chapter 1, but suffice it to say that if change is to come this is an area where early childhood teacher educators can have their greatest influence. Early childhood academics can legitimately point to their own lack of exposure to psychoanalysis as a cause for this major omission in the field. While a few academics have taken the opportunity to address this lacuna by engaging with psychoanalytic theory, as I and some others have done (cf. Britzman, 1998, 2003, 2006; Boldt & Salvio, 2006) child psychoanalysts, too, have a responsibility to reach across the disciplinary boundary from psychoanalysis and clinical psychology to interest themselves in the schooled lives of children. It certainly speaks volumes to the rigid disciplinary boundaries of academia, as well as to a status hierarchy in universities in which early childhood education is positioned at the lower end, that such outreach is an altogether rare occurrence.[6] The consequence is a lost opportunity for early childhood teacher education.

Parole vide ou parole pleine?

As my uses of psychoanalysis in some of the following chapters illustrate, different psychoanalytic concepts can be used to illuminate different facets of childhood. Here I will concentrate on the content of the child's language. In *Separation and creativity* Maud Mannoni (1999) draws a distinction between *parole vide* and *parole pleine*. "Parole vide", literally "empty talk," refers to the language used by a child whose meaning-making capacity is saturated with the symbols of parental knowledge and circumscribed by the constraints of parental anxiety. "Parole pleine", or "full speech" refers to the robustness of the expression of a child who can speak from a place of desire or being. I can recall from my childhood that on those rare occasions when relatives came to visit, our parents prevailed upon my siblings and I to rein in our desires and to politely decline when we were offered a half a crown, or even a precious sixpence. This tendency to inhibit my desires followed me throughout my life, as I discuss in Chapter 3, and caused me to tell myself and everybody else that I was enrolling in a masters degree program when I entered a Ph.D. program at Columbia University. I occasionally allowed myself to think full thoughts, to acknowledge fleeting glimpses of my dreams, but I could not let desire speak its name. As I write these words I am sitting in an office at Unitec Institute of

Technology in Auckland, in Aotearoa/New Zealand, where I have a summer teaching appointment. When a colleague in New York asked me how I had managed to get this appointment I replied that I had simply asked. Voici la parole pleine! At age fifty five I had come to voice a desire.

As Mannoni correctly notes, and this has been emphasized too in the writings of Alice Miller (e.g., 1997), children who occupy places in other's desires rather than coming to speech in their own right, often develop a severe sense of dutifulness. Paradoxically, they often are the best behaved, most industrious, and most accomplished students in our nurseries and schools. However, as Karen Horney illustrated in *Neurosis and human growth* (1991) these achievements come with a very heavy price tag, artfully labeled by Horney as "The tyranny of the should." If love can only be earned through continuous accomplishment we cannot rest. If nobody takes such children in hand and allows them to begin to name the unnamable and free themselves from the yoke of external demand and conditional love, how grim are the prospects for such children ever experiencing either happiness or creativity? And what if such children grow up to be teachers or parents? Will they be able to allow the children in their care to experience an unadulterated joy that they themselves have never known? Or will the grim specter of unrelenting demand claim another generation of dutiful children ruled by la parole vide?

More generally, As Mannoni explains in *The child, his "illness," and the others* (1970), a child whose capacity for genuine expression is stifled will often channel that desire into symptoms including physical illness and the usual disorders that bring children to therapy. Symptoms, therefore, are actually coded messages from the child of something seeking expression. The child's symptom conceals a question, and our task is to help the child uncover that question: "In treatment, the subject's question will replace the demand or anxiety of parents and child, a question that is his deepest wish, concealed hitherto in a symptom…" (1970, p. 61). Some children appear to be so attached to their symptoms, as I illustrate below and in Chapter 5, that experiencing desire is profoundly challenging. Others, such as Ponette, the four-year-old girl in Jacques Doillon's (1999) beautiful film of the same title, and Ludovic, the protagonist of Alain Berliner's (1997) enchanting *Ma vie en rose* are endowed with a resilience that allows them to ask their questions despite the concerted efforts of all of the adults in their worlds to silence them.

Mannoni notes that a primary goal of child therapy—and I would argue of early childhood education—is to assist each child to "refind the play spaces of childhood" (1999, p. 47). The writings of Vivian Paley (e.g., 1986, 1992,

2004b, 2008; Paley & Coles, 1991) and Max Van Manen (1986) represent very compelling examples of the kind of emotionally attuned pedagogy that can lift the burden of demand from a child's shoulders to allow desire to emerge. A key concept in Lacanian psychoanalysis, as I explain in Chapter 3, is the concept of *sujet supposé savoir* or "subject supposed to know." While the patient will impute knowledge—and perhaps even wisdom or omniscience—to the therapist, it is vital for the therapist to view the patient as the agent of his or her own coming to know. Thus, in psychoanalytic therapy, garrulousness is the enemy of knowledge, because it displaces the patient's curiosity or desire to know in favor of the analyst's blather. Similarly, in early childhood education, it is vital that teachers make a commitment to curiosity—and hence desire—as the most fundamental purpose of all pedagogical experiences. Without curiosity, as Paulo Freire (1972) wisely pointed out in *Pedagogy of the oppressed*, we enter a pedagogic space of oppression where the fundamental agency of the knowing person is denied. Or as noted radical American educator Myles Horton stated in *The long haul* (1990), teachers need to be experts in coming to know, rather than containers and dispensers of received knowledge.

Creativity, within this way of thinking, comes, in the first instance, from the provision of what is the inverse of schooling, namely a freeing space in which external demand and constraint are minimized in order to diminish the anxiety of children. Second, Mannoni recommends rather delightfully that we "listen to the nonsense of desire" (1999, p. 99). What a refreshing thought! Lewis Carroll, author of *Alice in Wonderland*, and J.M. Barrie, author of *Peter Pan*, had precisely this sensibility. School as a place for nonsense? Preposterous! Mannoni sums up this sensibility this way:

> The more painful reality is for the child, the more important is the ability of the parents to dream along with him of a different world in which the wondrous has its rightful place, its place as the inspiration for the poet and the storyteller in search of the lost language of childhood. (1999, p. 156)

In Search of the Lost Language of Childhood[7]

When she called me seeking an appointment five-year-old Myrna's mother told me that she had called me because Myrna's kindergarten teacher said that Myrna refused to speak at school. When the parents arrived at my office Myrna did not utter a word. She tentatively reached out and took a container of Polly Pocket dolls and played perfunctorily with them, but she did not speak.

I learned some of the family history from the parents, with Myrna listening. They were clearly uncomfortable speaking in her presence, and they came back another time on their own for more frank discussion. However, believing that the unconscious needs to receive the truth for the child to begin to heal (cf. Piontelli, 1992), I was frank with the parents about how such silences arise in children. The father had been successful in his profession, but when Myrna was three a crisis erupted in the family. The father left the family and was now remarried with a young baby. He also had suffered a business reversal that limited his ability to support Myrna, her mother and younger sibling. Myrna's mother had to move back in with her aging parents in a crowded apartment. Myrna had never verbalized an opinion about any of this, but her symptoms were clearly telegraphing some kind of traumatic response.

In session with Myrna I explained to her that I had no expectation as to what she might do while visiting with me each week. She could do anything she wished, or nothing at all, and I invited her to inspect the play materials, drawing materials etc. in my office. In subsequent weeks Myrna engaged in three activities. She occasionally drew; she played Candyland, a board game; and she played with dolls. In fact she and I spent most of the session on the floor where she dressed the various Polly Pocket dolls in outfits in preparation for a trip to the beach. During her play Myrna surprised me with a running commentary on what she was doing. Her speech flow was continuous but decidedly monological. Following techniques described by Laurent Danon-Boileau in *The silent child* (2001), I attempted to introduce conversational anomalies that would provoke dialogicality. Myrna was receptive and surprisingly playful. If I dressed a male doll, for example, in a female outfit she would exclaim "No" and laugh. Occasionally she ran to the waiting room to show off an item or an accomplishment to her waiting parent. With her parents separately she was sometimes voluble. With them together, she was silent. A conference with her teacher yielded information that she has never had a direct verbal interaction with her teacher in eighteen months together. She was voluble in the playground but silent inside the school, though she was willing to communicate through gestures.

This treatment is in its earliest stages. Myrna has begun to express some desires. Twice she asked if she might take the dolls home. Also, unlike Vanessa, whom I will discuss next, Myrna uses play therapy in a remarkably intuitive way. She has entered into a reciprocal relationship with me. Perhaps the most promising sign of all is that one day, while dressing the dolls, she half-whispered: "I have a little brother at my daddy's house but I can't see him because my mommy says the woman is bad." The unspeakable emerged for a tantalizing second. It has yet to return, but knowing this little girl's capabilities, I am confident that it will return, accompanied by her capacity for "full speech."

Vanessa was brought for therapy at age five with symptoms of self-injurious behavior. She repeatedly attempted to gouge her skin with the kindergarten scissors in school. When the teacher removed the scissors Vanessa repeatedly tried biting her hands and arms. Vanessa came from a highly stressed family— one in which all of the children in this extensive family are symptomatic, and the family has had protracted involvement with school counseling services, with social work services, and, on a few occasions with child protective services when some of the children had complained in school about episodes of domestic violence. Vanessa was not silent. However, though she could speak coherently at times, in more psychotic moments she spoke using guttural sounds and gestures. She pushed and shoved not only when aggressive, but also as a gesture of playfulness or affection. She lacked the capacity to symbolize her emotions. There was little rhythm to the three years of therapy I did with Vanessa. My office is filled with personal artifacts from my travels, etc. and Vanessa's favorite activity was picking up artifacts and simply asking "What's this?" She also repeatedly asked me if I had a daughter, what her name was, etc. She was struggling to imagine place, relatedness and connection.

In weeks when things were difficult at home Vanessa was in quite a psychotic state and she would spend much of the session throwing things aggressively or breaking the tips of markers and crayons by stabbing the drawing paper. I built a very nice rapport with Vanessa's mother but she seemed to be incapable of making any psychological adjustments to ease the pressure on Vanessa. In her world Vanessa was either obedient or disobedient. This lack of maternal holding was evident in Vanessa's drawings. She drew a picture of her mother that was dark and demonic. Her father was simply disengaged. Her own self-portraits vacillated between idealized pictures of a little girl reminiscent of Lucy in the *Peanuts* cartoon series and drawings of a little girl with the saddest imaginable face.

My office is rather small, and Vanessa surprised me by playing hide-and-seek regularly with me even though there was virtually no hiding places worth speaking of in the room. She would insist on hiding repeatedly, and she would demand that I search the room systematically until I located her. Just the tiniest bit of desire began to emerge in such moments. Vanessa lacked what Lacanians refer to as mirroring. As Lacan noted in *Ecrits* (2007) children gain a sense of their own existence through the affirmative gaze of caregivers. Lacking such recognition, a child experiences misrecognition and has difficulty developing a core sense of being. Vanessa tried to set up conditions for her own recognition in my presence, apparently unconsciously knowing that this vital function was lacking among her primary caretakers. She needed me to find her.

A major crisis emerged for Vanessa when her early adolescent sister became pregnant and had the first of two babies. The only tentative claim to identity and place that Vanessa had came from her status as the baby in the family, and the arrival of the first of these new babies was catastrophic for her. She filled sheet after sheet of paper with dense red crayon scribbles. The outline of a baby could vaguely be made out in one of the drawings: "The baby is sad and dying and there is blood all over the hospital," Vanessa explained. As the end of the school year rolled around, Vanessa sent a note to her teacher asking if she could please take her home for the summer. When I spoke with the teacher she was anguished at her powerlessness in the face of Vanessa's suffering. Vanessa's hold on reality was tentative and was very much predicated on the capacity of people such as this wonderful teacher, and hopefully me, in my therapeutic role, to endow her with a sense of *recognition* in a world where *misrecognition* was the story of her life.

Although I continually praised Vanessa's progress to her mother, the mother was not convinced. She took Vanessa from my care without notice to bring her for a neuropsychological evaluation, and thereafter decided to move her for treatment to a neuropsychological facility. My experience here is similar to Catherine Mathelin's, as described in *The broken piano* (1999), in that this was a parent who was only willing to invest in external solutions—magic bullets—that left the prevailing family dynamics intact.[8] I did manage to get her mother to bring Vanessa back for a leave taking, but, needless to say, the parting was so freighted with anxiety for Vanessa that she regressed to a psychotic state, with guttural speech and, at best, *parole vide*.

Lacking language to name her suffering, Vanessa is at risk of replicating both her mother's and sister's experience. Both had babies in early adolescence in what may well have been a futile attempt to reclaim the lost languages of their childhoods. As Selma Fraiberg and colleagues (1975) noted, and as I discuss in detail in Chapter 9, some children are haunted by ghosts that inhibit their capacity for full speech.

Little seven-year-old Alex is perhaps the saddest child I have met. He enters my office downcast, and he will not make eye contact or shake hands with me unless prompted. Alex is renowned for his rowdy behavior, foul tongue and abusive language, all of which he freely exhibits in my presence. The first self-portrait by this gifted and artistically talented child was of a boy shedding tears profusely. Most of his drawings have sharp jagged edges and creatures with large spiky teeth reminiscent of the creatures in Maurice Sendak's (1988) *Where the wild things are*. Alex's mom and dad had severe violent conflict during the prenatal period and during the first two years of his life before his father finally left. His father, a severely narcissistic individual, is inconsistently available, but sometimes showers Alex and his sibling with expensive gifts. Alex's mother bitterly encourages her children to take what they can from their father. His first picture of his father was as a money tree with dollar bills for leaves. Ventriloquating his mom, he also drew his dad as "an ugly, fat liar." In a fit of rage he drew his mom as a pile of excrement. He has made many spontaneous drawings of men with swords through their hearts. Angry at me, he put a sword through my heart too, and he has vented his rage on every piece of furniture in my office.

Alex currently resides with his mom, sibling and grandpa, in his maternal grandfather's home. On one poignant occasion he drew a series of four pictures, depicting his family members—or more accurately, depicting the turmoil in his object relational world. For his father he drew an unsmiling stick figure with the simple legend "Go" in the speech bubble. "He wants us to go away," Alex explained. For grandpa he drew a stick figure with a picture of a house in the speech bubble. When asked what this represented, he said "Grandpa wants us to get out of his house." For his mother, he drew a large somewhat witch-like creature, and in the speech bubble he drew a picture of a child. Commenting on the picture Alex explained that his mom was thinking of his brother (i.e., as opposed to Alex himself). Finally, he drew his older sibling (10 years old) and the child in the attached speech bubble was drawn with a sword through his heart. "My brother wants to kill me," he stated simply. Concerned with the lack of recognition in Alex's life, I conferred with his mother and explained to her the content of this sequence of pictures. She looked at me wearily and said: "Huh, what do you expect me to do?"

Having failed to develop a capacity for trust, and having lost all hope that he might ever be allowed to experience his own desires, Alex developed a severely oppositional personality. His school was taking steps to attempt to classify him as emotionally disturbed so that he might be moved to a more custodial school environment. Sadly, the only guaranteed outcome from such a strategy is probably that Alex will increase the level of oppositionality in his personality. In therapy he either contented himself with building highly imaginative but obses-sively constructed block buildings or he simply refused to participate at all and exhibited explosive anger. Lacking trust, he resisted emotional openness or any possibility of becoming vulnerable enough to build a relationship with me. On one occasion, engrossed in chess, at which he was much more adept than I, he complained when the session came to a close and he had to leave. Otherwise therapy was torture for him because, with all of its possibility, it simply served as a reminder to him of all the things in life that he could not have. Here was a seven-year-old whose life possibilities were foreclosed. It is hardly surprising that he experienced depression and suicidal thoughts.

Megan came to see me when she was ten. Megan was an endearing child but she presented as somewhat eccentric. Her private school had recommended therapy because they were concerned about her social adjustment at school. She had difficulty negotiating friendships, and she had special difficulty in accepting that Adrienne, who Megan regarded as an exclusive friend, could also be friends with other girls in her class. Megan had difficulty feeling part of the group, and she had difficulty taking part in group activities. For instance, when children in her class would go outdoors to play soccer Megan preferred to sit on the swings and read or write in her journal. If the children pressed her to play she would become angry and defensive. Ten-year-old girls are notorious for forming cliques and ganging up on particular children, a process professionals refer to as relational aggression. The girls responded to Megan's outsiderness by excluding her. Megan felt terrible and when her peers invariably did not respond to her overtures to rejoin the group she would grow agitated and hurl accusations at them. School was a decidedly unhappy place for Megan and her deep compassion, her warm sense of humor, her deep interest in literature, and the novel she was writing, all apparently went unnoticed. At school her symptoms of maladjustment were prominent, and response to those by teachers and peers pretty much defined Megan as a troubled child.

In session Megan spent a lot of her time playing with Polly Pocket dolls and gradually she built rapport with me and talked about her life. Over a period of a couple of years Megan and I untangled both her complex school situation and a home life in which there was considerable tension. Her parents argued a lot and Megan, agitated by their arguments and the residual tensions in the family, would become distraught. I encouraged Megan to call me when she was upset, and she did so quite often. Her phone messages to me invariably began: "Hi Michael O'Loughlin, this is Megan. I need to speak with you right now..." I worked with her parents on conflict reduction and emotional communication. On one occasion, Megan's parents called me in a crisis. Megan had become upset over some conflict with her parents and she locked herself in her parents' bedroom and began systematically breaking and throwing everything in sight.

When the parents called me they were standing helplessly outside her door pleading with her to stop. After some complex negotiations she opened the door sufficiently to allow the phone to be passed through and I talked with her until she calmed down.

The difficulty Megan had managing her emotions became all too apparent one day in session. We had been working together for more than a year when she suggested we play Candyland. As I noted above, while this board game is designed for very young children, it is often a surprisingly popular choice among older children. During the course of the game I noticed that Megan was cheating. At one point, using sleight of hand, she took the Ice Princess card and placed it in the deck so that it would come up on her turn thereby assuring her of victory. This stratagem is exceedingly common among children. However, curious to see how she would deal with frustration, I used similar sleight of hand to steal the Ice Princess card from the discard pile and place it so that it came up on my turn also. When the card turned up on my turn I expressed delight at my good fortune but Megan grew enraged. She (correctly) accused me of cheating and when I responded by saying I thought it might be fun if we both used the Ice Princess card to help us win she grew extremely upset and she started shredding the cards. She took special care to shred the Ice Princess into multiple pieces. She fled my office inconsolably upset, and climbed onto her mother's lap and curled up in a fetal position.

Therapy resumed and the Candyland incident was not mentioned again. At the end of the year Megan made a transition to a large public school where her parents and I felt she might have more success. She has been extraordinarily successful academically. We phased out therapy but she comes to see me or consults me on the phone from time to time to smooth out any socialization difficulties she encounters, though she has been remarkably successful socially. About ten months after the Candyland incident, as therapy was terminating, Megan came to see me. "I brought you this," she said, as she entered my office. She opened her hand and handed me an exquisitely hand-drawn picture of an ice princess, drawn exactly the same size as the original card in the Candyland game. I thanked her for her gracious gift and I told her that this gift was a symbol of her success: From now on, I said, Megan knew that when things went wrong they could be put right. Having grown up in a family where repair was never done, and where every fight led to anger and then existential despair, Megan had managed to discover the power of reparative processes, and in doing so, she had stopped accumulating angst and despair from so much unfinished business. She was ready to move on.

Conclusion: Return of the Question Child

In a recent paper Deborah Britzman (2007) articulates the concept of the question child in psychoanalysis and suggests, as I do here, that much childhood suffering comes from the displacement of childhood desire by the demands of adult expectation. While there are differences between early childhood educational settings and childhood therapy settings, it seems we might all agree on the importance of assisting children in asking questions that lead them to truths that allow children to live their lives with ease rather than dis-ease. Furthermore, if early childhood teachers understand how to engage children in freeing experiences less children might develop the egregious symptoms that require the services of a therapist for relief.

· 3 ·

THE CURIOUS SUBJECT
OF THE CHILD

On Coming to Be

The four pictures are quite unremarkable. Two were taken in a photographer's studio on the occasion of my initiation into First Communion and Confirmation in the Catholic Church. In these black and white prints, all of us are smiling stiffly. The other two, taken by visitors with cameras, provide extremely rare documentary evidence of my existence as a child. I was excited to receive digital copies of these prints from one of my sisters as a gift for Christmas 2007. However, after studying them intently for a few minutes a wave of discomfort washed over me, and then a feeling of depression. I put them back in the envelope and did not dare reopen them until today, two months later. To my wife's suggestion that I have them framed, I brusquely said no, without explanation.

Why is it so difficult for me to look at these childhood pictures? Is it part of normal mourning for a childhood that has passed, never to be recovered? I have noticed that when my students complete the sentence stem "As I look back on my childhood I feel…" by far the most common response among students is a sense of loss that their childhoods are gone, never to return. Perhaps this is the powerful allure of Peter Pan's perpetual youth. Then again, following Alice Miller (e.g., 1997), it could be that entry into the world of parental demand is so alienating that we spend our lives in mourning or in denial about the losses of our childhood. It is hard for me to tell if my losses are uniquely particular to me or banal in their commonness. Either way, these photographs remind me of the powerful pull of my past and cause me to search for a nuanced understanding of what constitutes my coming to be in the world. Perhaps Roland Barthes is correct when, in *Camera Lucida* (1981) he claims that every photograph contains that "rather terrible thing... the return of the dead" (p. 9), since photographs evoke a profound sense of otherness and an invocation of the spectral self (p. 14). Barthes goes on to suggest that interesting photographs contain a *punctum* (p. 42), a detail from which it is possible to re-view events from an angle that opens up expansive possibilities. In Barthes' terms, these photographs seem, therefore, to have metonymic significance for me in opening up a window into my childhood.

I have noticed that I have pursued an understanding of my subjectivity in different ways. I have a theoretical understanding which is evolving continually and which is currently anchored in psychoanalytic understandings, particularly ideas drawn from Lacanian theory. My theoretical understanding is fairly muddled but I gravitate to theoretical writing because it places me at a safe distance from myself and my own experience. Theoretical writing is also heavily valued in the academy and writing in this genre, therefore, assuages some of my anxieties about acceptance in the academic world.

I also have a practical/performative understanding of my own being, and this is readily evident both in my teaching and in my clinical work as a therapist, and most especially when I work with children. Parts of my being that are often hidden from view—the childish parts—emerge in both arenas. I am frank, playful, silly, and imaginative. I am unguarded. I lie on the floor and build blocks with child patients and play frenzied competitive bouts of Connect Four or Candyland with a child who needs to lose tentativeness and experience unabashed *being*.[1] In my office a little boy plays with female Polly Pockets dolls to his heart's content, and recently a very tentative twelve-year old boy ventured to ask, "Do you think we could play Candyland?"

As a psychoanalyst I have learned to be aware of and use my unconscious. As I have acquired this capacity it is increasingly obvious to me that I have always taught performatively and the "pull" of my teaching has been my capacity to lay bare my unconscious and thereby open up a space for dialogue with the unconscious of my students. With respect to my teaching and therapeutic work

I know that my desire to engage others with possibilities of healing, inquiring, and imagining is in large part reparative (see Chapter 4 below). In healing others I heal myself. In freeing others from demand I free myself. Are we not always either speaking or avoiding speaking to the child within?

My third mode of inquiry is autobiographical. Introspection allows me to seek understanding within. Without such capacities I could neither teach well nor be a competent therapist as each vocation is anchored in *being*. While there is sometimes useful synchronicity between theoretical and autobiographical ways of knowing, often they are at odds. Even theoretical ways of knowing that claim to have transcended Enlightenment and Positivist modes of knowing are necessarily constructed from language and hence part of the symbolic realm. Lacan (1968) reminds us that language is inherently alienating, and Bakhtin (1986) reminds us that the words we use necessarily come with previously established meanings. Thus, we *come to be* through the Other, and find our being in the recognitions/misrecognitions and in the language of the Other. In academia this seems to be even more true. Losing myself in prevailing discursive locutions and having the illusion of understanding because I can ventriloquate through, for example, Lacanian discourse, is an ever present temptation.

In this chapter, however, I will resist that temptation, and I will seek to illuminate the multi-faceted nature of subjectivity through the prism of my own experience. In this way I hope to show that the essentializing binaries we use to characterize children are simplistic and false. Can we separate emotion from cognition? Is there a divide between the intrapsyhic and the external? Is it useful to separate the unconscious from the conscious or the present from the past? I hope to show that we can conceptualize childhood subjectivity more inclusively using rubrics such as *desire* and *curiosity* that operate through subjective mechanisms that transcend binaries.

Becoming is multi-faceted and holistic. It is also over-determined. As Judith Butler (1997) noted, becoming a subject is in large part a process of becoming *subject to* prevailing discursive practices, particularly as mediated by language and culture, a process Althusser (1971a) referred to as interpellation. The picture becomes even gloomier if we factor into the equation unconsciously transmitted phantomic trauma from the individual and collective experiences of our ancestors. Selma Fraiberg and colleagues speak of families that are "possessed by their ghosts," intruders that "have been present at the christening for two or more generations. While no one has issued an invitation, the ghosts take up residence and conduct the rehearsal of the family tragedy from a tattered script" (1975, p. 165).[2] So, in seeking to understand my subjectivity, I need to pay close attention to the tattered script, the unconscious determinants that have shaped my being through my upbringing in particular familial and cultural contexts.

This is My Father's Story

I am a "resistant writer." Sometimes I cannot figure out what is blocking my capacity to put words on paper. I want and need to write so I am not resisting in any conscious sense. I am unable to grope through my *resistances*—oops, sorry, I guess I am resistant after all—to say what I need to say. The frustrating part of it is that I thought I had this problem solved recently when I worked through some of the emotional issues that seemed to hold me back. In a paper I wrote at that time (O'Loughlin, 2007a—see also Chapter 6 below) I spoke of originary losses pertaining to my early hospitalization and I latched onto my identification with my father as one probable cause of my writing paralysis.

My father left school at fourth grade, though his education even prior to that was perfunctory. In the rural Ireland of the 1920s all of the boys in my father's school worked on the teacher's farm...well, almost all. The teacher's son was exempt because he would become a doctor and therefore had need of an education. When I was four I can recall reading the local newspaper aloud to my father. An abiding memory from my childhood is the drone of my mother's voice drifting from the fireside to my bedroom. She read an entire book about the sinking of the Titanic aloud to my father in an attempt to respond to his genuinely puzzled query: "What are you reading all them books for?"

I did not think less of my father for his lack of access to literacy. I felt pain watching his labored script as he signed his name. I followed his lips as they moved from word to word as he laboriously read snippets from the local newspaper. I heard my father tell my mother, with abject humiliation, how a neighbor would draw his attention to something in the newspaper: "Patrick, have you read this?" and snicker and wink at her husband when he invariably replied, "I can't read it now. I forgot my glasses." In his later years, now on disability after a construction accident, my father had the means to buy a used car. A well-meaning neighbor suggested to him that they both attend the local technical school for a course on routine car maintenance. My father was excited, and then a week before the class was to begin, the neighbor said to him: "You can ride in with me on Wednesday. Just bring a notebook and a pen." Needless to say, my father had to make his excuses, and only my mother knew of his shame. He was ashamed. She was wrenched by his abjection. In speaking with my dad, especially once I began college, I worked very hard to modulate my vocabulary so as not to embarrass him. It is striking to me that one of the last topics my father discussed with me while suffering from terminal cancer, was his great regret that he had never learned to read well. What could I, privileged to be writing my Ph.D. dissertation in New York at that time, possibly say to him? In attempting to protect his feelings, did I acquire his shame? Can it be that the more I achieve, the more I need to hide my accomplishments?

The easy psychoanalytic explanation, then, is that my holding back is a mechanism to protect my father, or perhaps even a mechanism to protect myself from the kind of abject feelings that might come my way from criticism if I exposed my ignorance in public. All of this is actually true, but it is by no means the whole story. My identification with my father is troubled by the knowledge, gleaned from my mother just a few years ago, that my father was profoundly anti-intellectual. "Oh sure, he wanted you to be a teacher," she said, "but he thought you were mad to give up your teaching job to go back to school. To him that was a pure waste of time." I was stunned. I had always imagined his support. I replay these sentences as I try to understand my last conversations with my dad where I tried to find some way to explain to him the meaning of intellectual work, and particularly why my dissertation work was taking so long! I needed him to see value in the hill that I was struggling to climb.

I had left his world for a symbolic world and I lacked the tools to meta-phorize my experience in ways that might make any sense to him. I have to believe that he rooted for me to succeed even though he had no idea what I was trying to achieve. My desire to know and to share knowledge, today, is compromised by deep ambivalence about sharing my knowledge. *This* is my resistance. Heretically, sometimes I even have doubts about the merits of creating knowledge: Is this thing that I do *real work*? Where are the scars that might prove my worth?

Moving Up from the Bottom of the Class

My identifications are troubled too by the terrible wish from my parents that I grow up to *not* be like them. Reading Valerie Walkerdine's *Schoolgirl fictions* (1990) offers a painful reminder of the complexity of identification and the difficulty of holding onto a sense of belonging when you leave home.[3] My dad would show me the chemical burns on his hands from the cement after a long day spent finishing concrete floors. Workers like him had no protective gear, not even gloves. "You have to stay in school. You don't want to be like me," he would say, showing me his damaged hands and soiled clothes. He may have been unable to access intellectual discourses but he did not need to read Bourdieu or Foucault to comprehend the regimes of power associated with credentials in a highly class-stratified society. He wanted an easier and more dignified life for me. Having given up on me becoming a priest, he wanted me to become a teacher.

Being the ambivalent and dutiful child that I was, I tried to take both sides of the road. I worked diligently in school, and I also helped my father—perpetually busy in his spare time building and gardening—even though I loathed manual work. When he was building an extension on our house that made us, the poorest people in the neighborhood, the first ones with indoor plumbing I would talk with him and be his helper until late in frosty winter evenings. It was the vigil of my childhood. As an adolescent I worked on construction sites next to him feeling an odd mix of pride and shame. I was in his world, but not of his world. I was slipping away to another place. I found myself developing increasing contempt for our rural community and our working-class ways. Ours was the kind of household where, if an intellectual discussion came on television, somebody would turn down the volume. They would have changed the channel, but back then there was only a single channel! Aspiring to college, I won a scholarship to the better of the two nearby secondary schools where the bumpiness of my path to the middle-class became apparent on the first day.

On that day the head of the school, a priest, welcomed the new students, most of them robustly middle-class, with the admonition that he knew we were all *thick and rich*.[4] Instead of being an induction into the middle-class, this school was for me a perpetual reminder of my outsider status. I was neither thick nor rich. I was perpetually Other, and I think, perhaps, this marks one of the key points of my entry into alienation. I became a *stranger to myself* to use Kristeva's (1991) felicitous term. I was marked as Other by my poverty, marked as Other by my mode of speech, and while undoubtedly desiring of bourgeois success I felt completely lost. I did not want what I had, and I could not comprehend what was being offered to me, except I knew that I was instinctively suspicious of it. What happens if you desire something and resent the object of desire simultaneously because you see the pain that its absence has wrought for your parents?

Art Spiegelman's tale of his father's difficulty in adjusting to middle-class life post-Holocaust in Rego Park, New York (Spiegelman, 2003) points to the tragedy when somebody faces the end of life as they knew it and cannot find new subjective meaning in existence. The terrible crisis faced by Chief Plenty

Coups and the Crow Nation after the elimination of the buffalo and the only way of life they knew also points to the appalling prospects when the only life that gives meaning to existence is no longer possible (Lear, 2006).[5] While I would not want to measure my crisis against such events, nevertheless it was a crisis in subjectivity that left me bereft of certainty. Some children, faced with such loss react to the nothingness by constructing new subjective possibilities in a process Lear calls *radical hope*.[6] It is a pressing question for me why, in the face of such annihilation, I lacked the resilience to articulate an unflinching desire. It is not that I did not *feel* such desires. I did feel them. However, I consciously suppressed them or tended to them only in the most secret recesses of my being.

One day, in twelfth grade, the same redoubtable head of school came into my class. We were the "A" stream students, the highest achievers in the school. He asked each of us to fill out an application form, I think perhaps for a civil service competition. The forms were in Gaelic. When it came to entering the information on "father's occupation" I hesitated. The Gaelic word for "laborer" is *sclábhai*. It is also the Gaelic term for "slave." I did not want to write it. He saw the blank spot on my page and (knowing full well) said in a bullying tone "What does your father do?" I mumbled a reply and then he loudly ordered me to enter *sclábhai* on the form. I could have lied. Instead I chose to comply.

When the guidance counselor, another priest, invited students to sign up for meetings with him regarding their college plans I had the temerity to make an appointment. He upbraided me for wasting his time. Since I had no money, I needed to get a job as a civil servant or bank clerk, he said. Why was I wasting his time since university was out of the question? I retreated in confusion. Nevertheless, wanting to blend in, and, no doubt, nurturing some illusion of hope, I paid my £5 and went on a coach trip to University College Galway that year with the college-bound seniors. The bus passed right by my house on the way home and I asked the driver to stop a quarter mile further down the road so that my humble origins would not be evident to all.

What effect can such self-loathing have on a child? If you do not want to be what you are, and cannot allow yourself to be what you are becoming, what is your fate? In a world of binaries and non-porous boundaries, and particularly in a world where, because you cannot voice what you feel to anybody, a world where "the thread of speech has been radically cut" (Davoine & Gaudillière, 2004, p. 71), what hope is there for acquiring the comprehensive narrative of a particular subjectivity?

Shame came all too easily. We wore home-made clothes instead of store-bought clothes. We sometimes carried home-made schoolbags instead of store-bought backpacks. We ate sandwiches made from home-made bread with just butter in the center. We rarely had pocket money. Although we lived in a farming community we came from a publicly subsidized rural house instead of from a farmhouse. While there were plenty of children as economically marginal as we were, and some even worse, we were among those marked as Other by our residence, by our clothing, and by our lack of roots in the community.[7]

We were fortified by our mother's anger. She labeled people who inflicted petty humiliations on us "stinkers," and she vowed that we would live to see the day when "castles fall and dung hills rise." My father was a practical man who knew his place. He was excessively deferential to priests, doctors, and teachers, and whatever assertiveness he had in dealing with his peers, was subsumed once he encountered authority. My dad tiled bathrooms and did handyman work in his spare time for more affluent people. He was beloved, though poorly paid, by many. But, like Southern blacks in the U.S., he knew his place and was careful to use the back entrance.[8] I will not use the back entrance, but like Mr. Elliot, entering the Royal Ballet with trepidation for his son's audition (Daldry, 2001), I am not so sure I want to use the main door either.

A Haunted House

As I child I delighted in reading *Ireland's Own*, a popular magazine that always had a melodramatic spooky story as its centerpiece. In those days I did not think of our own modern house as haunted, but it is increasingly clear the ghosts were everywhere. In psychoanalysis and in the related field of hauntology[9] ghostly memories are thought of as those memories of traumatic events that were denied symbolization and pass on from generation to generation unless somebody brings them to the light of day and exposes them to the possibilities of being spoken and therefore symbolized and ultimately worked through. Referring to the trauma of the Aboriginal peoples of Australia, Judy Atkinson (2002) describes these kinds of unconscious memories as *trauma trails* that can be traced across generations.

There is a considerable literature on the mechanisms by which trauma transmission occurs.[10] A calamitous consequence of wars and genocides, and of many natural disasters, is that trauma goes unprocessed and unnamed and thereby creates a disastrous legacy for future generations. Consider, for example, Ellen, a patient whom therapist Annie Rogers describes in *The unsayable* (2006). Ellen was brought for therapy at age 11, having become the victim of repeated sexual abuse. During her treatment she began to have dreams about Nazi soldiers. Eventually it emerged that her step-aunt had been the victim of sexual assault by the Gestapo in Paris in 1945. Her mother had gone to great pains to keep this knowledge from Ellen to protect her from the horror. Little did she realize that Ellen had already unconsciously received the knowledge and was acting it out in her dreams and in her behavior.

Esther Rashkin notes in *Family Secrets* (1992) that secretiveness and shame drive traumatic knowledge underground where it continues to maintain its potency. In families not all children are necessarily trauma bearers. Some children appear to have unusual receptivity and these children then become the symptom bearers who are destined to carry this unconscious knowledge for their family or community. Traumatic ancestral memory can produce symptoms in successive generations or can apparently lie dormant until activated. The reactivation of ethnic hatreds in the former Yugoslavia, leading ultimately to the Bosnian war and ethnic cleansing, was powered by artfully reawakened memories of Serb losses at the Battle of Serbia in 1390. High levels of incidence of sexual abuse and domestic violence in indigenous communities in Australia and North America could similarly be argued to be manifestations of unprocessed ancestral trauma[11] and, though I have seen no evidence for this, I would not be surprised if the high incidence of alcohol consumption in Ireland had similar origins.

I have little knowledge of the familial history of my parents and their ancestors. I do, however, know a considerable amount about the many great tragedies of Irish history, and I received a stark reminder of perhaps the greatest of those tragedies, The Great Famine, when a mass grave filled with Famine era skeletons was discovered a few hundred yards from my home when I was ten. My parents were but three generations removed from our ancestors who watched a million compatriots die, and who somehow managed to survive genocide through starvation to perpetuate our family line to this day. While I have experienced profound sadness and despair reading and viewing accounts of the Holocaust (e.g., Amery, 1998; Lanzmann, 2000; Levi, 1989, 1996; Wiesel, 1982), nothing has approached the depth of sadness I felt the first time I read *The great hunger* (Woodham-Smith, 1962), the definitive account of the Great Famine of the 1840s, when I was sixteen. Is it because that work evokes ancestral memory within me that I had such a deep response? Is this why I have resisted revisiting *The great hunger* for thirty years? Were there any traces of that terrible catastrophe in my parents' lives, and if there were, what effect have they had on how I came to be as a child? Are the marks of such an event discernible in what might be called an *Irish subjectivity* in general and on my subjectivity in particular? Without memorial exercises to confront such losses will these phantoms continue to tumble through time, haunting future generations?[12]

One could argue that in some respects such questions are unanswerable. As a psychoanalyst I know there are two clues that are informative. First, we know that hidden trauma will make its presence felt through *symptoms*. Second, Lacanian psychoanalysts are trained to look for manifestations of unconscious events in signifiers disguised in the language of everyday life. With respect to symptoms, I know that throughout his life my father experienced debilitating panic attacks. Of course, during my childhood, we did not have the vocabulary of the DSM-IV (American Psychiatric Association, 2000) to assist us in naming them as such, but we knew for sure something highly abnormal was happening when my father would wake in the night with what looked like a heart attack, but which our mother insisted was not a heart attack. "It'll go away in a while, just wait," she would say with evident trepidation as my siblings and I gathered around my flailing father. And, indeed, after some hours of soothing, my father would become calm and life would return to a tentative normal until the next recurrence.

In my childhood days there were no community psychiatric hospitals or psychiatric doctors, not to mention therapists. There was, however, a *lunatic asylum* within two miles of my house. We would hear the blast of the industrial whistle that signaled the end of the work day for the inmates who worked outdoors tending the gardens and doing laundry behind nine-foot walls. To admit the possibility of mental disturbance was to admit to insanity and risk admission to the asylum, perhaps never to return. Therefore we maintained a furtive silence, not knowing then that the secrets and silence we so assiduously cultivated were insidious perpetuators of the mental trauma we sought to hide.

This is [a Fragment from] My Mother's Story

I gained further insight into the power of shame in creating walls of secrecy when I decided last year to interview my mother about her early life experiences. The anxiety I experienced at the prospect of asking her was surely indicative that I was aware of the taboo of ambient ghosts. My mother consented, but then she grew agitated. "There wouldn't be any point in me talking to you," she said, "because I couldn't tell you the bad things. They are too awful. I wouldn't want anyone to know them." She was not persuaded by my argument that it would be helpful to me in understanding myself, and understanding how I came to be. Her argument appeared to be partly composed of a suggestion that such painful memories are best forgotten, and partly that revelation of abject memories could only perpetuate shame. In *Holocaust testimonies* (1991) Lawrence Langer notes that not only could some Holocaust survivors not easily testify to their experience, but, for people with certain categories of traumatization, resurrection of the memories only lent itself to retraumatization.

Ethically, therefore, I needed to proceed carefully with my mother, and one of the assurances that I gave her is that I would not write about the specifics of her experience without first eliciting her approval of anything I might write. After this negotiation we proceeded, and what surprised me most, I think, was that the memories that were shameful to her were not for the most part memories of particular traumas, but simply memories of the everyday abjection of severe poverty. She reminisced about the fact that her sister and she shared one good frock, and therefore alternated days attending school, despite the fact that both loved learning intensely. She spoke repeatedly of the daily humiliations of rural poverty, repeatedly prefacing her remarks with "You won't believe this" or "I can't believe we had it that hard."

During my mother's childhood tuberculosis was rampant in Ireland. Since the disease was highly contagious, and since this was prior to the development of a vaccine, contraction of the disease was a death sentence, and sufferers were isolated in facilities known as workhouses. At the youthful age of thirty, having three children under ten, my mother's mother went to hospital to deliver her fourth baby, and was then transferred from there to the workhouse, where she died in due course from tuberculosis. My mother had one recollection of her mother prior to her illness. That was when she baked a cake for the children for some occasion. "I can't remember her face," she said, "but I remember pure kindness." She also recalls one visit to see her mother in the workhouse, but all she can remember is tears. My mother's older sister, aged 10, having eavesdropped on her father making plans to put the children in an orphanage after their mother's death, smuggled a letter into the workhouse to inform their mother of his intentions. Her mother then made their father swear to raise the children himself. In view of what we have since learned about Irish orphanages of the period, that was a most fortunate outcome.[13]

The children were never told of their mother's impending death. Rooting through a chest of clothing at home one day, the children found what they thought was a brown dress. When they asked their father about it, he told them to ask their grandmother. She harshly told them it was the habit in which their mother was to be buried. When their mother finally died, the children were not even informed. When I asked if any process was put in place to assist the children in mourning, my mother looked at me in amazement for making such a naïve inquiry: "It was awful hard...I can't think of anything like it...Every time we heard that someone died I felt like I was going to vomit...It had an awful effect on us...Don't talk of it." The regimen of domestic servitude and deprivation only intensified thereafter until finally she and her sister were old enough to enter domestic service for other families.

In my mother's family we have generations of a family of rural Irish people, victims of severe deprivation and suffering in the present, bearers of untold trauma from a genocidal famine, and apparently incapable of providing any kind of psychological sustenance for my mother and her siblings who had suffered such immediate catastrophic losses. There was a certain hardness in the Ireland of my youth and earlier when it came to children's emotions. This is evident, for example, in Frank McCourt's widely read *Angela's ashes* (1996), a work, that was received in parts of Ireland with considerable resentment. Writing in 1991, Anthony Clare, one of Ireland's leading psychiatrists, characterized Irish culture as "A culture heavily impregnated by an emphasis on physical control, original sin, cultural inferiority and psychological defensiveness" (p. 14), and he quotes an Irish psychiatrist writing on Irish child-rearing practices in 1976:

> The family home in Ireland is a novitiate for violence. Even from the cradle the child is made to feel rejection, hostility, and open physical pain. The infant is left to cry in his cot because his mother does not want to "give in to him." Later he is smacked with the hand or a stick. He is made to go to bed early. He is not allowed to have his tea. He is put in a room by himself...and in order to invite this morale breaking treatment from his parents, all the Irish child has to do is to be *normal*. It is the normality of childhood that sets parents' teeth on edge. They take no joy in childishness. (Quoted in Clare, 1991, pp. 15–16)

Sitting with my mother and attempting to wrap my mind around the indescribable nature of her unmourned losses was an unforgettable experience for me. Part of my heaviness of heart undoubtedly came from my empathy with my mothers' legacy of suffering, and part no doubt came from the indubitable realization that my subjectivity was formed in the crucible of my mother's losses. I also marvel that, despite her upbringing, and contrary to my father's more incommunicative and heavy-handed approach, my mother managed to transcend her pain and raise her children with fortitude, love and empathy.

So, in addition to structuring my being around fixing my father's intellectual deficiencies, without of course claiming so much credit that I might put him in the shade, it seems that I also have structured my emotional being around repairing my lonely mother's inner child through incessantly teaching teachers the importance of creating reparative experiences for children in school, and through my own direct efforts to create reparative experiences through my therapeutic work with children.

And then I Went to School

Although Western societies propagate the myth of the child as innocent, and of child development as a process of unfettered intrapsychic growth, the cynicism behind this view is evident in the ways in which even the most supposedly liberal and democratic societies control the process of schooling. The rhetoric of liberal and progressive education is wedded to a rhetoric of cultural transmission and ideological control that shapes the subjectivity of children in very specific ways. As Jonathan Lear (2006) noted, to be a member of the Crow nation required seeing the world in a particular Crow way. Cultural rituals, rites of initiation, and apprenticeships often serve this function for groups. For post-industrial societies, schooling serves as the major mechanism of cultural socialization and homogenization. There is considerable literature both on how western institutions foster a particular kind of consumer self-hood in people, and on how schools, in particular, socialize children into knowing their place in the particular segment of the social order made available to them.[14] Despite liberal hand-wringing over schooling, governments have continued to develop very specific accountability mechanisms for schools in order to control the aspirations and desires—and hence the subjectivities—of their citizens.

While freedom and desire may be possible, too often the constraints on subjectivity are such that children's horizons are foreshortened. As Gregory Jay noted, schools feature a pedagogy of *consumption* rather than a pedagogy of active *production* (1987, p. 798). This does not surprise me. If society's demand is that citizens become *consumers* (of ideas, goods) then it makes sense to apprenticeship them in consumption. If society wished for children to be *originators* (of ideas, inventions) educational experiences would be structured radically differently so that expansive narratives of self and society could be imagined and lived.

The workings of these processes can best be seen in the language of schooling. Does schooling speak to the unconscious and enable the articulation of desire and curiosity or is school a place where conversations about the subjective possibilities of the child's being are shut down? Too often, schools shut down subjective possibilities for children. Some children are lucky enough, either alone or with assistance, to transcend the palette of available identificatory possibilities so that they do not limit themselves to slots in predetermined narratives. Although subjugated, I made some efforts along those lines as a child.

For the most part, my schooling mirrored the kind of experience described by Charles Dickens (1854/1994) in *Hard times*. The teacher was not the *subject supposed to know*. The teacher *did* know. The children were ignorant recipients of the teacher's knowledge. As Oliver Goldsmith stated in *The village schoolmaster*, a poem from my childhood, "And still they gaz'd, and still the wonder grew, that one small head could carry all he knew" (Goldsmith, 1770/2003). The environment in which our mastery of skills and facts took place was crafted to maximize anxiety and fear so that we were neurotically focused entirely on the demand of the teacher. At first, avoidance of punishment and the winning of approval was all that mattered. Later, the emphasis deftly shifted to the pursuit of grades and credentials as means of satisfying external demand. Apart from acquiring a high capacity for conformity and a high level of the kind of neurotic personality characteristics described so ably by Karen Horney (1991) and Harry Stack Sullivan (1968), the subjective possibilities were abysmal. *Did you get it done? Did you get it right? How many did you get wrong?* These were the trembling queries we posed to each other. And as for the catastrophic consequences of failure, these came in the form of the daily ritual of *Sín amach do lábh!* [Open up the palm of your hand] as we waited for the delivery of slaps from the teacher's rod, a switch that one of us had personally been ordered to pluck for him from a nearby ash tree. Anxiety. Fear. Humiliation. Anxiety. Fear. Humiliation. Anxiety. Fear. Humiliation. Annihilation...

The subjective possibilities of schooling ultimately come down to the possibilities of language. If teachers *know* and students are thereby recipients of inert facts, then subjective possibilities are killed off. If teachers recognize that children contain unconscious knowledge, and that this can be brought into conversation so that curiosity and desire are engendered in the child this opens up possibilities for the construction of agentic narratives of their lives. In Lacanian terms,[15] in order for the child to become the *sujet-supposé-savoir* ("the-subject-supposed-to-know") the teacher must relinquish the position of omniscience and allow the student's *lack* to emerge in the form of questions. Recognition of the child's questions and an awareness by the teacher of the need to become a receptor for the child until the child can assume the *sujet-supposé-savoir* position creates an opportunity for the kind of agentic dialogue that allows the child to begin to construct a narrative of possibility for his or her own subjectivity. Judicious selection of literature that opens the possibilities of historical memory, and an invitation to adopt multiple subject positions relating to *difference*, to *knowing*, to *history*, and to *imagination* only serve to expand subjective possibilities further.

Some children appear willing to go to extraordinary lengths to fight *misrecognition* and come to be seen as beings-in-their-own-right. My two favorite examples are Billy Elliot, the main character in the move of the same title (Daldry, 2003) and Ludo, the main character of *Ma vie en rose* (Berliner, 1997). Billy fights valiantly to become a ballet dancer, despite growing up in a staunchly homophobic and sexist working-class British community, and Ludo battles gender stereotypes and familial and community prejudice so that he can lay claim to his feminine self. Notably, Billy received powerful affirmative mirroring from his deceased mother, and Ludovic received similar recognition from his oddly vibrant grandmother.

I was not so strong. It was not lack of indignation or imagination that hampered me, so much as sufficient *misrecognition* to cause me to feel that I needed to harbor my hopes and dreams internally. There were three notable exceptions, and each, though small, contributed in important ways to my capacity to claim my place as a *sujet-supposé-savoir*. The first occurred when I was seven. In our three-room schoolhouse we had the same teacher for grades 2–4. She was a young teacher, newly married, and she spent practically every day of the three years I spent in her room creating art and craft projects for her house. The only time she made an effort to teach was when the feared School Inspector arrived for his annual visit. Much as children are pressed into service today to do well on standardized tests to save the school's skin, we were pressed into service to save her from the wrath of Mr. Inspector.

The Inspector examined us orally for hours, and then, as he was writing up his observations, he summoned me to the front of the room. Quaking with fear, burning under the anxious gaze of my classmates, I walked forward. He spoke to me kindly. He asked me my name. Then he asked me what my father did in order to assess my economic status. He asked me if I intended to go to secondary school and university, and I was too embarrassed and confused to answer coherently. He told me I was a bright boy, and that I should think about this for the future. Later that evening, when I told my parents about the encounter, I cannot recall mentioning the university part. I think I had already acquired a disposition where the anticipation of that much entitlement was more than I could handle.

Our headmaster taught fifth and sixth grade, and he derived much of his social status from preparing sixth-graders for local exams that allowed top achievers to win scholarships to pay secondary school tuition. As his most promising student I was drilled by rote on all aspects of the test, and we prepared canned compositions so that there would be no surprises on the exam. We also had an Irish oral recitation requirement. In addition to the simple school poems, my mother had acquired from my uncle, a fluent Gaelic speaker, a lengthy mournful elegy to some child who had died in a snowstorm. It began: *"Is cuimhin liom an sneachta mór"* ["I remember the great snowfall"], and descended into misery from there. She insisted I memorize it so as to stand out during the competition. On the day of the recitation, when the examiner scrutinized my list he asked me to pick a poem. Instead of choosing the mournful poem, I said it didn't matter to me and asked him to choose. He picked the simplest poem on the list and I recited it perfectly. During the English exam I ignored the canned composition topic for which I had been so thoroughly prepared. Instead I wrote an essay on "Books," the topic of my choice.

My teacher met with me after the exam and when I told him my topic choice for the essay, and how I had handled the oral exam, he stalked off, got in his car, and drove immediately to see my mother to tell her that I had failed. "After all our preparation he wrote about 'Books'," he said contemptuously. When I arrived home on my bicycle an hour later, my mother was despondent. I explained what I did, though I felt despondent and unsure of myself. Needless to say, I did very well and earned a scholarship, but my teacher never apologized for his behavior.

My entire secondary school experience was forgettable except for Denis Canty. In my junior year, in what must have been a fit of temporary madness, my straitlaced school hired a drama teacher. Denis taught us improvisation, and was the only teacher I ever encountered who began each class with "Well boys, what would you like to do today?" It was an incredible gift.

So that is My Story

That is my story, and if I have succeeded I trust it will serve as an invitation to you, the reader, to engage in dialogue around the expansive possibilities of subjectivity.

· 4 ·

THE DEVELOPMENT OF
SUBJECTIVITY IN YOUNG CHILDREN:
THEORETICAL AND PEDAGOGICAL
CONSIDERATIONS

Subjectivity describes our sense of being in the world. Notions such as individual identity and autonomous self are problematic because they postulate static and essential notions of selfhood, and because they are premised on the assumption that we can separate ourselves from the world and define ourselves independently of it. Nothing could be further from the truth. Children are born into families and communities that embody specific languages and discursive practices. The challenge of developing our subjectivity, as Judith Butler (1997) noted, is in enabling ourselves to become vibrant living subjects who identify with particular cultures and discourse practices, without simultaneously becoming totally subject to those same ideologies and discursive practices. The line between subjectivity and subjection is a fine one. My interest, in this chapter, is in exploring the tension these factors produce in children as they come to name their own subjectivities. How much, I wonder, are children's emerging subjectivities circumscribed by the norms of family, community, and society, and how much by intrapsychic processes within each child, and in what ways are the tensions between these forces reconciled by individual children?

We become subjects through processes of identification and disidentification. We clarify our gender and ethnic identity, for example, by some combination of identification with desired gender- or ethnically-identified objects, and disidentification with objects that we perceive as other-than-what-we-desire. The idea that we clarify our subjectivity through identification is intuitive, but it is problematic, as Van Ausdale & Feagin's (2001) research indicates, to the extent that children identify with characteristics that are antisocial or socially retrogressive. Teachers are frequently troubled, for instance, at the prospect of working with young children who come to school with misogynist, homophobic, or racist identifications. The notion that disidentifications are involved in the development of subjectivity raises other troubling questions. If, as this notion suggests, some people define their subjectivity primarily in terms of what they are not, what does this suggest about the obstacles to developing harmonious intergroup relations in our society? For example, in early Freudian thought, possession of a penis was everything and masculinity was the norm by which gender was defined. Boys had a penis and girls envied them for it.

Now, however, some authors suggest that early identification with the mother is a key process in gender formation. These authors suggest that, early on, young boys begin to experience femaleness as the norm and apparently feel the need to disidentify with that norm in order to claim a male gender identity (e.g., Greenson, 1978; Stiver, 1991). If this is so, masculinity may develop primarily through disidentification with nurturance and other maternal characteristics, leaving us to wonder what effect such an inherent rejection of femaleness may have on the male psyche. A similar process appears to be at work in racial identity formation for some groups. While it would seem, intuitively, that identification with one's own racial or ethnic group is essential to identity formation, some writers suggest that, at least for Caucasians, the development of a white racial identity may depend as much on defining an Other that they are not, as on defining some essential characteristics of whiteness with which to identify (Cushman, 1995; Fanon, 1967; Roediger, 1998). Again, we are left to wonder what the long-term effects of such a polarizing process of identity formation might be.

Some elements of this way of thinking about subjectivity are well established and appear to constitute a canonical narrative of early personality development. Proponents of attachment theory argue that a child's personality develops in dialectical interaction with primary caregivers. Donald Winnicott (1965) once observed that there is no such thing as "a baby," meaning that babies can only be thought about in relation with primary caregivers. The standard narrative of child development (e.g., DeHart et al., 2000) uses a mixture of ideas from attachment theory (e.g., Ainsworth et al., 1978; Bowlby, 1982, 1988; Sroufe, 1995) and psychosocial theory (Erikson, 1963) to highlight issues such as the importance of early attachment in emotional development, the role of caregiver attunement in creating an effective holding environment for the infant, and the development of basic trust as the springboard from which a child launches her or his exploration of the world, an exploration that moves in ever-widening circles away from the central fulcrum provided by a reliable caregiver. Attachment theory has significant face validity. The experience of therapists working with adults with either personality disorders or significant relational difficulties (e.g., Kohut, 1971, 1977; Miller, 1987, 1997; Sullivan, 1968; Winnicott, 1965) points persistently to the long-term effects of failures in the early relational environment of the child. Nevertheless, attachment theory has its limitations, principal among which are insufficient attention to unconscious processes of identification, insufficient attention to the discursive and cultural contexts of children's lives, and failure to look beyond the child as an individual to the effect of group experiences on the development of children's subjectivities.

My purpose here is to present the outlines of a theory of subjectivity that is anchored in processes of identification. I begin by outlining Melanie Klein's theory of the development of individual subjectivity through early object relations. Klein's focus is unconscious forces within infants that cause them to seek out relationships in the world, and the consequences for a child's personality formation of the ways in which primary caregivers in the child's life respond to those basic needs and impulses. Then, using neo-Kleinian writings, I widen the inquiry to explore what happens to subject formation as the child begins to move from dyadic interaction with single caregivers to awareness of a sense of belonging to particular groups. Here I explore the effect of group membership on the child's evolving sense of subjectivity and capacity to define self both through processes of group identification and disidentification. In the concluding section, I explore ways in which specific discursive environments at home and at school can either open up possibilities for expanded subject identification for children or limit those possibilities.

A subtext to this inquiry is my concern about the development of hatred in children. Hatred appears to be premised on capacities for defining Others who are different from ourselves on whom we can vent our aggression and bad feelings. By understanding the processes by which children come to identify and disidentify with certain people, I am hopeful that we can understand more about such processes and perhaps understand better how to intervene to help children develop positive and empathic identifications. In this chapter, I use racial identifications as a prototypical case, but there is no reason to assume that similar mechanisms of identifying sameness and marking difference are not at work in the differentiation of gender, class, sexual orientation, and other aspects of subjectivity.

Caregiver–Child Relations and the Development of Early Identifications: a Kleinian perspective

Melanie Klein's theory is a story of the struggle between love and hate in human development. She explains human subjectivity, and the ways in which we manage love and hate, through a theory of object relations (e.g., Klein, 1964, 1984a, 1984b, 1984c, 1984d; Mitchell, 1987; Ogden, 1992; Segal, 1975). Her concern is with the ways in which infants organize their experience as they move from being totally merged with the mother at birth to eventually becoming aware of their own separate existences, and developing satisfying relations with the objects in their world. Evidence of successful relating, which Klein characterizes as the depressive position, can be seen in children and adults who have developed a fairly fixed sense of selfhood and who have a "capacity for guilt, mourning, empathy, gratitude, and so on" (Ogden, 1992, p. 614). The other pole of experience, referred to by Klein as the paranoid-schizoid position, refers to a less satisfactory state of relatedness, one in which people with inadequate means of negotiating the relational world grow "heavily reliant on splitting, idealization, denial, projective identification, and omnipotent thinking as modes of defense and ways of organizing experience" (Ogden, 1992, p. 614).

Although the more extreme paranoid-schizoid symptoms are seen only in people with significant personality disorders, all of us start out, in the first 6 months or so after birth, in a paranoid-schizoid position. We are likely to revert to that position whenever our ability to manage our relational world fragments. Klein's theory is not a linear or stage theory of development. She believed that throughout life we teeter on the edge of depressive and paranoid-schizoid modes of being depending on the context and the degree of persecutory anxiety or security it evokes.

Managing Feelings of Love and Hate

Klein (1984c) argues that from early infancy the infant experiences significant anxiety that must be discharged. The earliest object relation is a phantasied relation with the breast. Klein suggests that the ego splits the phantasied breast into good and bad breasts. Good feelings from the infant are projected onto the good breast, and are in turn introjected by the infant as evidence of its goodness. Klein notes, "the projection of good feelings and good parts of the self into the mother is essential for the infant's ability to develop good object relations and integrate his ego" (p. 9). She argues, "the introjection of the good object, first of all mother's breast, is a precondition for normal development" (p. 9). "The more often gratification at the breast is experienced and fully accepted," Klein tells us in her essay on envy and gratitude, "the more often enjoyment and gratitude, and accordingly the wish to return pleasure are felt. This recurrent experience makes possible gratitude on the deepest level and plays an important role in the capacity to make reparation" (p. 189).

As noted earlier, Klein characterizes the period immediately following birth as the paranoid-schizoid position. This period is presumed to be a very difficult period. Aggressive impulses threaten to overwhelm the infant, who resorts to a wide range of defensive mechanisms to protect itself from these frightening impulses. Among these are splitting, idealization, feelings of omnipotence and projective identification. One of the infant's impulses is to expel the bad parts of the self. Expulsion entails a splitting of the ego, so that the mother can serve as good and bad breast simultaneously. As Paula Heimann (1991) noted:

> Thus, "good" breast and "bad" breast, inner breast and outer breast appear in his [sic] feeling and phantasy in close alternation. The whole mental life of the infant revolves about and develops from the phantasies of a "good" and a "bad" breast in the inner and outer world. (p. 522)

Failure of early object relations leaves the infant to live with his own aggression. Having expelled this onto the mother, that is the bad breast, through a process known as projective identification, the infant identifies with the projected bad self, and experiences his own aggression coming back at him in persecutory ways. Klein (1964) summarized the process this way:

> Unpleasant experiences, and the lack of enjoyable ones, in the young child, especially lack of happy and close contact with loved people, increase ambivalence, diminish trust and hope, and confirm anxieties about inner annihilation and external persecution; moreover they slow down, and perhaps permanently check the beneficial processes through which in the long run security is achieved. (p. 347)

Such a child, struggling for wholeness, faces enormous obstacles. If early splitting and projection processes continue because of the unavailability of a consistently loving good object, or because of a child's failure to introject an available loving object, the child continues to project the bad parts of itself outward. Identifying with this projected part, the child then experiences its own aggression as persecutory, thus increasing its distrust of the world. At the same time, the adults in the child's world who experience the child's projected aggression are less likely to respond in consistently loving ways, thus further confirming the child's paranoid response. Klein (1984c) describes this destructive cycle as follows:

> If we contrast the individuals who are capable of bearing frustration without too great resentment and can soon regain their balance after a disappointment with those who are inclined to put the whole blame on to the outer world, we can see the detrimental effect of hostile projection. For projection of grievance rouses in other people a counter-feeling of hostility. Few of us have the tolerance to put up with the accusation, even if it is not expressed in words, that we are in some ways the guilty party. In fact, it very often makes us dislike such people, and we appear all the more as enemies to them; in consequence they regard us with increased persecutory feelings and suspicions, and relations become more and more disturbed. (p. 257)

Reparation, according to Klein, is a super-ego function that causes a child to experience feelings of guilt at its own destructive impulses and to make reparation to preserve its good objects. Klein sees the accompanying anxiety—an anxiety associated with the depressive position—as a productive anxiety in that it leads the child to develop the capacity for empathy that allows a child to enter into truly mutual loving object relations. Klein's theory is more complex than this brief summary might suggest, and it is also very suggestive. If we want children to grow up to be responsible, and caring, that is to exhibit reparative characteristics such as guilt, mourning, empathy, gratitude, love and a capacity for sharing and mutual sacrifice, it is important that we raise them in a mutually loving environment in which they have opportunities to express love and accept love from their surrounds. The expressing and accepting of love involves positive processes of projection and introjection. As Klein (1964) notes, both projection and introjection are critical identificatory processes. In projection, one identifies with the person into whom one projects, while in introjection, one absorbs into oneself the desired characteristics from the other. The presence of positive, loving objects in the child's—and adult's—life cannot, therefore, be overstated. Positive identification, arising out of mutually gratifying object relations, is at the heart of positive identity formation:

> To be genuinely considerate implies that we can put ourselves in the place of other people: we "identify" ourselves with them. Now, this capacity for identification with

another person is a most important element in human relationships in general, and is also a condition for real and strong feelings of love. We are only able to disregard or to some extent sacrifice our own feelings and desires, and thus for a time put the other person's interests and emotions first, if we have the capacity to identify ourselves with the loved person. (Klein, 1964, p. 66)

The other side of the coin is all too familiar—children who have failed to develop robust, mutually gratifying object relations. There are children in our schools who seem to exist within walled-off worlds of depression and alienation, and others who, filled with bottled up anger, are ready to vent their anger at adults or peers. These are the children whose potential for deep alienation or explicit violence is often a source of public concern.

Speaking specifically of racial hatred as one exemplar of this process, Michael Rustin (1991) argues that racism is, in part, a psychotic process for expelling bad and unwanted parts of the self in order to try to restore a feeling of wholeness:

Dichotomous versions of racial difference are paranoid in their structure, since they function mentally...as ways of condensing basic feelings of positive and negative identification...The effect of getting rid of bad feelings into the other is to allow the self to perceive itself as wholly good. (p. 66)

Rustin cautions us, however, not to assume that hatred can be fully explained by intrapsychic processes such as the projection of hated parts of the self into an Other in order to feel more fully whole, since group processes and prevailing discursive practices are also contributing factors (p. 70).

The Role of Group Processes in Subject Formation: A neo-Kleinian perspective

People derive much of their subjectivity from their sense of identification with specific groups. Group identification comes with a cost, however, because groups often take on a group mentality that individual members are expected to absorb if they wish to maintain their group identification. Even well-adjusted adults who do not ordinarily experience a lot of primitive anxiety, and hence do not activate paranoid-schizoid defenses in their personal lives very frequently, for example, are liable to experience paranoid-schizoid anxiety if a group with which they identify experiences a lot of this kind of anxiety. The collective paranoid-schizoid anxiety of the group can induce individuals to think and act in ways contrary to their own personal moral and ethical principles.

Applications of Kleinian theory to group processes are useful in understanding how this works. Writers in this area (e.g., Alford, 1989; Bion, 1961; Freud (1959); Kernberg, 1998; Rustin, 1991) argue that groups use processes identical to those that individuals use to consolidate group identity. Karen Lombardi and Naomi Rucker, for example, argue that while group psychology may differ somewhat from individual intrapsychic processes, the same mechanisms of dissociation and splitting occur in groups, so that group members come to define themselves precisely by what they are not: "The process of forming identifications simultaneously fosters the formation of disidentifications with those who do not share our identity" (Lombardi & Rucker, 1998, p. 154). They note that the kind of reparative and empathic functions that might help dissolve or mitigate the otherness that comes from disidentification appear to be particularly absent in racial groups in the USA. It is precisely the "empty" nature of race as a category, that is its lack of any basis in biological reality, that makes it such an ideal container for unwanted feelings and hated parts of the self (Lombardi & Rucker, 1998, p. 160). Echoing this view, Michael Rustin (1991) summarizes the application of Kleinian theory to subject formation this way:

> What is expelled by the group expressing prejudice or hatred, and what has to be borne (or resisted, or got rid of, if that is possible) by their recipients are powerful doses of bad psychic stuff…Expressions of prejudice, rejection, or distaste fulfil active, albeit unconscious, emotional needs for those who make them—they get rid of something unwanted and uncomfortable out of the self, where they cause mental conflict and pain, into some external container, whose pain is disregarded as of no account, or, worse still, has a perverse value for those who project it in its visible existence outside of themselves. One can easily see how social groups made to receive the projections of collectivities superior to them will be filled with the desire to push them on to some group still more vulnerable than they, and thus how maltreatment is passed down the social status ladder from group to group. Racism can thus be seen to involve states of projective identification, in which hated self-attributes of members of the group gripped by prejudice are phantasied to exist in members of the stigmatized race. (p. 68)

Fred Alford (1989) argues that the group that is hated or feared serves as a blank screen onto which members of the hating group can project their anxiety and hatred, much as the infant treats the mother as a blank container for his or her projections (p. 87). He points out that projection of hatred onto an Other serves a useful function in that the Other can then serve as a container for all of the aggression that otherwise might be employed in intragroup conflict: "Aggression against one's own group…is split off as aggression against other groups in order to allow a more secure, dependent attachment to one's own group" (p. 76). The problem, as Alford notes, is that a strategy that is useful in managing collective anxiety becomes, through processes of splitting, devaluation, and projective identification, a means of depersonalizing the Other, and hence a major obstacle to reparative morality and the possibility for intergroup understanding (p. 86). Alford goes on to point out that a paranoid-schizoid orientation toward the world:

> is not incompatible with genuine love and concern for parts of it. Indeed this is precisely what splitting and projection allow: namely that some groups may be treated well by exaggerating their differences from other groups, which become, via paranoid projection, the source of all evil. (p. 86)

One need only recall Ronald Reagan's invocation of the "Evil Empire," or the paranoia among US schoolchildren about Iraqi Scud missiles landing on their schools during the Gulf War, to realize how well government leaders understand how to exploit collective paranoid anxieties. Judith Shapiro (2000), reviewing David Chandler's book about the genocide at Tuol Sleng, a death camp in Cambodia in which 14,000 people were tortured and massacred by Pol Pot's followers, describes the ultimate effects of such dehumanization:

> By defining their victims as subhuman, interrogators became capable of shutting down empathy, and torture became routinized. "Turning the victims into 'others,' in a racist fashion—and using words associated with animals to describe them—made them easier to mistreat and easier to kill." The source of the evil enacted in Tuol Sleng, Chandler argues, lies within all of us. (Shapiro, 2000, p. 15)

Alford (1989) wistfully remarks:

> Responsible leaders will therefore not exaggerate the goodness of their own group and the badness of the other. Talk of the opposition as an "evil empire" only encourages splitting and projection...a political leader who recognizes that "the only thing we have to fear is fear itself" expresses deep insight into the political psychology of the group. By calling the enemy by its right name—not some evil group, but also our own anxiety—such a leader may help the group minimize its use of paranoid-schizoid defenses. (p. 90)

In working with young children, therefore, it is important to be sensitive to the ways in which they use group processes and accompanying identifications and disidentifications to consolidate aspects of their emerging subjectivities. While proscriptions such as Paley's (1992) "You can't say you can't play" are understandable in the kindergarten world, it is important to realize that a complex process of identity construction is under way and that simplistic prohibitions, while well intentioned, may serve to conceal what we most need to understand.

The Constitution of
Subjectivity through Discourses

Conventional psychological theories evade the complexity of human subjectivity by postulating an essential self that emerges from intrapsychic processes or, at best, a subjectivity that is shaped within very limited caregiver and familial contexts (see Chapter 1). A more complex view calls for a conceptualization of human subjectivity as inherently situated and constantly in the process of becoming. We are not subjects who become and are then influenced by pre-vailing ideologies and cultural practices. Rather, we constantly name ourselves through insertion into, identification—or possible disidentification—with, and performance of prevailing cultural practices and ideologies. Speaking of pre-school children and their understandings of race and racism in the USA, Van Ausdale and Feagin explain the importance of societal context in the formation of subjectivity as follows:

> As we have demonstrated in the survey in Chapter 1 and in our data, racist thought and practice remain strong in the United States, and young children cannot avoid participating in and perpetuating them. Racism surrounds us, permeates our ideas and conversations, focuses our relationships with one another, shapes our practices, and drives much in our personal, social, and political lives. There are few social forces so strong. Children are neither immune to it nor unaware of its power. A social reality this mighty is bound to become an integral part of their lives, and thus it endures from generation to generation, perhaps changing somewhat in form, but still strong in its impact. (2001, pp. 197–198)

They describe the interweaving of societal discourses (of race in this case) with pre-school children's subjectivities this way:

> Each child in our study possessed connections with family, friends, teachers, and play-mates at the center. They were part of even larger social circles and networks—and were thus part of the larger racialized society of which we are all members. How they have managed to create, re-create, and reinvent that racially stratified society in their own discourse and practices is at the center of our analysis. Racism intersects with their lives in a flood of elaborate, blatant, and subtle ways—from the definition of identity

and self, to the performance of hurtful practices, to various articulations of dominant group power. (p. 198)

Theoretical Understanding of the Role of Context in Subject Formation

A central concern of all discursive theories is understanding the relationship between subject formation and societal ideologies. Bakhtin's (1981, 1986) studies in the philosophy of language, Lacan's (1977, 1998) studies of subjectivity, and inquiry in the areas of cultural and post-colonial studies (Ashcroft et al., 1995; Bhabha, 1994; Chambers & Curti, 1996; During, 1993; Grossberg et al., 1992; Morley & Chen, 1996) are all concerned in some way with what Althusser (1971a) called interpellation, namely, the mechanisms by which cultural categories and taxonomies structure the subjectivity of individuals. Discourse theorists acknowledge that prior to ideology and culture there is no subject, merely a potential subject. It is not that ideology and culture influence our subjectivity, but that we become subjects through incorporation of the ideologies and discourse practices of our daily lives.

The difficulty is that ideology is as pervasive as water in the ocean. Do fish give thought to the water that surrounds them? Through the languages we speak and the normal everyday discursive practices we take for granted throughout our life, we swim in a sea of ideology that has a powerful implicit influence on how we are in our worlds. Scholars of culture tell us that strolling through a shopping mall, ordering from a mail-order catalog, purchasing gasoline, using everyday speech genres, or any of a thousand other daily practices contribute powerfully to our normalization of certain practices and viewpoints as good and acceptable, and the rejection of others as alien and undesirable. Not only do we continually construct our subjectivities through our everyday practices, we also contain within us socio-historically constructed notions of self and Other that emanate from our historical memory. Baldwin (1998) captures the tyranny of our unconsciously embodied histories this way:

> White man, hear me! History, as nearly no one seems to know, is not merely something to be read. And it does not refer merely, or even principally, to the past. On the contrary, the great force of history comes from the fact that we carry it within us, are unconsciously controlled by it in many ways, and history is literally present in all

that we do. It could scarcely be otherwise, since it is to history that we owe our frames of reference, our identities, and our aspirations. And it is with great pain and terror that one begins to realize this. In great pain and terror one begins to assess the history which has placed one where one is and formed one's point of view. In great pain and terror, therefore, one enters into battle with that historical creation, Oneself, and attempts to recreate something according to a principle more humane and liberating; one begins the attempt to achieve a level of personal maturity and freedom which robs history of its tyrannical power, and also changes history. (p. 321)

Possible Uses of Discursive Positionings in Subject Formation

My purpose here is not to advance a deterministic argument as Althusser might. While it is important to acknowledge the situated nature of our subjectivities, this does not mean that children or adults lack agency. In fact, an important virtue of our capacity to disidentify is that it endows us with the capacity to reject received ways of being. Being is, after all, a dynamic process. While the discursive climates in which children grow do matter, of greater interest to us as educators are: (1) the ways in which children choose to identify or disidentify with aspects of their discursive experiences, and (2) their openness to identifying with alternate discursive possibilities in constructing possible selves.

Mama's (1995) research into the racial formation of African origin women in Britain offers insight into the ways in which discursive positionings work through identity. Mama's research subjects drew upon different discursive positions in different contexts: "[I]ndividuals have many discourses and discursive positions available to them, and the positions they take up are momentary, changing with the different social contexts and relations they find themselves in" (p. 99). The availability of subaltern discourses, or the availability of people or texts that enabled them to read hegemonic discursive positionings oppositionally, enhanced the prospects for developing an oppositional stance toward hegemonic racial positionings:

> Discourses, as they are defined here, position individuals in relation to one another socially, politically, and culturally, as similar to or different from; as "one of us" or as 'Other'. They exist within and transmit networks of power, with dominant discourses exercising their hegemony by resonating with and echoing the institutionalized and formal knowledges, assumptions and ideologies of a given social and political order. On the other hand, subaltern discourses also exist in contradiction to hegemonic ones, which subvert the dominant symbolic order and empower oppressed groups

through their resonance with alternative ideologies and cultural practices. In other words, discourses do not only transmit cultural content but also power relations, both relations of oppression and subordination and relations of resistance. (Mama, 1995, p. 98)

Determinism is further mitigated, Mama notes, by the dialectical nature of discursive positions, i.e. that particular discursive positions necessarily contain within them the seeds of their opposite. Thus, while one person, exposed, for example, only to a racist, homophobic, or misogynist discursive positioning might unconsciously take on that position, another person in the same situation might take on an oppositional discourse, and use their resistance to develop a more empowered sense of self. One key to understanding racial formation, therefore, is the repertoire of discursive positions available to subjects, and the stances individuals adopt in relation to these discourses.

For instance, Mama's research participants appeared to have a choice between an assimilationist discourse, which Mama calls colonial-integrationist discourse, and an oppositional discourse, referred to by Mama as black radical discourse. Mama noted that, for black people, "Colonial-integrationist discourse conveys a message of conformity and an acceptance of white hegemony, while black radical discourse conveys a politics of resistance" (p. 100). Mama says that while racism clearly can have a deleterious impact on subjectivity, it may also produce oppositional racial discourses. The range of possible discursive positions available to a person is significant. A person for whom the only discourses available (e.g., at home, at school, in their community, and through literature and mass media) are racialized discourses, in which they are positioned as Other, is in a very different position to somebody for whom positive racial identifications are available:

Those raised in all-white environments (suburbia, care institutions, boarding schools, foster families) do not have black discursive positions readily available to them. One consequence of this is that they may be "unable" to perceive and respond to racism, even though it is part of their experience. Such people will have subjectivities that are racialized, but in ways that differ from those who have become part of the collective change heralded by black radicalism, because they have been subjected to racism without having access to any of the real or imaginary referents which we have seen the women in this study make use of. To cite an extreme example, black children raised in children's homes commonly develop a habit called "skin-scratching" in which they compulsively scratch away at their skin, as if to exfoliate themselves... These and other visible markers can be seen as the result of internalization of the derogatory images of black people that continue to prevail wherever they have not been sufficiently challenged. (Mama, 1995, p. 141)

In looking at the lives of children, therefore, it is not enough to survey the range of current and possible discursive positions available to them in domains such as gender, race, and other realms of subjectivity. We also need to pay close attention to the ways in which the children use these subject positions in the service of subject formation from moment to moment.

The Role of Caregivers and Teachers in Enhancing the Subjective Possibilities Available to Children in School

Children who project hatred and anger, and who experience persecutory anxiety, are psychically wounded. Teachers cannot replace parents and undo the relational wrongs of the past. Neither can they engage in the kinds of long-term psychotherapy that might enable children with damaged object relations to work through their persecutory anxieties and introject good objects to replace their internalized persecutory objects. That is the work of psychotherapists. However, there is much schools can do to provide non-persecutory, emotionally supportive environments to assist children in working through debilitating anxiety in order to develop healthy identifications. Klein (1984c) notes, for example, that the working through of emotions that is a central feature of psychoanalysis needs to be a part of the everyday experience of the child if the child is not to develop the kinds of persecutory anxiety that lead to pathological defenses and an absence of reparation:

> Freud has postulated the process of working through as an essential part of psycho-analytic procedure. To put it in a nutshell, this means enabling the patient to experience his [sic] emotions, anxieties, and past situations over and over again both in relation to the analyst and to different people and situations in the patient's present and past life. There is, however, a working through occurring to some extent in normal individual development. Adaptation to external reality increases and with it the infant achieves a less phantastic picture of the world around him [sic]. The recurrent experience of the mother going away and coming back to him [sic] makes her absence less frightening, and therefore his [sic] suspicion of her leaving him [sic] diminishes. In this way he [sic] gradually works through his [sic] early fears and comes to terms with his [sic] conflicting impulses and emotions. (Klein, 1984c, pp. 255–256)

It is but a short leap from this to the idea that schools should serve as emotionally facilitating spaces for children—places in which children might work through their feelings and anxieties so as to prevent them being flooded with persecutory anxieties that can lead to paranoid-schizoid responses and a flight from love. Regrettably, many schools actually contribute to paranoid-schizoid responses in children by creating climates in which children experience themselves as unlovable and unloved. The recent upsurge in "no touch" policies in US early childhood centers is a troubling example of a trend, at least in US society, toward withholding affirmation and ignoring the feelings and desires of young children (e.g., Tobin, 1997; Johnson, 2000), as is the extraordinary absence of children's voices from many US classrooms (Goodlad, 1983).

School as Reparative Community

Rustin (1991) notes that if we accept that hatred is related to the presence of persecutory anxiety and the use of mechanisms such as splitting, idealization, and projective identification, as well as the consolidation of identity through disidentification with Others onto whom we have projected the hateful parts of ourselves, then rational educative approaches that are aimed at changing attitudes are likely to "do no more than ruffle the surface" (p. 74). Furthermore, since racial hatred is a fundamentally irrational process—though readily exploited by rational leaders for their own ends—any approach that attempts to deal with the issue rationally is likely to exacerbate persecutory anxiety. As Rustin says, "persecution seems ill-advised as a technique for dealing with states of mind that are at root paranoid and persecutory" (p. 76). We might be well advised to rethink our notions of how to pursue anti-racist education in schools.

Instead of thinking of schools exclusively in functional and instrumental terms, we might want to think of schools as reparative communities—places in which teachers and caregivers work with students to diminish persecutory anxieties, and to create with students opportunities to engage in nonthreatening ways with the Others of their worlds so that the depersonalization that leads to hateful projection is minimized. If either a harsh persecutory climate pervades the institution, or if, in the process of developing anti-racist or anti-violence initiatives, we create a persecutory climate, then the likelihood of students bringing any of their fundamental anxieties to the surface for processing is remote.

The literature on group dynamics discussed earlier suggests that we need to be particularly attentive to the ways in which children use group processes in the construction of their subjectivities because of the likelihood that the consolidation of identity will be accompanied by the cultivation of admired in-groups and rejected out-groups. Schools are sites in which social engineering is a constant fact of life and there is no reason that an observant caregiver or teacher might not engineer her classroom to allow children to have experiences in groups that foster intergroup understanding and empathy. Likewise, through the use of field trips, visitors, films, and literature, a teacher can create opportunities for children to engage empathically with distant Others, far beyond their immediate experience. A note of caution is necessary, however. At this point we do not know enough about the workings of processes of identification and disidentification to cause us to seek to banish disidentificatory processes from children's lives. If disidentification is in some ways necessary, then we need to understand it better. The question, perhaps, is whether it is possible for children to develop parts of their subjectivity through disidentification, while simultaneously developing a capacity for empathy and mutual understanding across differences.

Expanding the Range of Identificatory Possibilities Available to Children in School

Children are continually in the process of becoming. Such becoming necessarily entails performing diverse societal discourses concerned with issues of gender, race, class and so on. Teachers and caregivers may find it worthwhile to pay close attention to the uses to which children put these various identificatory positions. Which subject positions seem to produce identifications in certain children? Which ones seem to invite disidentifications? Teachers and caregivers may wish to engage young children in conversations about both of these choices in order to expand the range of identificatory possibilities they might perform. In addition, a teacher or caregiver might wish to expand the realm of identificatory possibilities available to children, particularly by introducing subaltern ways of being that allow children to identify more revolutionary possibilities in their own lives, and perhaps to develop more empathic identifications with people from other communities. These issues not only invite pedagogical and research inquiry, but they also raise important questions about the ethical responsibilities of adults who work with children. The one thing we do not want to do, I think, is assume that subject formation is inconsequential, or that we need do nothing because the inherent innocence of children will protect them from performing hateful acts. The cautionary tale that opens Van Ausdale and Feagin's (2001) book serves as a pointed reminder:

> Carla, a three-year-old child, is preparing herself for resting time. She picks up her cot and starts to move it to the other side of the classroom. A teacher asks what she is doing. "I need to move this," explains Carla. "Why?" asks the teacher. "Because I can't sleep next to a nigger," Carla says, pointing to Nicole, a four-year-old Black child on a cot nearby. "Niggers are stinky. I can't sleep next to one." Stunned, the teacher, who is white, tells Carla to move her cot back and not use "hurting words." Carla looks amused, but complies. (p. 1)

· 5 ·

ON KNOWING AND DESIRING CHILDREN: THE SIGNIFICANCE OF THE UNTHOUGHT KNOWN

Psychoanalysis has a long tradition of understanding that ignorance is an active refusal to know. Ignorance in psychoanalysis is understood as a desire not to know and it should be considered an integral part of knowing rather than its opposite (Felman, 1987). My interest in this chapter is to explore the pedagogical and psychotherapeutic implications of working with these ignorances that Christopher Bollas (1987) refers to as "the unthought known" in the lives and desires of children—a latent subjectivity embodied in unconscious desires and ancestral memory. There is a rule of thumb in psychoanalytic practice which states that it is not what the patient says that matters; what merits attention is what the patient is *really* saying. A psychoanalyst pays relatively less attention to overt verbal utterances, listening instead for the unconscious communication that underlies the patient's words. The analyst gains knowledge of the patient from these communications and then returns this knowledge to the patient so that the patient can make use of it. Shoshana Felman, in *Jacques Lacan and the Adventure of Insight*, puts it this way: "...the analyst must be taught by the analysand's [patient's] unconscious. It is by structurally making himself a *student of the patient's knowledge*, that the analyst becomes the patient's teacher—makes the patient learn what would otherwise remain forever inaccessible to him" (1987, p. 83).

As any composition teacher who has helped a student to articulate "what you really want to say" in a piece of writing will readily recognize, the link between the analyst's task and school pedagogy is rather direct. Implicit in my discussion throughout this chapter is the idea that teachers err if they focus exclusively on rational, explicit, and memorable forms of knowledge. It is not in the ostensibly known and the to-be-known facts that creativity and desire are to be found. We ought to pay much more attention to the ignorance that lies beneath the façade of knowing because that which is ignored is also the source of unconscious desire and possibility. Felman presents the issue this way: "What is the riddle I pose here under the guise of my knowledge?" (p. 96).

Psychoanalysis can provide us a way to think about why thinking beyond knowledge might matter in the classroom. Arguing that pedagogy and curriculum should grow not only from a child's own questions about the world and her/ his place in it but also from knowledge present in the child's unconscious, I ask what it means to really listen to children. This is a question that positions the task of the teacher differently. Rather than assuming that s/he knows ahead of time what knowledge is worth pursuing, I am proposing that the teacher, like the analyst, should learn to listen for the questions that matter to the child, and behind the questions, to hear the unspoken desires that animate the child's life. I believe that as teachers we need to learn to construct curriculum and pedagogy that supports children in identifying the things that they desire to know and be in the world. For me to do this meant first learning to listen to my own questions and desires.

Troubling Childhood

I had a troubled childhood. When I was an infant I suffered from severe projectile vomiting and therefore had to spend most of the first two years of my life in the local county hospital. There were occasional interludes when I was allowed home. I had two siblings, both toddlers themselves, only one and two years older than me. My dad worked all day and the whole family was perched precariously on the precipice of poverty. The little time I spent at home, my mother tells me was frenetic. When I vomited there were no spare linens and my mother had no running water, washer or dryer. My illness caused serious domestic upheaval as well as lots of worry.

Meanwhile, at the hospital, my mother and father were advised to visit me as little as possible, as their presence invariably upset me, and times when they could actually hold me were strictly limited. My mother tells me that when she visited, she would peer longingly at me through the glass window. The hospital was so anxiety-producing for me that to this day, when I hear an ambulance, I experience anxiety. I have been left with an abiding sense of vulnerability.

My subjectivity has been constructed, then, through the absences, losses, anxieties, and dread that surrounded my tenuous grasp on life, as well as by my prolonged exposure to institutional "care." I was fragile. I was different. I was alone. Yet I also experienced myself as desired, and this was enough to inspire in me a struggle to live. This, of course, is not my past. It is very much my present. My anxiety in the company of strangers; my difficulty in putting myself forward in my writing (see Chapter 3); my difficulty functioning in impersonal institutional environments; and my pleasure in working with children all have a plausible correlation with my earliest experiences. My childhood is not a historical remnant. It is very much who I am today. I live my childhood anew each day. As Rose (1992) noted in the context of a discussion of children's fiction: "The most crucial aspect of psychoanalysis for discussing children's fiction is its insistence that childhood is something in which we continue to be implicated, and which is never simply left behind. Childhood persists..." (p. 12).

In *Women Hollering Creek* Cisneros captures the notion of the embeddedness of childhood within us rather whimsically:

What they don't understand about birthdays and what they never tell you is that when you're eleven you're also ten, and nine, and eight, and seven, and six, and five, and four, and three, and two, and one... Like some days you might say something stupid, and that's the part of you that's still ten. Or maybe some days you might need to sit on your mama's lap because you're scared, and that's the part of you that's five. And maybe one day, when you're all grown up, maybe you will need to cry like you're three, and that's okay. That's what I tell mama when she's sad and she needs to cry. Maybe she's feeling three.

Because the way you grow old is kind of like an onion or like the rings inside a tree trunk or like my little wooden dolls that fit one inside the other, each year inside the next one. (1991, pp. 6–7)

A popular view is that psychoanalytic psychotherapy is designed to help people transcend their pasts. I think not. I believe I need to embrace the forgotten or unnamed knowledge of my past, so that I may use it to express my desire more fully.

The idea of the enduring nature of childhood was greatly reinforced when I began to practice as a psychoanalyst. My initial determination was to confine my practice to adults. I had begun my professional life as a first-grade teacher, and I had spent much of my adult life visiting schools and writing and teaching about children's issues. Having reached middle-age with my own children entering adulthood, I thought that perhaps it was time I worked with an adult population with whom I imagined I had a shared life experience. It was time I grew up. To my surprise, from the moment I began my clinical practice I was plunged into untangling the minutiae of childhood—the aspirations, losses, disappointments, hopes, attachments etc. that constituted my adult patients' lives. I enjoyed this very much, and soon I decided to devote a significant portion of my practice to seeing actual children so that I could engage with children's unfolding subjectivities.

In working with children I am in many respects a child. I work childishly. I have a playful consulting room, labeled recently by a perceptive parent of a toddler as the "it's okay to knock the blocks over room." Yet, I am also the adult analyst intent on reading child's play as an expression of the unsymbolized aspects of a child's unconscious expression of desire. As Mathelin (1999) documents so unequivocally in *The Broken Piano*, children's desires are inextricably constructed in the matrix of parental desire. Thus, paradoxically, to have a child in therapy is clearly to have their parents in therapy too. In *History Beyond Trauma* Davoine and Gaudillière (2004) take the argument further, suggesting that humans also embody unconscious memories of the unresolved trauma of their ancestors. The consulting room is a very crowded place indeed, and the separation of life into childhood and adulthood is troubled by these shadows of past-into-present and present-into-past.

In other words, parents impose upon their children not only their own wishes and anxieties but also the wishes and anxieties that were passed down to them from their parents and their parents' parents. Perhaps the most common challenge facing any child analyst is the fact that adults, sometimes consciously and often unconsciously, demand that their children perform identities, behaviors and even desires that emerge not from the children's needs and wishes but from those of the adult. In *The Case of Peter Pan*, Rose (1992) cites adults' vested interest in proclaiming childhood innocence as an example of this. This insistence on seeing childhood as innocent, Rose argues, gives adults a way of avoiding awareness of the complexity their own identities. "If we do not know what a child is," Rose states, "then it becomes impossible to invest in their sweet self-evidence, impossible to use the translucent clarity of childhood to deny the anxieties we have about our psychic, sexual, and social being in the world" (p. xvii).

What makes *Peter Pan* such a controversial and interesting work is precisely the blurring of boundaries between the world of children and adults. As Rose explains, J.M. Barrie, the author of *Peter Pan,* was far from a disinterested observer of children. His love of boys is well established. *Peter Pan* was originally penned as a tale within a larger story, *The Little White Bird* (Barrie, 1902). In that work the male adult character narrates the story of Peter Pan to a young boy as part of a seduction ploy. Rose's book is a study of how *Peter Pan* has been plucked out of this context and sanitized as the archetypal narrative of childish innocence. It is possible though, to trouble this putatively innocent tale, as Rose does, by raising the tricky question of desire:

> Suppose, therefore, that Peter Pan is a little boy who does not grow up, not because he doesn't want to, but because someone else prefers that he shouldn't. Suppose, therefore, that what is at stake in *Peter Pan* is the adult's desire for the child…I am using desire to refer to a form of investment by the adult in the child, and to the demand made by the adult on the child as to the effect of that investment, a demand which fixes the child and then holds it in place. A turning to the child, or a circulating around the child— what is at stake here is not so much something which could be enacted as something which cannot be spoken. (pp. 3–4)

So, in constructing childhood as discrete from adulthood, and as innocent, the motives of adults may be suspect. The ascription of childhood innocence may represent a manic attempt to deny the unacknowledgeable history of our own subjective experience and unnamable desires. It may also represent an adult projection of unnamable desires. We subject children to mixed messages. We want them to grow up, yet we tell them to act their age. We proudly celebrate childhood innocence, yet we live with a legacy of colonialism that continues to infantilize and inferiorize ethnically and racially different persons as *minor(ity)*. We ascribe purity of motives to children, yet we create technologies of care and education that discipline their bodies and minds (cf. Donzelot, 1979; Rousmaniere et al., 1997) and work to conceal from children the unconscious knowledges, especially unthought memories of trauma, that could allow children to name their histories and release their creativity. In what follows, I turn to my analytic practice to demonstrate the importance of helping children to symbolize their histories, their questions, and their desires.

Naming the Unthought Known

I am returned to an episode in therapy. "If this therapy isn't working," the father says, staring pointedly at me, "and if *you* don't do what I need *you* to do [now pointing an accusatory finger at his twelve-year-old son] then I am going to send *you* away to boarding school like your brother."[1] This father had placed me in an impossible bind. Speaking with me on the phone before he ever brought his son for therapy he asked me how I worked with children in therapy. I gave a brief explanation and added that sometimes, if the child finds it helpful, one or both parents would become partners in the therapy and participate in sessions with their child on an as needed basis. He replied tersely, "I don't think that will be necessary." In any event, he allowed his child to enter therapy, but he intruded periodically when he felt that his son was not adjusting sufficiently to the demands of family and school life. The bind for me of course continues to be figuring out how to accomplish the "adjustment" goals the father demands, at least sufficiently to allow the boy to remain in therapy, while simultaneously liberating the child from excessive parental demand. What if, as is the case here, the boy's inability to mourn his biological mother, who died many years ago, is now emerging in the form of resistance to his father and new stepmother? What if the father himself failed to mourn his dead wife, and his son's rebelliousness constantly raises the specter that the wall he has carefully constructed against his own emotions will come crashing down? As Brenkman (1999) notes, in the introduction to Maud Mannoni's *Separation and Creativity*, contrary to psychiatric and educational approaches which focus on symptom removal and behavioral adjustment, one purpose of psychoanalytically informed therapy with a child is to engage the child in understanding the process by which that child's desires have become spoken for him/her through parental and/or institutional (e.g., school) demand:

> [W]hat can the child discover in the analytic dialogue about what it means, within his or her own psychic reality, to be in the eyes of others the bearer of a "symptom," "illness," or "deficiency" and to be treated with a mood-altering drug? The power of psychoanalysis lies in its specificity and even its limits. Its task is to expand the area of experience that can be articulated in the individual's own terms and own name, and therefore must leave open, case by case, how that project will mesh or not with the medical and educational goals of normalizing children's behavior. (p. xx)

As Mannoni herself earlier noted, echoing Bakhtin's (1986) notion of how the social ventriloquates through individual speech, "we must also realize who is speaking, because the subject of the words is not necessarily the child" (1970, p. 20). To the extent that Judith Butler (1997) is correct that *subjectivity* may be synonymous with *subjection* because the child inherits the demands, desires, and language of parents and society, then the task of psychoanalysis is to liberate: to enable the child to name the unconscious external forces shaping his or her desires and thereby producing "symptoms," so that the child can then get out from under that yoke to experience creativity and possibility. As Mannoni (1970) stated, we need to help the child remove "the screens the adult erects to keep the child in a state of *unknowing*" (p. 27).

Framing psychoanalysis from a Lacanian perspective, Mannoni argues (cf. also Mathelin, 1999) that the symptom or presenting problem which brings the child to therapy needs to be understood as having been produced by circumstances. If all capacity for meaning is precluded for the child, then the emergence of the repressed desire through somatized illness is a likely consequence:

> The reality of the "illness" is never underestimated in psychoanalysis, but an attempt is made to pinpoint how the real situation is lived by the child and his family. It is then that the symbolic value that the subject attaches to the situation, re-echoing a given family history takes on a meaning. For the child it is the words spoken by those around him about his "illness" that assume importance…Whatever the child's real state of deficiency or disturbance may be, the analyst endeavors to understand the words that remain petrified in an anxiety or encased in a physical disorder. In treatment, the subject's questions will replace the demand or anxiety of parents and child, a question that is his deepest wish, concealed hitherto in a symptom or in a particular type of relationship with his surroundings. What will become clear is the manner in which the child bears the imprint not only of the way his birth was awaited, but also of what he is going to represent for each parent as a function of their respective past histories. His real existence will thus come into conflict with the unconscious projections of his parents, and this is where the misunderstandings arise. If the child gets the impression that every access is barred to a true word, he can in some cases search for a possibility of expressing himself in illness. (1970, p. 61)

So how does one reveal to the child the truth that others would unconsciously wish to conceal? Mannoni invokes Winnicott's notion of potential space, arguing that a play space opens up the possibility of truth and creativity. As Winnicott noted, "If there is no play and no maternal counter-play the transition from dependence to independence is impaired" (cited in Mannoni, 1999, p. 4). Lacking the ability to "name the unnamable" (Mannoni, 1999, p. 7), the child is encased within the shell of an imposed parental identity and remains trapped in an alienated and painful existence; as a result, Mannoni suggests, the child lacks the capacity for creativity and fantasy. Intergenerational trauma compounds the problem. If a child continues to lack the capacity to metabolize traumatic losses into adulthood, then there is a high probability that a similar silence about emotional loss will be bequeathed to ensuing generations. Speaking of those concentration camp survivors who were unable to express and transform their initial trauma, Mannoni notes: "What remains unspoken is a wound that is handed down from generation to generation, a wound of memory the effect of which is to rob the victim of pleasure in life." (1999, p. 31). Echoing Alice Miller (1997), Mannoni argues that parents (and, of course, early childhood professionals too) who attempt to repair their *own* childhoods by being excessively rule bound, dutiful, or achievement oriented, unconsciously impose similar values on their children and thereby deprive them of the *fantastic* space that would allow them to grow up as playful, creative beings, instead of the "slaves to duty" (Mannoni, 1999, p. 36) who end up all too well prepared for long-term incarceration in rule-bound schools and workplaces later in life.

"Creativity," Mannoni notes, "is motivated by a present event combined with what of the past can be transposed, recreated, on an Other stage" (1999, p. 65). It is to be noted that the Other that is the catalyst is a therapist, teacher, or other mirroring individual who has developed the capacity to speak truth with the child. The twelve-year-old boy mentioned above gets through life wearing a mask. He is a clown, a funny man. He laughs and jokes his way through school. He evades my invitations to speak about his emotions by being silly. In my office he plays with the toys my younger patients use. He is childish in resistance to the adult demand that he grow up *in a certain way*. I have made only one promise to him: I will take him seriously.

Analysts use the term *symbolization* to describe the process of assisting patients in transforming their feelings into truth. Mannoni describes the role of the child's coming to voice in this process:

> Shut off from communication with others, lodged in a retreat to the point of thwarting all personal development, the subject has trouble with speech: he lacks the words to say what is happening with his state of being. . . . the aim of analysis is to give the subject access to full speech and thereby to a fuller authenticity, which can only occur through speech that has been loosened from its moorings. When the subject's speech is thus reworked in analysis, it becomes possible for him to recognize desire. (1999, p. 94)

Davoine and Gaudillière (2004) also approach the issue of silenced trauma from a Lacanian perspective. Their concern is with the intergenerational transmission of traumatic events that have been blanketed in silence through processes of dissociation. They argue that people we deem *mad* are the victims of just such processes of erasure of the historical origins of their suffering:

> These cases of trauma and madness are a challenge hurled at clinical treatment, since the analyst comes up against a piece of the Real [i.e., the *unconscious* in Lacanian

terms]. Because signifying speech was lacking, nothing could be inscribed, on this point, in the unconscious. The customary tools of treatment are thwarted, since, in this regard, the subject of speech, even repressed speech, has not been constituted. What is at stake then, is precisely the coming into being of the subject, the subject of a history not so much censored as erased, reduced to nothing, yet somehow existing. (p. 47)

Davoine and Gaudillière suggest that at moments of trauma in a child's life it is vital that adults not get so caught up in the traumatic response as to forget to provide verbal reassurance to a child of the order of "Something serious has happened, but you are not responsible for this sudden upheaval. Trust us." (p. 72). If this kind of reassurance is not provided, they note, "the thread of speech may be radically cut" (p. 71), leaving the child with no way to name or metabolize the traumatic feelings. The unconscious trauma is thereby encased in silence and, if unnamed, it will be transmitted in mute form to ensuing generations. The solution, they argue, is to render the unsaid sayable:

> As the child psychiatrist Lionel Bailly puts it, when "children hear the voices of the dead" they are most often those who died without burial, without a rite. This brief illusion will cease as soon as it is heard by a therapist in whom the voices of the dead can resonate instead of remaining a dead letter. (p. 145)

If the encased trauma is not given voice, Davoine and Gaudillière note, "a seed of psychosis" (p. 145) is planted because the child is left on its own holding this "terrible knowledge" (p. 146).

Before looking at some clinical examples of these phenomena among children, one final point must be noted: A child does not necessarily need to be exposed to a concrete traumatic event in order to be left with the silent burden of unsymbolized experience. All it takes is for the parents to pass on their own unconscious, unmetabolized psychic pain to the child. As Davoine and Gaudillière note, "a baby may be assigned the role of *therapôn*, keeper of the mind for its parents, the boundary of their irrationality, remaining welded to them by a bond that may prevent any other attachment." (p. 157). An example of this in Lacanian thought (e.g., Fink, 1997; Mannoni, 1999; Mathelin, 1999) is the situation where a child is confronted with a one parent who is absent or passive and another who is emotionally engulfing. In such cases, the child may not develop the capacity to own or verbalize his or her own experience. The outcome is predictable. We can expect such children to exhibit deep silence, unsymbolized emotions, severe anxiety, or symptoms of somatized illnesses as a response to the unnamable burdens imposed on their psyches.

Symptomatology of
Misdirected Desire and Unmetabolized Loss:
Some Clinical Examples

Gabe—the silent scream

Gabe began seeing me when he was ten. He is an affable boy with a tremendous talent for mimicry. He bonded well with me and took with relish to playing card games, drawing, and telling tall tales. Despite having a flexible and accommo-dating fifth-grade teacher, Gabe began to refuse school. This happened only sporadically and with a little crisis intervention the moment passed. It was obvious, though, that Gabe was carrying a heavy emotional load. Any attempt to probe his emotions or offer an interpretation of his experience caused him to freeze. Sometimes he came to session and sat with his arms tightly folded for the entire hour, unable to speak or participate. He exemplified *The Silent Child* described by Danon-Boileau (2001) in the book of that title. He had an emotional crisis in sixth-grade. What exactly precipitated this is unclear. The transition from the smaller elementary school, where he had a strong bond with a single teacher, to the larger and more impersonal middle school may have been a factor. More likely, escalating tensions in the home increased Gabe's need to scream, except of course he was unable to. His father is emotionally unavailable and *unreasonable*. In a recent altercation his father dressed him down verbally and left Gabe feeling emotionally devastated. His mom, who, as a child, had experiences with school refusal and emotional constriction that remarkably mirror Gabe's own symptoms, is anxious, depressed and hopeless in the face of his resistance. Both parents are unable to provide a reconstitutive mirroring experience that might reassure him in the face of terror. Gabe now refused to go to school at all. I met with the school psychologist and Gabe's teachers. I found them to be empathic and emotionally supportive. Yet Gabe spurned all offers of help. He stayed home, ran out of the school building, or spent the day in the student support office under the eye of the psychologist.

He became increasingly depressed and angry. A crisis was building. He tore his room apart. He kicked the furniture in my office. He drew a series of self-portraits reminiscent of the ones in *The Silent Child* in which he depicted himself as terror-stricken, and with a series of bars drawn harshly across his mouth powerfully depicting his muted scream. In one picture, in addition to the barred mouth, he added layers of vibrating lines around his body as if he were in a state of shock. I have constructed an image of Gabe at home, both parents screaming at him to go to school, and his only method of voicing his trauma is refusal. This of course merely exacerbates their desperation and his flight from reality. Gabe eventually began voicing threats to himself and others. He ran away. He climbed out of his bedroom window and threatened to jump from the roof. He ordered most of his valuable possessions removed from his room. A child psychiatrist was consulted, and Gabe was placed on medication to stabilize his mood. He resumed school—for the most part. His affable self returned—more or less.

Yet, he is still struck dumb. Ironically, for a boy who can speak in so many other people's voices, his own voice is often muted. Just recently he left me in no doubt as to how he feels about my inability to name the pain that is tearing up his insides. He arrived at my office in good humor, carrying an adult brief-case. He opened it with a flourish and took out a toy gun and pointed it at me. "Bang. You're dead." True to form, he ignored my interpretation that he was expressing disappointment with me for failing to name his trauma. We played some games and he talked about events in his life, and then, before leaving, he offered to draw a picture. He took out the pistol again and traced its shape on the paper. He wrote the caption "19 caliber" on top of the drawing of the gun. Directly across from the barrel of the pistol he drew a stick figure with a look of terror on its face, and with blood pouring from its head and stomach onto a large pool on the floor. "You don't have to guess who this is," he told me amiably, as he wrote the legend "Mike O." underneath the figure. Then he left.

I have some urgent unfinished business with this young man. Fink (1995) describes Lacan's definition of psychosis thus:

> Psychosis, according to Lacan, results from a child's failure to assimilate a "primordial" signifier which would otherwise structure the child's symbolic universe, that failure leaving the child unanchored in language, without a compass reading on the basis of which to adopt an orientation. A psychotic child may very well *assimilate*, but cannot *come to be in* language in the same way as a neurotic child. Lacking the fundamental anchoring point, the remainder of the signifiers assimilated are condemned to drift. (p. 55)

His case is an agonizing reminder that, as Lawrence Langer (1991) illustrates so deftly in *Holocaust Testimonies*, sometimes a trauma cannot be spoken. Or, perhaps it is the case that the talking that takes place in therapy can never truly name certain traumas. Primo Levi's suicide, years after apparently working through his Auschwitz experience by writing *Survival in Auschwitz* (1996) and other memoirs, suggests that we need to be cautious about the reach of our influence or the power of the "talking cure." Is it always possible to use language to rescue somebody who is more spoken than speaking? Gabe will leave his local school this year to attend a psychiatric day treatment center.

Perry—lacking nom du père

Perry is ten. The psychologist who referred him to me told me that she feared he was on the verge of a psychotic break. At our first session Perry presented as a precocious, adultified child who inserted himself readily into his parents conversations, finished his parents sentences, and like a Greek chorus, offered wise and cautionary coda to their remarks. I could hear the parents ventriloquating through Perry, better than I could hear either their own words or his voice. It felt like an orthopedic consultation in that they spent most of the session talking about Perry's physical fragility. Perry had indeed broken some bones and spent a few months in traction, but this whole family felt fragile—as if everybody could fall apart at any moment. His mother had recently completed hospitalization for a nervous breakdown, and the whole family looked like they were terrified of disintegration. Perry's drawings were stick figures of the kind a much younger child might draw—both parents were depicted with smiling but overpowering faces, and little else. At our second session he took a little stuffed tiger, removed it from the doll house, and placed it outside at the back of the house because it was dangerous. Then he built a large Lego containment fence. Having removed the menacing tiger, Perry arranged the figures in the doll house meticulously. He then took the baby and placed it in a clear space in the bedroom, and built a large Lego wall all around the baby to keep it safe. Suddenly, the tiger was roused from its slumber. It crashed through the fragile walls of its enclosure, tore into the house and killed all the people inside. The following week the doll house went on fire and Perry marshaled his fire trucks to attempt a rescue. Perry's world was a fragile and dangerous place indeed.

Both parents agreed to come for consultations at a time separate from Perry's therapy. I soon learned that while his younger sibling would sleep over at a grandparent's home, Perry refused because he did not want to leave his mother. I had learned from my referral source that after dropping her children at school, Perry's mother often stayed in the school building or its vicinity all day as she could not bear to leave her children. It soon was evident that this mother had an overwhelming longing for her children and was using them to assuage some deep, unfulfilled need from her own childhood. She lay in bed with them for at least an hour each night before they went to sleep. She had resisted toilet training them and hence both her children were persistent bed wetters. When her husband traveled, quite frequently, both children slept with her, and when he was home, they displaced their father from the parental bed in the middle of every night and consigned him to the couch so that they could sleep with mother. She had projected her own needs so compellingly into her children that she was convinced that she was experiencing *their* needs. She felt lonely and abandoned, and she was convinced that this was what her children experienced. Her children needed to be babies to assuage mother's desire. When I explored this in session with the parents, Perry's mother told me that Perry's favorite activity was to curl up in her lap in the fetal position with a bottle of water. The recent death of her sister, who had been this mother's *de facto* caregiver, had precipitated a major psychotic break and hospitalization for the mother. The family sought me out immediately after she was discharged as the psychiatric team had advised her of the danger to her children, particularly Perry, whom they recognized as carrying an inordinate psychic burden.

Probing gently into his relationship with mom, I asked Perry to depict his night-time experience. He drew two bunk beds. His mom stood next to his little brother in the lower bunk. His mother was smiling beatifically while embracing his sleeping brother. Meanwhile, Perry, in the upper bunk, was standing fully erect, with his arms raised in supplication, apparently screaming for mommy. Perry then took a dark purple marker and created a dense colored scrawl that almost obscured his own figure entirely. Turning the paper over, he continued by drawing himself again, this time dwarfed by a very large ghost. He hastily reassured me that he knew ghosts weren't real. On another occasion Perry spoke with me about being in college. "Will you miss mom when you are in college?" I inquired. "Oh yes," he replied, "but I will call her everyday on my cell phone and I will come back and sneak in at night when daddy isn't looking, and I will go into bed with mommy and stick my b-i-i-i-g penis in her." The obliteration of himself in his drawing, the shadow of the ghost, and the oedipal fantasy are all indicative of the awareness that this young boy has of the terrifying power he is being asked to wield in his family. This young boy was rushing headlong for a full-blown oedipal victory with all of its catastrophic consequences.

The heart of the Oedipal crisis, Lacan tells us, is that children must come to understand that they can neither possess nor be possessed by their parents. While both children and parents may struggle with this reality, children must learn to turn to find comfort and engagement outside of the fantasy of remaining forever at the center of their parents' world. This reality is what Lacan named "The Law of the Father." Neither Perry nor his parents had learned how Perry might name his own desires separate from those of his parents. In Lacanian terms, The Law of the Father had collapsed entirely in this family.

The most critical part of my work has been to reestablish this Law so that Perry has the space and the invitation to leave behind the psychosis of his infancy—or more precisely, of his parents' infancy. The consequence of not doing so for Perry, the symptom bearer of his family (cf. Mathelin, 1999; Winnicott, 2002), is that he will have to continue to live the psychotic life of a baby in order to keep his parents sane. Perry and his parents have done well in therapy. In weekly parent counseling sessions, I have worked through the parents to engineer changes in the family dynamics by enabling them to become conscious of how their desires are manifesting themselves in Perry's symptoms and assisted them in creating emotional boundaries and rebalancing the distribution of parental authority and demand.

Lacan, Fink reminds us, "emphasizes the fact that patients' lives are determined by their 'purloined letters'—the snatches of their parents' conversation (that is, of the other's discourse), often not intended for their ears, that were indelibly etched in their memories and sealed their fate. Patients bring those letters to analysis, and analysts attempt to render them legible to their patients, to uncover the hidden determinants of their desire" (1997, p. 206). In therapy Perry has begun to deal with these issues in his transferential relationship with me. He acts out his rescue scenarios and uses me as a prop in his plays. As Mannoni would suggest, Perry is beginning to use fantasy and play in a way that he has never had the luxury of doing before. I provide him with vocabulary that names his struggle with enmeshment and names the battles against anxiety that are revealed weekly in his play. He strides into my office confidently, sits on my therapist's chair, and says "Mike, I think I know what we need to work on today." I become an instrument of his desire and he is master, at least of this micro-universe. His teachers report that Perry is also a lot more comfortable in his own skin at school (cf. Briggs, 2002). As Derek Wolcott, speaking of the fragmentation of the Antilles through colonial conquest, remarked in his Nobel acceptance speech, sometimes the vase that is shattered and rebuilt possesses a very special beauty: "Break a vase, and the love that reassembles the fragments is stronger than the love which took its symmetry for granted when it was whole. The glue that fits the pieces is the sealing of its original shape . . . and if the pieces are disparate, ill-fitting, they contain more pain than their original sculpture." (1992, unpaged). Perry is beginning to piece together a life in which he can make meanings of the troubles he has experienced, naming his own desires while coping with a world not of his making.

Educators and the Unthought Known

Having considered in some detail the existential plight of children who have encountered obstacles to claiming their own subjectivities, it only remains to clearly enunciate the underlying purpose of adults who work in professional capacities with young children. As Fink (1995) notes, Lacan views trauma as a blockage in the child's capacity to symbolize, to turn unnamed experience, embedded in the unconscious real, into language. This, of course, can only happen through dialogue and symbolization. Felman defines dialogue as "the radical condition of learning and of knowledge" (1987, p. 83). Dialogue, here, however, has a special meaning. It refers to the capacity of the Other (teacher, parent, therapist) to bring into the symbolic realm aspects of the child's subjectivity that are unarticulated. The subject, paradoxically, can only become a subject, through dialogue with the other. However, if this dialogue is of the catastrophic type often practiced by parents and teachers, in which their own demands are forced on the child, then it will produce only alienation. This, Fink reminds us, occurs because the focus is on the Other's demands (e.g., for achievement, conformity, duty) rather than on the kind of desire that will bring into being the child's subjective sense of self. To elicit desire the analyst must take care not to offer too much understanding or clarification even though the patient demands it. Feeding demand only leads to the negation of the kind of desire that leads to creativity and the growth of fantasy. As Fink noted, "[t]he more you try to understand, the less you hear—the less you can hear something new and different" (1995, p. 149).

In my clinical practice, I have worked against imagining that I can know ahead of time what a particular child needs and have rather devoted myself to listening for the child's desire and to trying to understand my own desire in relation to the child. I believe that it is possible to likewise construct a school curriculum and a pedagogy wherein children might engage in play and learning that would create the potential for them to articulate and bring forth their inner desires and fantasies. Such a curriculum could provide the space to name and unlock traumatic knowledges that can lead to crippling inferiority and an inhibition of the child's subjective possibilities. Play (cf. S. Fraiberg, 1996; L. Fraiberg, 1987; Paley, 2004a), open ended and emotionally grounded conversation, and the use of children's literature allow children to experience the multiple dimensions of their subject selves and to get in touch with their "unthought knowns" through encountering openly evocative emotionality (cf. Bettelheim, 1989; Coats, 2004; Sendak, 1970, 1988). These practices have the capacity to assist children in symbolizing their unconscious knowledges and releasing their imaginations.

A major obstacle to radically creative teaching that values fantasy and play is the emotional baggage that adults bring to their work with children. If adults are to nurture freeing dialogue with children, then the adults must first free themselves from barriers to their own feelings so that they avoid restricting the child's creativity with excessive demand (cf. Field, Cohler & Wool, 1989; Jersild, 1955). Psychoanalysts commonly refer to this as the problem of countertransference. Mannoni (1970) argues that in an ideal world all teachers would experience psychoanalysis so that they might better get in touch with the traumas and blockages of their own inner child and thereby be more open to emotionally freeing dialogue with the children in their care. Phenomenologist Max Van Manen, for example, argues in *The tone of teaching* that adults need to approach children with tact and thoughtfulness to bring forth each child's unexpressed possibility. As Van Manen notes, children bring us the gift of "experiencing the possible" (1986, p. 13). We merely have to allow ourselves to be free enough to receive that gift and reciprocate, a point that Buddhist thinkers have repeatedly made (cf. Epstein, 2004).

This, of course, is an unabashedly romantic notion of pedagogy as freeing children—and adults—to explore their inner beings in an unfettered manner. In *A child's work: The importance of fantasy play*, Vivian Paley (2004a) brings us back to reality with a harsh reminder of the drastic decline in fantasy play in early childhood curricula in the past decade in the United States. Paley's text offers powerful illustrations of the emotions that fantasy play elicits in children and the ways in which through natural storytelling processes children move from emotional expression, through language, to symbolization of their experiences and the construction of empathic learning communities in early childhood classrooms. In the analysis of young children's fantasy play that has emerged from decades of acutely attuned eavesdropping, Paley arrives at a startlingly psychoanalytic observation: "Had I listened more closely," Paley notes, "I would have heard among other secrets, that when one is young almost every story begins with and returns to a mother and child" (p. 18). Paley delightfully describes how she and her children "use fantasy to calm our anxieties and reassemble ourselves along promising paths" (p. 19), and laments greatly the academicization of early childhood education, a movement that denies children the opportunity to become the subjects of their own experiences: "The potential for surprise is largely gone. We no longer wonder "Who are you?" but instead decide quickly "What can we do to fix you?" (p. 47).

What then of the great progressive tradition of educators as guardians of the possibility for children to live whole lives, unrestricted by either the demands of parents or the sociopolitical limitations of our societies? I spoke just today with the kindergarten teacher of Vanessa, a beautiful five-year old patient of mine who is suffering acute stress.[2] Vanessa gouged her arms with a scissors at school, and when her teacher denied her access to scissors, she alternately chewed or scratched her arms to shreds. This little girl lives in an intolerably stressful situation at home—so much so that if she were a little older she would be considered at risk for suicide. Her sole refuge is school. Her teacher told me that Vanessa, who can barely write, leaves a stream of notes on the teacher's desk every day telling her teacher how much she loves her. Just this week, the teacher told me through her tears, Vanessa asked if she could come live at the teacher's home. School ends in three weeks, and we both fear for this beautiful child when she says goodbye to one of the few anchors in her unstable world. The love this teacher offers is inspiring, as is her capacity to see beauty and possibility in this truly vulnerable little girl. In my estimation, it is our ethical responsibility as educators to offer our students spaces in which to name and realize the *unthought knowns* that are pathways to their desires. The corollary of this, of course, is that we have to be prepared to stoutly resist initiatives that are designed to erase children's desires and limit their imaginations.

· 6 ·

ON LOSSES THAT ARE NOT
EASILY MOURNED

At the beginning of his book *On private madness*, André Green (1986a) ruminates on why he writes. Apart from the obvious reasons, which he gleaned from his own analysis, Green states that fundamentally he has no choice: His writing is driven by his own sublimated urges. In my case the answer is much less clear. While those who know me intimately will affirm that I use intellectual pursuits, especially reading, in a sublimating manner, my relationship with writing is much more tortured. It seems that I write to seek answers, but the act of writing is so fraught with resistance that it would appear that I have a strong aversion to whatever truths I might find. Ironically, I find my work as analyst and professor performative and vivifying. It is only in the totally solitary act of writing, in which my mirror image gazes back at me from the screen of my computer, that I face an inner emptiness that paralyzes me.

I am the sad clown. Those who encounter me in performative mode are moved to new emotional places and I experience a lightness of being in the interpersonal milieu that I have evoked. Yet, left to face myself, everything seems flat. This summer, for example, I taught a weeklong institute for teachers and psychologists on the emotional lives of children. As a capstone project on the final day, one group of students set up a playroom and all thirty-three of us played with children's toys for an hour. I felt transcendent. And then I came home to write...to write this promised chapter about depression...or rather to ruminate about depression and to flee back into reading others' writings because the prospect of placing my own words on paper became too anxiety provoking.

I am drawn to psychoanalytic writers who have the capacity to locate themselves explicitly in their work. It is somehow comforting to know that what Green termed "private madness"—the mirror image of my inner psychosis–is not mine alone. Perhaps all clowns are sad, and perhaps it is a clown's capacity to elicit an uncanny connection in audience members to their inner psychosis that is the true source of the clown's pathos. Green (1986a) notes that Harold Searles was preeminent among analysts in his capacity to "break the law of silence" (p. 15) and bring to life the dialogical relationship between his private madness and his capacity to work with patients. Paradoxically, while Searles was astute at using his own "private madness" as a therapeutic foil for his patients, he was also acutely aware of how easily the therapeutic encounter—much like the writing encounter for Green—could provide a sublimating escape from the analyst's own psychosis rather than an opportunity for new analytic inquiry:

> I surmise that not a few work-addicted analysts tend, as I do, to unconsciously defend themselves against an undeniably sustained experiencing of their own individual life by keeping themselves immersed in the collective lives of their patients. (1979, p. 159)

Perhaps, then, the opportunity to confront my own emptiness is a gift. I imagine myself as the clown meditating in his dressing room prior to a show. It is by reaching inward that I find ways of connecting to what, following Green (1999), I will refer to as the "objectalising/disobjectalising functions" that keep me connected yet leaves me alone among people. I have no way of knowing precisely what inaugural loss or deprivation might serve as the source of this emptiness, but, just as my patients do, I can imaginatively reconstruct links between known experiences and potential early correlates of those experiences that, at a minimum, provide me with an imaginary narrative of my life that "explains" my sense of loss and that names the unnamable, free-floating worry I experience when I leave myself free enough of intellectual pursuits to allow it to surface.

The crux is that all writing is autobiographical. I am no longer willing to hide myself in my writing because that makes me feel like an impostor. Therefore, when I stare at my reflection I recognize that I am compelled to come clean. Perhaps I am finally beginning to experience what my analytic training taught me at an implicit level, that becoming an analyst is really about being able to construct a narrative of one's journey into analysis. Thus, what set out to be a chapter on depression, an intellectual discourse on loss of vitality and feelings of emptiness, ends up, inevitably, as a tale of the intrapsychic encounter between self and other in the consulting room. More fundamentally, it is a tale of my reluctant journey as an analyst to confront the deeper and darker layers of my own psychic formation driven by my recognition that analytic insight and self-understanding are deeply intertwined.

Circa 1952—On Absence in Presence— An Abject Hospital Tale

When I was an infant I suffered from severe projectile vomiting for a period of two or more years. I spent most of that time in the local county hospital. There were occasional interludes when I was allowed home. I had two siblings, one and two years older, respectively. My dad worked all day, and my whole family was perched precariously on the precipice of poverty. The little time that I spent at home, my mother tells me, was frenetic. When I vomited at home there were no spare linens, and my mother did not have running water, let alone a washer or dryer. Thus, my illness caused serious domestic upheaval as well as lots of worry. It was far from the idyllic holding relationship Winnicott might have hoped for.

Meanwhile, at the hospital, my mom and dad were advised to visit me as infrequently as possible, as their presence invariably upset me and times when they could actually hold me were strictly limited. My mom tells me that when she visited she would peer longingly at me through the window. The hospital was so anxiety provoking for me that, to this day, I experience anxiety when I hear or see an ambulance. As a child I would stand paralyzed and "go white as a sheet" whenever an ambulance passed by. This experience resulted in arrested development and I reached all of my early developmental milestones about two years behind schedule. My life was saved when my dad, ignoring the doctor's advice to order a coffin for me, transferred me to the only other hospital in town where, in due course, I responded to treatment. The taxi driver who picked me up for my final trip home at age two was convinced that I was a newborn.

Today, my son and daughter are both emergency medical technicians, and both are embarking on careers in medical fields. Meanwhile, hanging in my office is a photograph given to me in 1987 by one of my students, a gifted amateur photographer. The picture is a headshot of a chalk statuette of an elegantly coiffed 1940's style woman staring wistfully at the world through the grimy window of an antiques shop. At the time I did not make much of it, but today I stand in awe of my student's uncanny sensibilities. Why did he shoot this particular image? Why, of the thousands of images in his portfolio, did he choose this one as his parting gift to me? I perform my emotions expressively in my teaching and in this course on human development I had focused particularly on loss, death and dying. I suspect that in so doing I worked through some of my own experiences of loss, and thereby unconsciously allowed him a window into the absence within.

My childhood illness was not easily forgotten. I lived on a restricted diet until I was fourteen and, reminiscent of the invalid boy, Colin, in Hodgson Burnett's (2003) *The secret garden*, I was labeled *delicate* throughout my childhood. I lived much of my childhood vicariously, envying the heartiness of Dickon in *The secret garden*, but identifying much more with the suffering children that peopled Dickens' novels. I bled for characters such as Smike, David Copperfield and Bob Cratchit's invalid son Tiny Tim. Although my early losses were intellectualized and sublimated to some extent, I never had the opportunity to name and symbolize them fully. They were part of my make-up in some nameless sort of way.

Poltergeists are invisible. Yet they have a way of making their presence felt. So too with my inner losses. They are my perpetual companions, a spectral and silent presence in my subjective experience of self. That is the part of me that gives off an aura of sadness and that causes me to feel dislocated and not belonging in the presence of others. It is often quiescent. Yet, like the poltergeist that is disturbed by new inhabitants occupying its ghostly mansion, excessive gaiety, loss, or loneliness, evoke intimations of unease and loss in my consciousness, insofar as experiences as unanchored and nameless as these can be said to be conscious at all.

March 1985—The Leave-Taking

When my father entered his final illness in the winter of 1985 I was still a graduate student in New York. I abandoned school for six weeks to return to

Ireland to be at his bedside. He had a terribly painful illness, yet the leave-taking, though lonely, was tranquil. Buttressed by his enviable religious faith in a better after-life and by the comforting presence of his family at his hospital bedside, my dad left this physical world. After the funeral an inordinate crowd of mourners came back to our house to eat, drink, and remember my dad. The revelry and absence of any *naming of loss* became unbearable for me, and I fled to my childhood bedroom to escape or perhaps indulge the *unspeakableness of my loss*.

Circa 1987—On Absence in Loss— Another Leave-Taking

Those among us who are exiles or emigrants know the dislocations that come with crossing borders and developing hybrid identities. I found an anchor to help me sustain myself through this struggle in a fellow traveler named Patrick. He was a year or two older than me and a veteran border crosser. Patrick died of leukemia when he was thirty-seven. His doctor and a small group of us stood at his death bed and granted his last wish that we share parting sips from a six-pack of Budweiser as he put the best face he could on what neither he nor any of us could name—his imminent death. Fifteen years later I was finally able to visit Patrick's wife at their home without being suffused by depression and a desire to flee. During those years I have never had the courage to listen to the audiotape of my remarks at the memorial service. The speech, as best I recall it, was a manic effort to protect all of us from annihilating grief by recreating the antic dynamic between Patrick and myself. Why do I now have the urge to listen to it?

June 22, 2002—Extract from a Dream

Dreams, of course, are the true poltergeists of the unconscious. Although I have revisited my family many times since I emigrated from Ireland, the trip I had planned for summer 2002 had some special significance as it was the occasion for a rare family reunion. Capitalizing on my return after an absence of five years, my sisters organized a surprise birthday party for my mom. My mom was seventy-six years old that summer, and this was the first time in her life that there has been a surprise party in her honor. I anticipated that my three sisters and I would attend, as well as grandchildren and relatives. My brother, who resided elsewhere in Europe, was noncommittal. The latest word I had was that he was too busy either to attend this event or to fly over to meet me during my visit. My brother had always resented the unearned privilege that accompanied my *delicate* status. The night before I departed I had a dream that included the following:

> We are attending a lavishly catered event. I greet my brother-in-law, Jackie—who, in real life is older—and I note that he looks much younger and happier than I. The table is all set and ready for dining and the moment comes for all of us to sit down. In my usual hesitant way I hold back a little to see where others choose to sit before taking my own seat. However, when I go to sit, all of the seats around the banquet table are occupied and there is no room for my brother and I. Everybody is eating and drinking with gusto. Nobody seems to notice that we are left out. I am holding a bowl of hearty chicken soup which, despite this being a catered affair, I know is made by my mother. Having no table on which to rest it, I balance it on my knee and try to break up one of the chunks of chicken. The chunk flies through the air and lands on my pants. In trying to catch it, I dribble the soup all over my clothes. I flee the room in confusion and change my clothes. My brother continues to eat his soup, and the others do not notice.

The actual party went according to plan, of course, and I derived some secret pleasure from my own sociability on that occasion. Nevertheless my dream is a reminder that I have periodically approached an abyss of primitive dread, a sense of non-belonging. In the days following the World Trade Center collapse, for example, I experienced a form of abject depression that I can only assume accurately mirrors my earliest experience. As Kristeva (1982) notes, failing to find anything outside with which to identify—and unwilling or unable to convert my melancholy into rage that I might expel onto Arabs, Afghanis, or any demonized Other—I turned inward and encountered the loss at the center of my being.

Inaugural Loss and its Consequences

My interest is in free-floating forms of primitive dread and emptiness, their origins, and their manifestations in psychic experience. Inaugural losses occur during the presymbolic period and continue to live within us as unsymbolized experience. While I have had little difficulty in recognizing split-off experiences in my patients, it took me a long time to recognize that the nameless, free floating feelings of worry and dread that I experienced were actually markers for unsymbolized and inaccessible aspects of my own experience. Psychoanalysis, Freud's pessimism notwithstanding, tends toward the optimistic and is often unreceptive to notions such as *inaugural loss* (Kristeva, 1982), *negativity* (Green, 1999), and the kinds of destructive impulses that Klein (1984c) described as underlying the paranoid schizoid position. As Joan Riviere noted, "The concept of a destructive force within every individual, leading toward the annihilation of life, is naturally one which arouses extreme emotional resistance" (Quoted in Rose, 1993, p. 134). Lacan's writings (e.g., 1968, 1977) leave us in no doubt, however, that the entry of humans into the symbolic realm, most particularly through language, is a painful process. Rose reminds us that, for Lacan, psychic negativity is simply "the price that all human subjects pay for the cruel passage of the psyche into words" (p. 131). The writings of Tustin and others at the Tavistock Clinic on the effects of autism (e.g., Tustin, 1992; Alvarez, 1992; Alvarez & Reid, 1999) and the work of others such as Bick (e.g., Briggs, 2002) and Bion (1989, 1993) reveal the cataclysmic psychic consequences of an incapacity to enter the world of the other through symbols. Overwhelming dread appears to be at the core of the everyday presymbolic psychic experience of autistic people. They appear to lack the capacity to gain even the temporary reprieve from terror that non-autistic infants accomplish through projection and that can, as Bion (1993) notes, ultimately lead to the reintrojection of metabolized, and hence less terrifying emotions.

Many analysts do not routinely work with significantly autistic or psychotic patients. Our population typically includes patients who have entered the world of the symbolic. Nevertheless, all analysts still have the opportunity to work with the unsymbolized parts of their patients' psychic experiences. Our capacity to work with these unsymbolized parts is what distinguishes psychoanalysis from other treatment modalities. More precisely, it is the capacity of the analyst to get in touch with unsymbolized or psychotic aspects of his or her own psyche and to use those therapeutically in the service of the patient that makes psychoanalysis distinctive. The repeated opportunity analysts have for working through their losses is surely at the root of the comforting adage that even if we do not improve our patients, we are no doubt helping to cure ourselves.

Depression without an Apparent Object

In her essay, *Negativity in the work of Melanie Klein*, Jacqueline Rose (1993) describes Klein as the "high priestess of negativity" because of her willingness to postulate a destructive or death instinct at the origins of psychic life. Contrary to "the idyll of early fusion with the mother" advocated, for example, by Winnicott, Rose tells us that "Klein offers proximity as something which devours" (p. 140). It is difficult to read Klein without experiencing a visceral response to the rage and destructiveness inherent in her vision of psychic development. Klein argues that it is *withholding* rather than symbiosis that is the catalyst for the delineation of subjectivity. Merger with an object produces tremendous narcissistic gratification. When this gratification is withheld, as it must inevitably be, the infant experiences a fundamental sense of loss. "For," Rose notes, "the loss of the object forces a breach in the primitive narcissism of the subject, a breach which, in a twist, produces the object as its effect." (p. 151). The earliest object relations, therefore are negative, arising from an infant's need to find an object to contain its projections. Experiencing a surge of negative emotion, and lacking the capacity to process these feelings, the infant seizes upon an object not for comfort but to expel negative feelings. Rose summarizes Klein's inscription of subjectivity in the negative as follows:

> In these earlier papers it is stated over and over that the subject first comes to experience itself negatively. Self-alienation gives the colour of the subject's coming-to-be: 'nothing good within *lasts*... the first conscious idea of 'me' is largely coloured by painful associations.' (Rose, p. 152, quoting from Riviere)

Rose points out that "For Klein the mother rapidly comes to be experienced as bad" (p. 153). In the ordinary course of things, Rose suggests, object relations "are 'improvements' on and 'protections against' primordial narcissistic anxiety; distrust of the object is better than despair." (p. 152). This is a dark view of the psychic life of the infant, a view that suggests that suffering is inevitable. Object relations from a Kleinian perspective are not idealized. While Klein does discuss reparative functions, her work does not allow us to imagine a relational world without suffering, disappointment, and inevitable loneliness. In the best of relational worlds, with an available good-enough-mother, the infant projects psychotic anxieties. These anxieties are returned with reasonable reliability in metabolized form by an attuned caregiver. In situations where "maternal reverie" fails, and where the infant is instead exposed to "a willfully misunderstanding object" (Bion, 1993) or, as happened with my mom, an absent object, the consequences, while not as calamitous as an autistic psychosis, are significant:

> Normal development follows if the relationship between infant and breast permits the infant to project a feeling, say, that it is dying, into the mother and reintroject it after its sojourn in the breast has made it tolerable to the psyche. If the projection is not

accepted by the mother the infant feels that its feeling that its dying is stripped of such meaning as it has. It therefore reintrojects, not a fear of dying made tolerable, but a nameless dread. (p. 116)

In her recent work, *Melanie Klein*, Kristeva (2001) notes Klein's point that even in the depressive position complete integration of the ego is never possible, and therefore loneliness and feelings of separation from the maternal object are inevitable. She cites Bion's fantasy of having a twin as a fantasy of integration of the ego that eliminates these splits. However, as Kristeva notes, when integration fails we are liable to experience a sense of non-belonging, a feeling with which I am all too familiar. Alternately, Kristeva notes, "one can defend oneself against too great a dependence on the external object by thrusting oneself upon the internal object," and this results in solitude being transformed into "an omnipresent feeling of forlorness." (p. 112)

Using a phenomenological approach, Kristeva has attempted to elucidate the psychic consequences of these kinds of losses. In a variety of writings, Kristeva (1982, 1989, 1991) focuses variously on manifestations of loss as expressed in symptoms of uncanny strangeness, abjection, and melancholia. In *Powers of horror*, for example, Kristeva describes how formless feelings of loss lead to an experience of abjection:

> There looms, within abjection, one of those violent, dark revolts of being, directed against a threat that seems to emanate from an exorbitant outside or inside, ejected beyond the scope of the possible, the tolerable the thinkable. It lies there quite close but it cannot be assimilated...When I am beset by abjection, the twisted braids of affects and thoughts I call by such a name does not have, properly speaking, a definable *object*. (1982, p. 1)

Kristeva conceptualizes this type of abject loss as arising from the inability to identify with an object in the world. This leads to a turn inward, a turn toward the emptiness that Kristeva theorizes as arising from an inaugural loss of significant proportions:

> If it be true that the abject simultaneously beseeches and pulverizes the subject, one can understand that it is experienced at the peak of its strength when that subject, weary of fruitless attempts to identify with something on the outside, finds the impossible within; when it finds that the impossible constitutes its very *being*, then it is none other than abject. The abjection of self would be the culminating form of that experience of the subject to which it is revealed that all its objects are based merely on the inaugural *loss* that laid the foundations of its own being. (1982, p. 5)

In *Black sun*, an examination of melancholia, Kristeva distinguishes two forms of depression. According to classical psychoanalytic theory, Kristeva notes, "depression, like mourning, conceals an aggressiveness toward the lost object" (1989, p. 11). An act such as suicide, therefore, is not only an act of aggression against the self but a reflection of hatred for the introjected object. Of more relevance, here, is the second form of melancholia posited by Kristeva. She suggests that often in narcissistic individuals, "sadness would point to a primitive self—wounded, incomplete, empty" (p. 12). This sadness is the "archaic expression of an unsymbolizable, unnameable, narcissistic wound" (p. 13). For such persons sadness itself becomes the object, and suicide merely a merger with sadness (p. 12). The center of mourning for a depressed narcissist, Kristeva says, is not an object, but rather an archaic attachment to an unsymbolizable object, which she refers to simply as the "Thing." The "Thing" is "an insistence without desire" (p. 13), that leaves the depressed person with a profound sense of having lost something supremely good but having no name for that lost object. Such a person, steeped in melancholia, is left without memory, without words, without desire, and could easily seek relief through suicide: "The Thing is inscribed within us without memory, the buried accomplice of our unspeakable anguish. One can imagine the delights of reunion that a regressive daydream promises itself through the nuptials of suicide" (p. 14).

Kristeva's ideas are consistent with the Kleinian perspective articulated above, and her broad-brush approach offers a useful window into the phenomenology of formless loss. It should be noted, however, that except in her recent work on Klein (Kristeva, 2001), Kristeva argues that the inaccessibility of unsymbolized experience is due to repression. I believe, following Klein, that splitting is a more likely explanation because of the inaccessibility, and non-neurotic characteristics of this nameless anguish. Green (1986a) clarifies the distinction this way: "The return of the repressed gives rise to signal anxiety. The return of the split-off elements is accompanied by feelings of severe threat, of 'helplessness' (Freud's *Hilfosigkeit*), 'annihilation' (Klein), 'nameless dread' (Bion), 'disintegration' or 'agonies' (Winnicott)" (Green, 1986a, pp. 77–78).

Green (e.g., 1986a, 1999; Kohon, 1999) has devoted a considerable amount of his writing to exploring this phenomenon. He speaks of blank psychosis as a radical solution to catastrophic object loss. Such a loss, rather than leading to repression results instead in a massive decathexis of emotion and a blank state of mind. Green's discussion of introjected maternal depression, the dead mother syndrome, is illustrative. By dead mother, Green is not referring to literal death, but rather to the effects on an infant of an emotionally dead mother.

A catastrophic event such as the death of a child or a miscarriage is liable to throw the mother into a deep depression. The effect on the infant is "a brutal change in the maternal imago" (1986b, p. 149), in which the vitality of the mother disappears. The blankness comes from the loss of meaning that occurs, in particular if the infant has nowhere else to turn to seek a metablolic outlet for his or her emotions. The crisis deepens when the infant, having exhausted available psychic defenses such as "agitation, insomnia, and nocturnal terrors" (p. 150) turns instead to "decathexis of the maternal object and the unconscious identification with the dead mother" (p. 150). Green characterized this not as a psychotic break, but as a breakdown only in a very specific area of emotional functioning, "a hole in the texture of object-relations with the mother" (p. 151). Modell (1999) offers another example. He describes a mother who, by virtue of her own psychic difficulties was unable to allow her child a mind of his own. The merger between the mother's mind and her son's mind caused the child to fail to identify his own psychic uniqueness and to feel psychically alive. As Green notes, the child may simply feel "forbidden for him to be" (p. 152).

The ego's attempts at repair involve the construction of what Green calls a "patched breast," a splitting off of the emptiness—the hole in the ego—and an attempt to replace it with sublimatory activities such as intellectual achievement, and an attempt to seek pleasure through auto-erotic excitation which allows for the sensation of pleasure without engagement with an other. In the area of intimate relations, predictably, the person remains vulnerable. "In this area," Green notes, "a wound will awaken a psychical pain and one will witness the resurrection of the dead mother, who, for the entire critical period that she remains in the foreground, dissolves all of the subject's sublimatory acquisitions, which are not lost, but which remain momentarily blocked" (p. 153). The patient, upon meeting a new love object may feel ready to love, believing that the dead mother trauma is excised, but the patient will fail, Green tells us, "because his love is still mortgaged to the dead mother" (p. 156). In a worst-case scenario, the emptiness the patient feels becomes the only alive part of the self—the absence becomes the presence, the dead becomes the living:

> Arrested in their capacity to love, subjects who are under the empire of the dead mother can only aspire to autonomy. Sharing remains forbidden to them. Thus solitude, which was a situation creating anxiety and to be avoided, changes sign. From negative it becomes positive. Having previously been shunned, it is now sought after. The subject nestles into it. He becomes his own mother, but remains prisoner to her economy of survival. He thinks he has got rid of his dead mother. In fact she only leaves him in peace in the measure that she herself is left in peace. As long as there is no candidate to

the succession, she can well let her child survive, certain to be the only one to possess that inaccessible love. (p. 156)

Shades of Norman Bates and his darling mother in Hitchcock's *Psycho*! Indeed, as was the case with Norman Bates' enactment, Green tells us that behind the blank mourning there is a "mad passion" of which the dead mother remains the object. The eternal fantasy of such patients is "to nourish the dead mother, to maintain her perpetually embalmed" (p. 162).

In more recent work, Green (1999, 2000) has attempted to situate his thinking about blank mourning within a larger structural theory of the work of the negative in psychic formation. Citing clinical instances such as the ones discussed, and the increasing prevalence of threats of mass destruction in the world, Green argues for the need to re-articulate the death drive as the motor of self-destruction. Green conceptualizes a life drive and a death drive. He argues that the purpose of the life drive is to ensure an "objectalising function" (1999, p. 85), by which he means the capacity to create and invest in meaningful object relations. In terms of the death drive, he cites clinical instances of the type discussed earlier, including "catastrophic or unthinkable anxieties, fears of annihilation or breakdown, feelings of futility, of devitalisation or of psychic death, sensations of a gap, of a bottomless hole, of an abyss" (p. 84). The purpose of the death drive, then is decathexis, a process Green labels "deobjectalisation." Contrary to the kind of mourning that sometimes accompanies loss, Green argues that this decathexis is characterized by an inhibition of the mourning function. This process, which involves what Bion would call attacks on linking, is at the heart of what Green (1999, 2000) terms negative narcissism—negative, because of the presence of significant self-abasement, and what Green calls "an aspiration to nothingness" (2000, p. 6).

Clinical Implications

Decathexis, splitting, and attacks on linking, symptoms of the kind of blank or formless depression under discussion here, make analysis challenging. In addition, the analytic relationship requires the co-construction of a new relational experience, and this requires the suffering person to turn away from solitude and toward acknowledging an other. Since wordless and formless anguish is presymbolic, the task of the analyst, as Kristeva (2001) notes, drawing on Segal and Bion, is for the analyst to use symbolism to enable the patient to transform unformulated *beta* elements into thinkable *alpha* elements, to experience mourning for an unnamable and unrepresentable archaic object. From the perspective of countertransference this requires the analyst to stay with the patient's unsymbolized experience long enough to work with it symbolically. This, of course, makes demands on the analyst's archaic objects and the analyst's capacity to live with his or her archaic experiences yet not be bound by them in the same unsymbolized manner as the patient.

Nancy

When Nancy presented for treatment she was in her thirties. Early in the treatment she brought in a childhood picture of herself, at about age three, gazing adoringly at her father who was working under the hood of the family car. She produced no picture of her mother. The definitive crisis in Nancy's life came when, in her early teens, her parents, long in a conflicted marriage, divorced. Nancy's father left during a bitter dispute and Nancy was forced to live with her mother. She could not handle the abandonment by her father. She went through periods of blank despair; a flight into drugs for a year; hospitalization for a psychotic break; and the development of severe schizoaffective symptoms accompanied by bouts of self-abasement, severe paranoid ideation, ideas of reference, and occasional delusions. Nancy abandoned her therapist of thirteen years without accepting a single session to explore termination issues. She sat in my office three times weekly and almost never made eye contact. She usually stared fixedly at the floor and said she really had nothing to say. She appeared to experience the most profound anger, but it always came out verbally as the mildest of recriminations—most often directed towards her mother or herself, but never at her idealized father.

By the time she began treatment with me Nancy had resumed an exquisitely delicate relationship with her father, some fifteen years after the catastrophic break. As we began to flesh out her family history she was explicit that we could talk about anything and change anything as long as it did not affect her relationship with either of her parents. These parameters, designed to protect her attachment to the emptiness that replaced the object, were to eventually prove fatal to the therapy. The predominant mode in our sessions was silence, punctuated by bouts of self-abasement, and anxiety lest I attack her. I found the silences extremely hard to bear. I began to doubt my competence and I constantly feared that she would abandon therapy. It took a considerable amount of work in supervision for me to recognize that her extreme isolation was evoking my own inner losses. I often experienced relief when she canceled a session. She showed little desire to speak of the external world, and she seemed terrified of her internal world. My supervisor's exhortations to me to join in her paranoid state rather than interpret from outside were initially puzzling and frightening to me. I often found myself perceiving her as waif-like and marginal, and for a long time I walked on eggshells in her presence. She was constantly fearful that I would take over her mind. I was fearful she would flee. Then I began to wonder if I was feeling her paranoia and I wondered if it was really me who wanted to flee the paranoid isolation we created. As I became more comfortable living in the deathly shadow of her paranoid structures some life entered the room. I caught a furtive smile from time to time, flirted a little, and pursued her when she canceled sessions. We even shared an occasional joke. I began to see a determined, interesting, and competent woman hiding behind the fragile shell she showed the world, and eventually I began to wonder if the fragility was an artful construction.

My suspicions about her fragility as an artifice were reinforced when Mother induced her to move back home under her care. The dynamic of their relationship was such that whenever Nancy exhibited signs of illness, Mother became solicitous and adopted a good mother role. However, whenever Nancy exhibited signs of thinking her own thoughts, Mother became extremely fragmented, enraged, and controlling. At such times, Mother would goad her until Nancy began to scream. After the fight, Nancy would eventually experience remorse and resolve to be a more caring and dutiful daughter. During their worst fights Nancy, lacking any self-soothing capabilities, would flee to the bathroom screaming and retreat into paranoid isolation. Mother would eventually remind her that she, Nancy, was sick and Mother was only doing things for Nancy's "own good." Mother suffered from severe anxiety and depression and had tremendous difficulties with boundaries. I referred Nancy to a new psychiatrist for medication management and Mother accompanied her to make sure, in Nancy's words, that she "got her story straight." I began to work with Nancy to help her distinguish her own thoughts from the overflow of psychotic anxieties she received daily from Mother. Gradually Nancy began to set her own boundaries and she began to use me as a resource to figure out where to draw the lines and to understand which psychosis belonged to her, and which belonged to Mother.

Nancy's professional life stabilized. She began dating casually, joined a sports league, and started interacting socially with long forgotten friends. She negotiated typically complex social situations such as family weddings and parties with greater ease. However, the more Nancy improved, the more Mother appeared to descend into rage-filled tirades, accusing Nancy of being ungrateful for all that Mother did for her. Did she not know how much Mother sacrificed on her behalf? Mother urged Nancy to resign her professional position and stay home all day. Feeling torn by guilt and pressed by Mother, Nancy agreed to accompany her on a vacation to a foreign country. During the vacation, Mother was extremely fragmented, and complained continuously. Nancy struggled valiantly to maintain boundaries but finally she reached breaking point. She called me from a foreign city and I reminded her of how to hold on to herself in the presence of Mother. She did, but she was wracked with guilt at thinking her own thoughts and not absorbing Mother's stuff. She was a bad girl, a failed daughter. The only way to make things up to Mother would be to become more dutiful and obedient. The therapy was making her life harder, highlighting the splits she experienced between self and Mother.

Nancy terminated therapy at that point, after eighteen months of treatment. She did agree to a few sessions for termination. Feeling that I had conceded defeat to Mother, I was rather depressed. I later learned that Nancy had moved out from home shortly thereafter, and was again living independently.

Not knowing Nancy's early history, it is impossible to delineate a possible relationship between early losses and later trauma. However, even from the brief description offered here it is evident that Nancy suffered serious ego disintegration as a result of a traumatic abandonment. Her situation was compounded by the absence of a metabolizing figure. Instead, her mother compounded the problem, further negating Nancy's existence by using her as a container for her own psychosis. Nancy's identification with her father may have precipitated her mother's persistent attacks on her. The end result was that Nancy suffered attacks on her capacity to make meaning, entered deep melancholia, and for many years lived in unspeakable anguish, having the kind of nameless loss at the center of her psyche that Green discusses as characteristic of negative narcissism. As noted earlier, Nancy lacked a capacity for mourning, due to her inability to symbolize her experience. In many respects, she was "forbidden to be." Her lengthy treatment, of which her work with me was only a small part, consisted of (1) encouraging Nancy's capacity to symbolize her experience; (2) engaging her in the kinds of dialogue that restored her capacity to think for herself and to restore absent links; and (3) fostering her desire and capacity for autonomous living. An ultimate goal, toward which small steps were taken, was to assist Nancy with engaging the possibility of moving from her terrified, distrustful object-relational state to a new form of objectalization in which mutual relations might become possible.

Nicole

Nicole entered once weekly therapy in her late twenties. She has no recollection of her mother as other than depressed. Disappointed in love both from her own mother and from the man she had hoped to marry, Nicole's mother then chose a marriage partner based on practical considerations. Nicole reports that her mother has lived her whole life in depression and suppressed anger, bitter toward men, burdened by her two daughters, and soothed only by alcohol. At age twenty, Nicole entered a relationship with an obsessive, alcoholic man. This relationship endured for a number of years and Nicole reports that she soothed herself through eating and heavy marijuana smoking. Her relationship ended under rather traumatic circumstances. Nicole returned home very depressed and sought therapy. Her relationship with her mother immediately reverted to its old pattern. Her mother, as always, was hypercritical and resentful of her presence in the home. Her mother resented the unspoken bond between Nicole and her father. Nicole had a deep longing for sexual and emotional intimacy but was terrified of entering a new relationship.

For three years our sessions had a numbing sameness. Nicole loved to come to sessions, and found in them a source of relief. She poured out the events of her week reportorial style and I felt induced to sleep. Sometimes her thoughts poured out in a jumble, as if she were thought disordered. I noticed that there was almost a direct correlation between Nicole's mental state and her mother's. When her mother has a bad week, Nicole was depressed and fragmented. When mother was occasionally solicitous, Nicole was elated, but this rapidly turned to depression, as she knew that this was temporary. It served only as a reminder of longing and loss. While she was cowed by her mother at home—and not helped by a docile and largely emotionally absent father—at work Nicole was very aggressive, suggesting that beneath the depression and fragmentation there was anger and life.

Many sessions had a manic quality to them. It was as if Nicole was desperately trying to connect, but even more desperately trying to keep me at bay. I had difficulty helping her symbolize her experience. My "dead mother" interpretations were of little help. "I know, that's why I hate my mother" was the typical response. By absorbing her experience without retaliation I managed to keep her engaged in therapy, though I felt little accomplishment in this. I felt that I was kept at arm's length.

In the past two years significant change has occurred in Nicole's life. She has earned a credential for a new profession, she has spent a year living on her own, she has taken a new professional position, and she has moved into a new apartment with her partner with whom she has shared a relationship for more than a year. This is not to suggest that all of her issues have been resolved. Her relationship with her mother may have improved on the surface largely because they now see each other infrequently. She continues to experience considerable levels of self-abasement and melancholy and she is still quite very fearful of touching that loss at the center of her being, even though she is well aware that metabolizing that loss is necessary to mitigate the pain. In addition, despite her bad first partner experience, she appears to have chosen a new partner who needs considerable care-taking. Nicole has some identification with her passive father, a man who has devoted his life to caring for her disconsolate mother.

Nicole's life has many elements that are suggestive of a dead mother introject. She has considerable difficulties with intimate relations, and rather than a securely introjected object, her thought confusions and bouts of melancholia and self-abasement suggest an internalized emptiness of the kind discussed earlier as negative narcissism. Nicole has been deeply wounded, but has lacked a capacity to symbolize that injury. She devotes considerable effort still to defending her mother, Nicole still has to struggle with intrusions from a decathected object. Despite these difficulties Nicole has struggled to create a new "third" in her relation with me. This co-construction has been hindered by her need to keep me at a distance. Yet, given the space to use the relationship on her own terms, Nicole has shown a capacity to develop and maintain a mutual relationship and is continuing in therapy.

Bringing Analysis to Life

Green (1986a) suggests that the analyst should strive to create a revivifying experience for the patient with unmourned losses. He cautions against silence on the analysts' part, as this is likely to cause the patient to retreat into solitude. Staying with such patients, however, is not easy. People who have negative narcissistic qualities and who experience blank mourning will come to sessions filled with feelings of self-abasement and unspeakable sadness. They will work to create a relationship in therapy that allows the confirmation and reproduction of those feelings despite a conscious desire to be healed. The likelihood is that the analyst who interprets from outside the patient's experience will contribute to the alienation of the patient and the objectification of their anguish. As the autobiographical introduction to this chapter suggests, it is my belief that the analyst needs to journey into his or her own losses in order to have the fortitude and sensitivity to engage the patient on a similar journey. What is needed is not didactic talk from an intrepid explorer who has already plumbed the depths and extracted nuggets of wisdom about inaugural loss. Instead, the humility of understanding the anguish of our own losses will allow us to tune our analytic ears to a register that allows us to absorb the patient's unconscious losses without the urge to either flee from or fix the patient.

· 7 ·

STRANGERS TO OURSELVES:
ON THE DISPLACEMENT, LOSS,
AND "HOMELESSNESS" OF
MIGRANT EXPERIENCES

"And what about your origins? Tell us about them, it must be fascinating!" Blundering fools never fail to ask the question. Their surface kindness hides the sticky clumsiness that so exasperates the foreigner.

—KRISTEVA (1991, P. 29)

My father lived all of his life in rural Ireland. Having lost all of his siblings as emigrants to London in the worst of circumstances, he stacked up the economic benefits of exile against the lifelong loss he knew would ensue and it just simply didn't add up. I never could find the words to explain my decision to emigrate to my dad. He wept profusely every time I left. I, in turn, am left perpetually to wonder if Kristeva wasn't correct when, in *Strangers to ourselves* (1991) she suggested that all of us who choose the path of exile are running away from, and toward, alienation: "Or should one recognize that one becomes a foreigner in another country because one is already a foreigner from within?" (1991, p. 14). Speaking of her own parents, Kristeva—an immigrant from Bulgaria to France—captured the violent alienation of this loss as follows:

And nevertheless, no, I have nothing to say to them, to any parents. Nothing. Nothing and everything, as always. If I tried—out of boldness, through luck, or in distress—to share with them some of the violence that causes me to be so totally on my own, they would not know where I am, who I am, what it is, in others, that rubs me the wrong way. I am henceforth foreign to them. (1991, pp. 22–23)

Philip Noyce's film, *Rabbit-Proof Fence* (Noyce, 2003; see also Pilkington, 2002), tells the story of the flight of three aboriginal girls from Moore River Settlement, a mission school for *half caste* children born as the result of liaisons between white fencers and aboriginal women. They were members of Australia's *stolen generation* of aboriginal and mixed-race children who were forcibly removed from their homes in an attempt at cultural annihilation and forced assimilation.[1]

As I watched this story of the systematic attempt by the Australian government to *whiten* Aboriginal people I was struck by the layers of complexity and complicity in the colonizing enterprise. The three girls are tracked relentlessly by the Australian police, and while they are betrayed by some whites on their twelve hundred mile trek, they are assisted materially by others. Their most formidable opponent is one of their own, Moodoo, an Aboriginal tracker who gives them a run for their money. Yet he, himself, is coerced into working for the government, and his daughter, too, is incarcerated in the school. Like all *good natives*, he has cultivated an inscrutability that makes it impossible to tell if he is working faithfully for the government or secretly subverting the pursuit. The inscrutable native allows us to project onto him whatever we choose.[2] Consistent with the colonial narrative, Christianity, and racism are conjoined in the persons of the angelic white nuns who run the mission school, scrubbing the children white, policing their language use, and tutoring them in Kiplingesque ditties for the benefit of their white benefactor, the ironically titled Chief Protector of Aborigines, Mr. Neville, named by the children "Mr. Devil."

As I read postcolonial reconstructions of the history of India, the Caribbean, the Pacific, countries in Africa, histories of indigenous peoples around the world, and of course the history of Ireland itself, I am increasingly struck by the unvarying sameness of the narrative, including economic colonization and military repression in the service of capitalism; racism through processes of inferiorization, dehumanization, and even enslavement; cultural and literal genocide; prohibition on access to schooling and the banning of native language and cultural practices; the development of a planter class, a local bourgeoisie, who through mimicry crudely ape their masters, implement their will, and aspire to inherit their power; the use of Christianization as a tool of subjugation, except in Ireland, where Otherness had to be reinforced through the attempted imposition of Anglican Christianity on a Roman Catholic population; and the elimination of indigenous knowledge-making through installation of a univocal, Eurocentric worldview and master discourse. All of this has ultimately led to participation of the oppressed in their own subjugation, frequently in late capitalist "democracies," in which the colonized people in what are now often called postcolonial societies are taught to believe that they are free. Gramsci (1971), who claimed there was no more powerful form of oppression than that which occurs with the consent of the oppressed, would be proud![3]

I come from Ireland and I spend a great deal of time meditating on the ways in which colonization, class subjugation, and Catholicism have interpellated and split my being. I will begin with some autobiographical meditations that will hopefully help locate myself. I will then introduce a few brief excerpts from writers whose capacity to capture some of the splits in Irish identity I find useful. I will then offer some meditations on history, memory, subjectivity, and the possibility of occupying the pedagogical margin subversively.

But first, a cautionary note from Trinh Minh-ha about the trickiness of this enterprise:

> How do you inscribe difference without bursting into a series of euphoric narcissistic accounts of yourself and your own kind? Without indulging in a marketable romanticism or in a naïve whining about your condition? . . . Between the twin chasms of navel-gazing and navel-erasing the ground is narrow and slippery. (Trinh, 1989, p. 28)

My God! I'm Split!

In 1940, one of my father's five sisters became pregnant out of wedlock at age sixteen. As was the custom then, as Peter Mullan details in his film *The Magdalene Sisters* (Mullan, 2004), girls who had sinned in this way were essentially ordered into permanent servitude under the auspices of Catholic nuns. They lived out their lives scrubbing floors and operating commercial ventures such as hand laundries on behalf of the nuns, in conditions that were appalling. Many children were physically and sexually abused in these institutions.[4] Their bastard children were either fostered to Irish families or sent as adoptees to Catholic families in the U.S. My father's sister was thus consigned to the local workhouse as an indentured-for-life servant. My dad saved enough money from his own meager income for her boat passage to England. He bribed the night watchman, climbed the gate, extracted her from the workhouse, and sent her to England. He never set eyes on her again. Her child, fostered out to a farm family in another abject form of indentured service in the Ireland of the period, died in his teenage years. My father continued to be a devoutly observant Catholic to the very end of his life. His sister's child was fostered to a family less than five miles from my family home...but we were not to learn of this until well after his death.

> *"C'mon. Hurry up. We'll miss our lift to school," my brother urged. I ran furiously. P.J. and Frances, older than I, knew that if we were there he'd let us pile in with all the other kids. What kid wanted to walk the mile to school in the frosty winter of 1958? We arrived at the van out of breath, with thank-yous on the tips of our tongues. We were on the tail end of the group as I scrambled after my brother and sister into the back of the blue Ford van. That was when the hand shot out and Hogan's voice rasped: "Are you an O'Loughlin? Get out. No O'Loughlins or Macs. I don't want to see the likes of you again."*

The story of my early life is in large part a battle against sanctioned inferiorization. I grew up as a member of the working poor in a rigidly class-stratified society. In the Ireland of my youth, local county councils bought plots of land from farmers and built subsidized *council houses*, commonly called laborer's cottages, for the working poor. They put special red tiled clay roofs on the houses so that they were distinctive. *A ghetto of red-roofed houses scattered across the rural landscape.* I guess they felt that we were not sufficiently marked by poverty, and God forbid we might rise above it and conceal our origins. The red roofs served as a powerful reminder to all of our abject origins. My mother lives in that house to this day. She is still marked as Other by the tyranny of bureaucratic architecture. I can recall returning from the only college visit I ever made, and asking the coach driver to stop a quarter of a mile from my home so that my abject origins would not be evident to my classmates.

I grew up in a society that endured British colonization for over eight hundred years. British colonialism in Ireland continues to this day. Since the British erased our language in a purposeful campaign of cultural genocide, most of us grew up speaking only English. However, as Homi Bhabha reminds us in his discussion of mimicry, while the British forced us to speak their language for purposes of domination, there were limits to how well we should speak it: "[T]o be Anglicized is *emphatically* not to be English" (Bhabha, 1994, p. 87). Our English was actually meant to mark us as inferior, in the same way that Indian English and Caribbean Englishes mark their speakers as Other. It worked. I can recall attending a conference a few years ago and, by chance, sitting next to a colleague from Oxford University who spoke in the perfect cadences of Oxford English. In spite of my best efforts to carry on a collegial conversation, I became overwhelmed with a sense of inferiority and was tongue-tied throughout the meal.

Growing up working-class, I often feel mystified as I try to live the life of an academic and try to understand the pretensions, aspirations, and mysterious ways of my academic colleagues. Ryan and Sackrey's (1995) *Strangers in Paradise* and Sennett and Cobb's (1993) *The hidden injuries of class* comfort me that the class dislocations I experience are not uniquely mine, but are in fact typical of the contradictions and tensions people experience as they try to cross boundaries in a class stratified society. Must we hide? Do we have to become impostors to ourselves? Or can we make room in our society for hybrid identities that allow us to minimize loss as we move across class, gender, race, and national boundaries?

Although I was not conscious of my racial formation, I now realize that the signs of otherness were always present. In our small town people commonly referred to the occasional Nigerian intern at the county hospital as "the black doctor." The Catholic Church abetted our racial formation through ubiquitous collection boxes soliciting pennies for "black babies" in Africa. There was a collection box in every classroom, with a destitute "black baby" staring vacantly from the photograph pasted on the front. Colonialist images of African black-ness as destitute, ignorant, and *other* were promulgated in glossy missionary magazines such as *The Far East* and *Africa*, which we sold door to door to help Irish missionaries in "darkest Africa" and South America. When television came to Ireland we also received our share of images of exotic black otherness from National Geographic type documentaries. I would go to a neighbor's house on summer evenings to watch television. In a country in which Catholic bishops had the power to suppress all images of sexuality, we were permitted to gaze without shame on the dark nakedness of the African Other in National Geographic specials. As Franz Fanon remarks in his analysis of the effects of colonialism on the black psyche: "In Europe, that is to say, in every civilized and civilizing country, the Negro is the symbol of sin. The Negro represents the archetype of the lowest values." (1967, p. 189).

I sit here, more than forty years later, and wonder what effect these unexamined representations of otherness have on my psyche. When my mom was in New York for her annual visit a few years ago we got to speaking of my sister and her newly adopted child from India. We were discussing how well my sister was prepared for raising an ethnically Indian child in Ireland. My mother acknowledged that the child would have problems, and went on to cite widely publicized incidents of racial harassment involving a family of Indian origin. Then, to my surprise, she said: *"It's just as well your father is not alive. He'd never speak to her again.*" She went on: "*The baby's too dark. Dad would never accept him. He was always dead set against blacks.*" My father had only a fourth-grade formal education. He had limited access to literacy and no interest in television. He rarely traveled beyond a forty mile radius of home. Living in a racially homogenous society what could be the source of his hatred of "blacks"? Did his father before him hate "blacks" too? Did his neighbors and friends? What effect did this unacknowledged hatred have on my racial formation? Are such sentiments handed down unconsciously from one generation to the next through the inferiorization of the psyche and the transmission of historical memory? What does knowing this do to me? As for my nephew, he was beaten up on the first day of kindergarten that Fall in his neighborhood school in a small town in Ireland.

Shadows of Memories: Exactly Who Do You/I Think I am?

History matters. Traumatic events in history and in families matter even more. There is considerable literature in psychoanalysis on the effects of ghosts (Fraiberg, Adelson & Shapiro, 1975; Gordon, 1997) phantoms (Abraham & Torok, 1994), unspoken secrets (Rashkin, 1992; Rogers, 2006), specters (Derrida, 1994; Venn, 2002) and catastrophic histories (Davoine & Gaudillière, 2004) on the psyches of people.[5] Selma Fraiberg, for example, suggests that pathological responses in the present can often be traced back across multiple generations, and Davoine and Gaudillière offer compelling evidence of a relationship between madness in the present and unspoken ancestral trauma. In attempting to understand myself, and particularly the unquiet aspects of my being, I have attempted to reach into my past and retrieve not only individual and familial narratives, but also narratives from the larger sweep of history that may serve to help explain my passions, disquietudes, and inhibitions to myself.

Reading *The Irish mind* (1985) by Richard Kearney, for example, I cringe anew at the characterization of my ancestors and wonder how this disrespect was internalized by them and whether remnants of it are still lurking in my psyche producing potential for inferiority, rage, and even racism:

> The British historian Charles Kingsley provided further justification for the cultural and military oppression of his Irish neighbours, when he composed this racist portrait in 1860: "I am daunted by the human chimpanzees I saw along that hundred miles of

horrible country. I don't believe they are our fault. I believe that there are not only many more of them than of old, but that they are happier, better and more comfortably fed and lodged under our rule than they ever were. But to see white chimpanzees is dreadful; if they were black, one would not feel it so much, but their skins, except where tanned by exposure, are as white as ours." So much for the colonial calibanization of the Irish. (1985, p. 7)

When I was a child a mass grave with a large number of skeletons was discovered a few hundred yards from my home. These were the remains of victims of the Great Famine which overtook Ireland in the mid-1800s. In her epic work on the Irish Famine, *The great hunger* (1962), Cecil Woodham-Smith offers vivid and depressing descriptions of the genocidal famines that yielded over a million deaths in Ireland and forced millions more into exile as indentured servants, while Great Britain exported Irish grain and livestock. Many of those who fled traveled in dreadful conditions in the holds of sailing ships. So many died that the ships became known as *coffin ships*. From a passenger's journal here is how one such voyage was described:

> Most of the passengers were from the South of Ireland; provisions and water were short and of execrable quality, but the captain, Thompson, was kind. Ship fever appeared before the *India* was a week out and Captain Thompson caught it and died; twenty six passengers also died, water ran short and the ration was reduced to a pint a day, three of the passengers became lunatics, and one threw himself overboard. Two ships were hailed and implored for a little water; they replied that they had none to spare—ship fever was raging in their own holds...when, after a voyage of more than eight weeks the *India* arrived at Staten Island he [the journal author] and 122 others were taken to the hospital...the patients were cruelly treated: the beds, grids of iron bars with a little straw laid on the top inflicted torture on the sick, who were reduced by fever to skin and bone; the doctors were negligent and indifferent, the male nurses took a delight in abusing and thwarting the helpless and struck patients for innocent errors; food was uneatable and conditions horribly insanitary. (Woodham-Smith, p. 251)

What phantom might dwell within me from the suffering of my ancestors who evidently survived such wrenching events? At what psychic cost did they survive, and did those psychic scars have an opportunity to heal or are they still haunting contemporary descendants such as I? I do know that I experienced Cecil Woodham-Smith's *The great hunger* as profoundly haunting from the first time I read it at age sixteen.

While there is tragedy aplenty in my Irish heritage, it is possible, nevertheless, to fashion redemptive narratives from Irish history that induce stirrings of patriotism, creativity and pride. Much of the great literary output of Ireland may well be associated with the ready juxtaposition of tragedy, comedy and hope. The story of my encounter with Irish-American history is a much more difficult tale however. Tragically, the Irish who made it to the U.S. were greeted with an onslaught of nativist prejudice and xenophobia.[6] Irish immigrants might have responded to this by making common cause with free Negroes and by supporting the movement for abolition. Instead, they edged out blacks at the bottom of the social ladder, and, on the basis of racial bonding, claimed domestic and laboring jobs as their right by virtue of their whiteness. As Frederick Douglass noted in 1853, "The Irish, who at home readily sympathize with the oppressed everywhere, are instantly taught when they step upon our soil to hate and despise the Negro" (cited in Ignatiev, 1995, frontispiece). Douglass also commented: "Every hour sees us elbowed out of some employment to make room for some newly-arrived emigrant from the Emerald Isle, whose hunger and color entitle him to special favor..." (cited in Ignatiev, 1995, pp. 111–112). Ignatiev concludes: "To be acknowledged as white, it was not enough for the Irish to have a competitive advantage over Afro-Americans in the labor market; in order for them to avoid the taint of blackness it was necessary that no Negro be allowed to work in occupations where Irish were to be found." (pp. 111–112). Scholarship on whiteness (Fine et al., 1996; Frankenberg, 1993; McIntosh, 1988; Roediger, 2006, 2007; Seshadri-Crooks, 2000; Tuckwell, 2002) has established the responsibilities white people bear for historical inequalities and oppression, and for the perpetuation of those inequities through implicit systems of privilege. My awareness of the strategic role Irish Americans played in declaring themselves white troubles further my engagement with my white privilege. It is very difficult for me to square my progressive politics, which are in part a product of the kind of privilege that access to cultural capital such as my advanced education provides, with the historical inequalities on which such privilege is constructed.

As I rummage in my cultural/historical backpack a few other elements are worthy of scrutiny. Growing up in southern Ireland, I was raised in an ultra-Catholic environment, and while it would probably take many years on an analyst's couch to disentangle the interpellative effects of that experience on my being, I will content myself with this brief satirical thumbnail sketch from the pen of Anglo Irish social critic Terry Eagelton. In *The gatekeeper*, Eagelton, raised in an Irish family in England, summarizes his experience of Catholicism, this way:

> Just as the convent bore only a tenuous relation to reality, so did Catholicism as a whole. Its esoteric doctrines seemed no more applicable to everyday life than trigonometry was applicable to pressing your trousers. Like magic, it was a highly determinate system, but entirely self-confirming, with all the exceptional clarity of an hallucination.

Catholicism was less about good deeds than about how to keep the charcoal in your thurible alight or knock about fifty years off your allotted time in purgatory. It was less about charity than candelabras. We were pious and heartless, strict-minded and mean, pure-living and pagan. There was a crazed precision about the Church's doctrinal system…It resembled the insane exactitude of the psychotic whose mathematical calculations are impeccable, but who is carrying them out perched on a window ledge thirty floors up. (2002, pp. 30–31)

Another deeply embedded dimension of Irish culture, one not so removed from the Catholic Puritanism of that era in Ireland, is a certain hardness when it comes to children's emotions. This is evident, for example, in Frank McCourt's widely read *Angela's ashes* (1996), a work, that was received in parts of Ireland with considerable resentment. Writing in 1991, Anthony Clare, one of Ireland's leading psychiatrists, characterized Irish culture as "A culture heavily impregnated by an emphasis on physical control, original sin, cultural inferiority and psychological defensiveness" (p. 14), and he quotes an Irish psychiatrist writing on Irish child-rearing practices in 1976:

The family home in Ireland is a novitiate for violence. Even from the cradle the child is made to feel rejection, hostility, and open physical pain. The infant is left to cry in his cot because his mother does not want to 'give in to him.' Later he is smacked with the hand or a stick. He is made to go to bed early. He is not allowed to have his tea. He is put in a room by himself…and in order to invite this morale breaking treatment from his parents, all the Irish child has to do is to be *normal*. It is the normality of childhood that sets parents' teeth on edge. They take no joy in childishness. (1991, pp. 15–16).

I am a child therapist, I teach courses on children's emotional well-being, and I consider myself an advocate for children. I spend a large portion of my life working with parents and teachers to create the possibility of healing and caring communities for children at home and at school (e.g., O'Loughlin, 2006; see also Chapter 4 in this volume). As I explained in Chapter 3, I am in little doubt that these activities are fueled by a reparative impulse based on the tone-deafness to children's needs in my Irish childhood.

On Homelessness, Marginality and the Decolonizing Potential of Loss and Otherness

My return to my native Ireland a few summers ago was unsettling. I went home—yes, I still call it "home"—but everywhere I went I felt that people silently coded me as Other. I wandered through Dublin trying fruitlessly to find myself in a sea of Irish faces. At the conference I attended I felt pierced by an Irish gaze. This contemptuous gaze, with which I was all too familiar, was the one that we—oops, "they"—reserve for pathetic Yanks coming back to find their roots. As Eva Hoffman (1990) and others (e.g., Aciman, 1999) have noted, a journey into subjectivity is also a wrenching journey away from subjectivity. Gains come through losses. Voice emerges from muteness. Movement stems from paralysis. As Kristeva (1991) notes, border crossers—and here I include gender, class, and ethnic border crossers as well as migrants and exiles—become strangers to themselves. This painful location, one of displacement, ambiguity, hybridity and loss, is increasingly a feature of the alienated global capitalist world all of us inhabit (cf. Augé, 1995; Cushman, 1995). While alienation structures all of our subjectivities, it is etched in sharpest relief in the migrant's futile search for home.

The Possibilities of Subaltern Memory and the Perils of Autobiography

> Eventually, of course, one does stop being an exile. But even a "reformed" exile will continue to practice the one thing exiles do almost as a matter of instinct: compulsive retrospection. With their memories perpetually on overload, exiles see double, feel double, are double. When exiles see one place they're also seeing—or looking for—another behind it. Everything bears two faces, everything is shifty because everything is mobile, the point being that exile, like love, is not just a condition of pain, it's a condition of deceit. (Aciman, 1999, p. 13)

From a theoretical perspective, my interest is in exploring what Leo Spitzer (1989) calls "the predicament of marginality" engendered by multiple border crossings and suppressed memories. In *The burden of memory*, Wole Soyinka (1999) describes the capacity of an ancient piece of Yoruba music played on the legendary Sosso-Balo to call up fossil memories from deep within his psyche:

> It was a dirge of ancestral severance, of loss too great to quantify...The Sosso-Bala becomes an unsolicited metaphor for the near intolerable burden of memory, a muse for the poetry of identity and that elusive "leaven" in the dough of humanity—forgiveness, the remission of wrongs, and a recovery of lost innocence. (pp. 193–194)

I share Soyinka's faith in the possibility of memory and I have found books such as Toni Morrison's *Beloved* (1988; see also Plasa, 1999) and Elie Wiesel's

Night (1982) pedagogically valuable for stirring unconscious memories and engaging students with their own historical constitutedness.[7] It would be naïve, however, to assume that stepping out of a Westernized/Eurocentric/enlightenment/rational bubble is an easy task. In asking "Can the subaltern speak?" Gayatri Spivak (1988) raises the critical question: Can we ever create conditions that allow non-dominant cultural identities and historical narratives to surface and claim their space in national discourses and educational practices? Trinh Minh-Ha (1989) is skeptical of the pervasive rhetorics of inclusive multiculturalisms. She worries about the dangers of "hegemonic dis-ease" embedded in such rhetorics: "A conversation of 'us' with 'us' about 'them' is a conversation in which 'them' are silenced. 'Them' always stands on the other side of the hill, naked and speechless, barely present in its absence" (p. 67). How might a teacher address this predicament of marginality?

In *The intimate enemy*, Ashis Nandy (1983) points out that the greatest obstacle to truly embracing subaltern Others has to do with *the enemy within*. Western, and perhaps non-Western, people's subjectivities have been interpellated with an *imperial consciousness* which prevents acknowledgment of subaltern identities. In meeting an Indian, for example, Nandy suggests that instead of understanding that Indian a Westerner is more likely to project onto that person his or her own fantasies of Indianness.

> India has always been a separate world, hard for any outsider, *Eastern or Western*, to penetrate. Such a culture becomes a projective test; it invites one not only to project onto it one's deepest fantasies, but also to reveal, through such self-projection, the interpreter rather than the interpreted. All interpretations of India are ultimately autobiographical. (pp. 79–80)

Dipesh Chakrabarty (2000) makes a similar argument regarding Western epistemology (cf. also Chatterjee 1993). He suggests that Western ways of knowing are so ingrained in how we think about knowledge that in school contexts it is virtually impossible to think otherwise. Referring to history, for example, he states that "Europe remains the sovereign theoretical subject of all histories, including the ones we call 'Indian,' 'Chinese,' 'Kenyan,' and so on. There is a peculiar way in which all these histories become variations on a master narrative that could be called 'the history of Europe'" (p. 27).

The issue is further troubled in that Western modes of being are tied up with "the practices, institutions, and discourses of bourgeois individualism," such that for an Indian "to be a 'modern individual' was to be European" (Chakrabarty, p. 33). Chakrabarty argues that the kind of confessional, private archeological inquiry that typifies Western subjectivity (and that some of the chapters in this book represent)—and that is inherent in bourgeois psychoanalysis, for example, of which I am a practitioner[8]—is alien to Indian epistemology and subjectivity.[9] Can all of this mirror-gazing and projection ever get us outside the circle of imperial consciousness? Is our interiority, the very thing we call *self*, peculiarly a Western illusion? He frames the issue thus:

> This modern individual, however, whose political/public life is lived in citizenship, is also supposed to have an interiorized "private" self that pours out incessantly in diaries, letters, autobiographies, novels, and, of course, in what we say to our analysts. The bourgeois individual is not born until one discovers the pleasures of privacy.... It is not that the forms of the bourgeois private self did not come with European rule. There have been since the middle of the nineteenth century, Indian novels, diaries, letters, and autobiographies, but they seldom yield pictures of an endlessly interiorized subject. (Chakrabarty, p. 35)

In teaching children from subaltern cultures, therefore, we are faced with two enormous challenges. How can we see the enculturated child in front of us for who he or she is, when our subjectivity predicates us to see them as projections and fantasies of our own cultural experiences? How can we embrace diverse ways of knowing and being if the worldview of Westernized education is saturated with forms of knowing that are ideologically imperial, rational, individualist, capitalist, and ultimately silencing of diverse viewpoints and historical narratives?

The Anxiety of the Foreigner, the Double Bind of Exile, and the Risks of Assimilation

> I belong nowhere, and everywhere am a stranger, a guest at best. Stefan Zweig (quoted in Spitzer, 1989, p. 171)

> This means that settled within himself, the foreigner has no self...I do what they want me to, but it is not "me"—"me" is elsewhere, "me" belongs to no one, "me" does not belong to "me,"...does "me" exist? Julia Kristeva (1991, p. 8)

What is to be the fate of the exile, the migrant, the hybrid, the border crosser? Are these writers unduly pessimistic? The in-depth case studies of the lives of three very successful nineteenth century border crossers, Stefan Zweig, Cornelius May, and André Rebouças, as reported by Leo Spitzer (1989), offer little comfort that even assimilated second-generation migrants can stop looking over their shoulders. Spitzer tells us that despite the extraordinary success of these men in their adopted lands, assimilation and acceptance were highly contingent. Cornelius May, son of a freed slave, was raised in bourgeois respectability in Freetown, Sierra Leone, and accomplished his parents' dream of assimilation by becoming a newspaper publisher as well as mayor of Freetown. "Throughout his formative years," Spizer notes, "Cornelius May found the British colonial system, of which he was a subject, generally acceptable, and viewed himself as different from and superior to Africans who had not experienced or taken advantage of prolonged cultural contact with Europeans in order to 'better' themselves" (p. 143).

André Rebouças, a mulatto child in Brazil, rose to a position of major importance in Brazil's government as well as in industry through a "willingness to become totally identified with the values of the predominantly white Brazilian elite" (Spitzer, p. 115). Stefan Zweig, one of the most widely read and translated authors of his time (Spitzer, p. 73) was a Viennese Jew who experienced immense success until the rise of Hitler, when "for perhaps the first time…Stefan Zweig, European, was being *defined from without* as Stefan Zweig Jew" (Spitzer, p. 167). Two of these highly accomplished men (Rebouças & Zweig) became despondent at their ultimate rejection on racial grounds after years of apparently successful assimilation and committed suicide, and the other (May) was turned upon and imprisoned for being an outspoken Black man in a British colony.

What these case studies demonstrate is the permanent insecurity many border crossers feel. Otherness and difference are continually marked and the *race/gender/sexual orientation/class/religion/migrant/exile alien/terrorist/Muslim/of Middle Eastern descent/illegal alien/suspicious looking/shifty/different…* cards can be sprung at a moment's notice. The illusions of assimilation are easily shattered. Spitzer notes that despite the apparently successful assimilation of Zweig, May, and Rebouças, they were only one incident away from being "plunged into a period of considerable psychological uncertainty about their identity: a crisis period of inner conflict and disorientation during which they became conscious of their marginal position between two worlds" (p. 145). How many of our children must live thus vigilant in putatively "multicultural" societies?

Kristeva sums up the perpetual anxiety of the foreigner thus in *Strangers to ourselves*: "Civilized people need not be gentle with foreigners. 'That's it, and if you don't like it why don't you go back where you came from!' " (1991, p. 14). A graduate student in my class on multicultural education one year sent me a note with similar sentiments after a class discussion that explored social inequalities and the workings of white privilege in the U.S. "If you are so critical of U.S. society why don't you just leave?" she queried. Small wonder we keep looking over our shoulders.

The Origins of Subjectivity in Alienation

"Therefore the Lord God sent him forth from the garden of Eden, to till the ground from whence he was taken. So he drove out the man; and he placed at the east of the garden of Eden Cherubims, and a flaming sword which turned every way, to keep the way of the tree of life." Thus Genesis, on humankind's first exiles. Since then, is there anyone who does not—in some way on some level—feel that they are in exile? We feel ejected from our first homes and landscapes, from childhood, from our first family romance, from our authentic self. We feel there is an ideal sense of belonging, of community, of attunement with others, and at homeness with ourselves, that keeps eluding us. (Hoffman, 1999, p. 39)

While my remarks thus far may have induced in you, the reader, reverie about your own border crossings, or speculations about the challenges facing indigenous, bicultural, and migrant children, and facing all children who are seen as other in our world, Eva Hoffman's statement is a reminder that this comes much closer to home for all of us. Both Kleinian theory (cf. Rose, 1993) and Lacanian theory (Apollon et al., 2002; Fink, 1995; Homer, 2005; Lacan, 1968, 1977, 1998; Nobus, 1998; Van Haute, 2002) address the onset of otherness in the formation of subjectivity, though, in this respect, Klein's emphasis is more narrowly on the psychic scars of the birth trauma itself.[10] Here I will discuss Lacan's understanding of the alienation caused by entry into the social world, beginning perhaps at six months of age.

For Lacan, the journey into self is, in many respects, a journey away from our originary sense of being, such as it is. Lacan argues (cf., also Althusser, 1971b; Butler, 1997) that becoming a subject is a process of becoming subject to the prevailing discursive practices of society. The paradox is that what we consider to be a self requires giving up much of whatever primordial sense of self we are born with and constructing a socially constituted sense of self by entering the linguistic and discursive practices of society. Thus, self is shaped through the responses of others, and is thereby a fundamentally alienating experience.

More precisely, a child's subjectivity is shaped both by the explicit demand and the unconscious desires of the Others in a child's life. When the infant first encounters its own image in a mirror it sees the primordial I. The mirror image rapidly becomes objectified through the linguistic structuring of the Other who basically tells the child what it sees. "Look. There's Joseph. Say Joseph. J O S E P H!" Gradually the child internalizes identification with the objectified image of itself and eventually becomes a speaking and indeed spoken—hence alienated—subject:

> The *mirror-stage* is a drama whose internal thrust is precipitated from insufficiency to anticipation—and which manufactures for the subject, caught up in the lure of spatial identification, the succession of phantasies that extends from a fragmented body-image to a form of its totality that I shall call orthopaedic—and, lastly, to the assumption of the armour of an alienating identity, which will mark with its rigid structure the subject's entire mental development. (Lacan, 1977, p. 4)

The young child is in an impossible position. To refuse to enter the world of language and to refuse identification with the Other in an attempt to preserve the primordial I leaves the child in an autistic/psychotic state of the kind described by Alvarez (1992) and Tustin (1992). As Bruce Fink notes, "A psychotic child may very well *assimilate* language, but cannot *come to be* in language the same way as a neurotic child" (1995, p. 55). Accepting language, however, and entering the symbolic world, while clearly necessary for interpersonal functioning, as well as for the symbolization of subjective psychic experience, comes with a high price tag—alienation. The *coming to be* of the child is in response to the linguistic structuring and recognitions/misrecognitions of the child by its parents. Lacan suggests that it is the sum of these collective linguistic structurings that causes a child to build up a sense of its own subjective self.

While a mother, for example, may repeatedly tell her son that he is a model son, this is not necessarily what enters the child's unconscious. As Fink, from whom this example is drawn, notes, " 'You're a model son'—is, like all communication, prone to miscommunication: the son may understand/misunderstand that appraisal in terms of model cars and planes, viewing himself thereafter as but a miniaturized, plastic version of the real thing, instead of a genuine son" (1995, p. 37). In addition, since the child is taking in mirror images of reality through the Other's discursive practices and desires, many distortions, are incorporated in the child's construction of self. Thus, each of us gains a sense of existence by subscribing to a symbolic order that has begun structuring our subjectivities well before we are born, and even before we are conceived. Lacan is clear, however, that while we develop a sense of subjective being through entry into language and the capacity to symbolize, human agency rests not with an essential *self* or ego, but resides in the unconscious. He gives numerous examples of how the unconscious plays with language to express meanings and desires through slips and slides that offer tiny windows to our inner subjectivity or state of being (cf. Apollon et al., 2002).

Lacan also believes that a child's unconscious desires are structured through the Other's—often mOther's—desires and that in effect *"the subject is caused by the Other's desire"* (Fink, 1995, p. 50). Philippe Van Haute summarizes the workings of desire in the child this way:

> What then does the mother want? What makes her repeated absences necessary? Or yet again: What does she desire that apparently I cannot give her. To the degree that the little child remains caught in the logic of the unconditional demand for love, it can think of only one solution to this situation—it tries to be or become the object that can fulfill the desire of the mother, and thereby tries to finally assure itself of the mother's love. (2002, p. 113)

The price the child pays for this, as Van Haute notes, is that in unconsciously pursuing the Other's desire, the child loses sight of its own desires (p. 114). Lacan suggests that the omnipotence of the mOther's desire is a significant source of anxiety, and that the child needs to break free from the mOther in order to develop its own desires. Lacan argues that through entering the symbolic the child can break free from this reality, and he suggests that a transitional object serves the function of symbolizing this break—a rupture that is inevitably accompanied by alienation.

In *Desiring whiteness* (2000) Kalpana Seshadri-Crooks uses this theory to show how, because of the dominance of whiteness as a racial signifier, the racial identities that children acquire as they grow up are inherently colored by whiteness. If Seshadri-Crooks is correct, then notions of racial difference are absorbed into our subejctivities very early, and are therefore very difficult to change later.

Rending the Fabric of Multicultural Discourses

> Trying to find the other by defining otherness or by explaining the other through laws and generalities is, as Zen says, like beating the moon with a pole or scratching an itchy foot from the outside of a shoe. There is no such thing as a "coming face to face once and for all with objects"; the real remains foreclosed from the analytic experience, which is an experience of speech. In writing close to the other of the other, I can only choose to maintain a self-reflexively critical relationship toward the material, a relationship that defines both the subject written and the writing subject, undoing the I while asking "what do I want wanting to know you or me?" Trinh (1989, p. 76)

Multicultural discourses, like all other aspects of schooling, are premised on information and reason. What if Trinh is correct that rational reason cannot get the job done because we are dealing with deeply unconscious aspects of the psyche? What if, instead of trying to persuade children to be *tolerant* and *inclusive*, we recognize that we must turn reason on its head and teach to the unconscious? Lacan argues for using a hysterical sensibility to detect the tears in the fabric of the symbolic order and to reach through for revolutionary possibilities. I suspect that the late Spike Milligan (2003, 2006) with his mad capacity for seeing the world from upside down and inside out, or maverick comic book illustrator Robert Crumb (Zwigoff, 2006), might serve as better guides to getting close to the unconscious than the kind of intellectual imprisonment that much of the discourses of schooling and multiculturalism offer.

Those of us who live consciously with the predicament of marginality can work to complexify and decolonize our students' understandings of these processes. By becoming sensitive to the exquisite losses involved in border crossings we can engage our migrant, ethnic and class border crossing students and our gender bending students in hysterical conversations that rupture rationality and reveal the socially constructed and hence hegemonic nature of the symbolic realm of language use. We will never be able to assure them of comfort but at least we can let them know that they are not alone (cf. hooks, 1990). The margin is actually a pretty crowded place—thankfully!

· 8 ·

HELPING POOR AND WORKING-CLASS CHILDREN MAKE SOMETHING OF THEMSELVES: THE CONTRADICTIONS AND POSSIBILITIES OF TEACHING FOR EQUITY AND DEMOCRACY

Educators pursue their life's work at the point of intersection between individuals and society. Hired by institutions to pursue institutional goals, but often drawn to teaching by a desire to make a difference in student's lives, many teachers resolve the tension by pursuing their goals behind frosted windows and closed doors. Some teachers go further. They fight for services for students, defend students' rights, and shield students from the worst excesses of bureaucratic schooling—excesses such as those involved in testing and labeling, for example. Acting as advocates for students is an important part of our work as teachers. Students need people who will humanize schooling and help them negotiate its power structures.

Institutional norms and values that support social dominance are often so embedded in the ways we do schooling that they seem natural. When I conduct workshops on racism, for example, many participating teachers become dismayed at the extent of institutional racism in U.S. society and disconcerted at the role schools play in reproducing racial inequalities. It is deeply disturbing to realize that one acts in complicity with a social evil such as racism, yet it is only through such awareness that we can grope towards ways in which schools might become sites for anti-racist action. It is no different for forms of social oppression based on gender, sexual orientation, physical ability, and social class.

My purpose is to inquire into some key aspects of the relationship between social class and schooling. Official rhetoric to the contrary, schools reproduce social class dominance. The challenge for socially conscious educators is to imagine and enact forms of schooling that do not reproduce existing inequalities. Acting alone, teachers do not have the power to transform school structures that oppress low-income and working-class students. Neither can they alone change societal discourses that pathologize poor and working class people as welfare cheats and freeloaders. Socially aware teachers can, however, create affirming school climate that gives students the space to explore the constraints of their lives and the ways in which they might act to challenge the limiting assumptions of society.

The Inferiorization of Working-Class Children

One of the most troubling aspects of my experience working with student teachers is how little they see the injustice, understand the exclusion, or empathize with the pain experienced by poor and working-class families. Given the hostile political rhetoric that has shaped public discourses about poverty and welfare in recent years, it is not surprising that many college students view low-income families as inferior, condemn them as welfare cheats, and assume that they neglect their children. Conversations with working-class people led Sennett and Cobb (1993) to conclude that teachers generally are prejudiced against working-class families. Ellen Brantlinger reached a similar conclusion. One of the mothers interviewed for her study expressed it this way:

> Well, you can see the difference between the people that come by the money—they're treated different and that's not right...I think all kids should be treated equal whether they've got anything or not, and I felt they're not (treating them equal). They're differencing them. (1985, p. 93)

Another one of Brantlingers's interviewees was even more explicit: "Teachers favor ones more like themselves, or people they feel is respectable, or whatever you want to call it." (1985, p. 95).

I am no stranger to being "differenced." As I grew up in Ireland, nobody ever made a pretence to classlessness. From the ubiquitous inquiry, "What does your father do?" to state birth certificates which recorded "Father's rank or profession," class and patriarchy were firmly inscribed in Irish society. Growing up as children of a construction laborer and living in one of the red-roofed houses built by the local county to house the working poor, my siblings and I were steeped in difference even before we got to school.

> I ran furiously. "C'mon, hurry up! We'll miss our lift to school." P.J. and Frances, older than I, knew that if we were there he'd let us pile in with all the other kids. What kid wanted to walk the mile to school in the frosty winter of 1958? We arrived at the van out of breath, with thank-yous on our tongues. We were on the tail-end of the group as I scrambled after Frances and P.J. into the back of the blue Ford. That was when the hand shot out and Hogan's voice rasped: "Are you an O'Loughlin? Get out. No O'Loughlins or Macs. I don't want to see the likes of you again."

Many of the children in my three-teacher rural school were working poor. But they were respectable poor. My family was not. Plonked in a farming community in subsidized housing, we suffered persecution from children and patronizing remarks from teachers. We also observed the lifelong humiliation our parents endured at the hands of teachers, priests, doctors, unemployment clerks and shopkeepers. My parents were usually deferential. At times they were painfully obsequious. When my brother and I remonstrated, they told us they had no choice. And they did not.

In the course of a lifetime such experiences have a corrosive effect on the psyches of individuals and communities. They create and ingrained sense of inferiority and shame. Frantz Fanon, writing about the impact of racism on the psyche, explains how the experience of being permanently treated as a racial Other leads to a deep sense of alienation from self. My own experiences with class persecution in Irish society, and the systemic exploitation and degradation of my parents, suggest that Fanon's suggestion is apt too for people who are marginalized, disrespected, and exploited because of their social class. Fanon says the effect of systemic racial inferiorization is to cause recipients to experience self-hatred:

> In other words, I begin to suffer from not being a white man to the degree that the white man imposes discrimination on me, makes me a colonized native, robs me of all worth, all individuality, tells me that I am a parasite on the world, that I must bring myself as quickly as possible into step with the white world, "that I am a brute beast, that my people and I are like a walking dung-heap that disgustingly fertilizes sweet sugar cane and silky cotton, that I have no use in the world." (1967, p. 68, including quote from Aime Césaire).

Self-hatred produces enormous psychological pain. Those who continue to identify with the subordinated group of which they are ashamed develop an ingrained sense of inferiority. Teachers and schools contribute to this sense of inferiority among many working-class students. Oppressive schools set children up for failure. The many students who will inevitably fail in such circumstances then become subject to the judgment of society that they caused their own failure. The combined effects of racial and social-class othering leaves psychic scars on poor and working-class people of color. What can the future hold for the many children like Alicia, an eight-year-old Latina student who was the victim of such abuse:

> Alicia was most engaged when she was sweeping. On several occasions Alicia was sweeping the classroom floor when we came for our sessions. "This one is not cut out for anything else," we were informed by the teacher in a loud voice. "She can't do the work." Alicia, head down, continued sweeping around our feet. "This is her vocation. And she's good. She could be my maid when she's old enough." (O'Loughlin, Bierwiler, & Serra, 1996)[1]

The tragedy of the situation is further compounded in that many teachers are themselves of working-class origin. Teaching is often a stepping-stone into the middle-class. When we make this transition do we turn our back on our roots? Sennett and Cobb (1993) suggest that most people who make it out of the lower classes are filled with ambivalence. While feeling superior to the ones left behind, they also feel guilty and filled with self-doubt. To handle these feelings they distance themselves emotionally from working-class children and their families. Through their own self-hatred they thereby create alienating experiences for the children in their care.

More often, though, teachers aspire to raise the aspirations and life chances of working-class students. They want to help them move up to the middle-class. They believe that if their students work hard enough they will pull themselves up by their bootstraps and make something of themselves. Such teachers see themselves as purveyors of hope. They are more accurately understood as marketers of the American Dream.

> Like Original Sin, working-class origin is a state from which we are saved— by working hard and being good (Americans). (Miner, 1993, p. 74)

In Pursuit of the American Dream: Hallucination, Delusion and Desire

The American Dream titillates desire: "All of this could be yours." It beckons seductively. Most poor and working-class people aspire to become something other than what they are. They want to move up in the world. Often this desire is expressed in the hope that their children will make something of themselves. Sennett and Cobb explained it this way: "Working-class fathers...see the whole point of sacrificing for their children to be that they *will* become unlike them-selves...the father doesn't ask the child to take the parents' lives as a model, but as a warning" (1993, p. 128). This is how it was for my father too. He would show me his bleeding hands and his rain-soaked work clothes. It was not just a warning; it was an object lesson in desire. My vision of upward mobility was given substance when a visiting school inspector stopped by my second-grade classroom:

> Then he beckoned, inviting me forward. My heart sank. What had I said wrong? I hesitated,
>   and he called me over. All eyes followed me. My peers looked on in trepidation.
> "What is your name?" he asked me kindly.
> "Michael O'Loughlin, sir." I replied
> "You're a clever boy, Michael," he said again kindly. "I noticed how well you answered my
>   questions".
> "Thank you, sir," I managed to stutter the words.
> "What do you want to do when you grow up?"
> "I don't know, sir," I replied, still tongue-tied.
> "What does your father do?" he asked.
> "He's a laborer, sir," I answered.
> "You should be sure to go to secondary school, and on to university some day. Do you think
>   you will?"
> "I will try to, sir."
> "Good boy."
> "Thank you, sir."
> I fled back to my seat in confusion. I was peppered with questions. "What did he say?" "Why
>   did he call you up?" I just said that he told me that I was doing alright in school. I then went
>   home and told the full story to my parents. I told nobody of the vision of university newly
>   planted in my head.

I should be the last person to complain. The hopes and desires that were nurtured within me in my youth still drive me. Nine years after completion of my Ph.D., I am back in school once again, pursuing unrealized hopes and dreams.

But there are down sides to the Dream of which I was not always aware. In my early years as a teacher educator I seduced student teachers with the Dream. In my naïve idealism I urged them to see their students as capable of lifting themselves up by their bootstraps. I was producing desire for a better life. It had worked for me, or so I believed. It seemed to have worked for my college students too. I gave little thought to the constraints working-class and poor children face in society. Like many teachers I preferred to deny societal constraints that neglected my ability to make a difference in my student's lives. I needed to believe that I was making that difference. But then I began to learn.

While working as a consultant in urban schools I witnessed communities of poor children locked into cycles of low expectations and failure. Their lives were discounted, their families pathologized. Schools passed blame for dismal test scores to children and their families. Refrain:

> *"These children can't learn."*
> *"These children can't behave."*
> *"You can't teach these children."*
> *"They should be behind bars... all of them should be behind bars."*
> *Blame... Blame... Blame...*

Jonathon Kozol's *Savage Inequalities* (1991) taught me how inequalities in the distribution of funding across communities lead to major disparities in life chances for children of the poor. Jeannie Oakes (1985) demonstrated how schools perpetuate social stratification by filtering poor and working-class children into less challenging tracks while reserving better academic preparation for children of elites. Despite a distinguished literature spanning many years (e.g., Delpit, 1995; DuBois, 1903/1990; Hale, 1994; Hilliard, 1995; Kohl, 1967; Kozol, 1967; Woodson, 1933/1990), documenting the unjust privations of school for low-income students and ethnically and linguistically diverse students, little has changed. Kozol argues that with the rightward shift in U.S. social policy in the past two decades "(i)n public schooling, social policy has been turned back almost one hundred years" (1991, p. 4). The current assault on welfare recipients, part of what Herbert Gans calls "the war against the poor" (1995), threatens to set the clock back further.

The American Dream is not a promise. It is a fraud. Schools are complicit with other forces in our class-stratified society in ensuring that most students will never attain the upward mobility that schools claim is theirs for the taking. Walkerdine's research (1984, 1990) demonstrates how schools promote middle-class ways of speaking, acting disciplining, and mothering, and pathologize working-class and ethnically diverse ways of knowing. Even our most "liberal," "humanistic," and "progressive-looking" schools seem designed to maintain the gap between white middle-class people and the Others that threaten their privilege (Counts, 1932/1969; O'Loughlin, 1995b). The cruelty of the Dream is that it nurtures the belief that individual ability and effort are all it takes to succeed. Having been taught by society that success is within their grasp, those who fail—and fail they must—internalize blame for their failure (Brantlinger, 1985). No wonder they wish for something better for their children.

But some children do succeed. Just as state lotteries produce impressive winners regularly to maintain the faith of players, schools must produce enough winners so that people do not lose hope in the system. As long as winners can be produced in each community, those who are not chosen have little option but to accept responsibility for their failure. Teachers of poor and working-class children, therefore, act as gatekeepers, selecting those children who will make it to the promised land.

"And now, the Lucky Winner is ... !"

Once the chosen few are identified, a split occurs between those children and their peers (Sennett & Cobb, 1993, p. 82). The chosen few ally themselves with teachers while the ordinary mass of children resign themselves to punching-in time in school, thus fulfilling society's—and teachers'—expectations for them. This system produces winners and losers among the poor and working-class. The losers risk inheriting the sense of inferiority their parents possess. For the winners victory is at best bittersweet. It carries within it the seeds of future pain and estrangement. Reflecting on her passage into the middle-class, Saundra Gardner noted:

> In America we are taught from our earliest years, that upward mobility is the essence of the American Dream. Growing up in a white working-class family, I equated such mobility with the "good life," "making it," and middle class respectability...It was clear that I not only wanted to move up but out. By getting a "good education" I would be able to leave my past behind and create a life for myself which was radically different from that of my parents.

> During those early years my own classism prohibited me from questioning the "dream" or the "rewards" education would bring. I was also unprepared for the marginality and estrangement I would feel as my dream came true. These feelings initially surfaced during college and intensified as I moved up the educational hierarchy. Thus, the more successful I became, the more "marginal" I felt. (Gardner, 1993, p. 49)

Writings by working-class people who have "made something of themselves" are replete with ambivalence about their accomplishments and the costs of their success (e.g., Dews & Law, 1995; Ryan & Sackrey, 1995; Tokarczyk & Fay, 1993; Walkerdine, 1990). The chosen few face a difficult task. We induce in them a desire for success and the good life. But we fail to inform them that the good life cannot simply be worn like a new coat or picked up like a lottery check. What is required is the progressive rejection of working-class identity as one increasingly identifies with middle class values and professional norms. This process can be excruciatingly painful. As Walkerdine notes, the "desire for identification" with middle-class values is accompanied by fear of "total loss and annihilation" of the working-class person's identity (1990, p. 47). The chosen few live complicated lives. Return to their origins is impossible, yet their lease in the middle-class world—what Ryan and Sackrey (1995) facetiously call "paradise"—is tenuous. Many report feelings of inadequacy; fears that they will put a foot wrong; discomfort with the individualism and competitiveness of middle-class life; and a fear of being found out and sent back where they came from. These feelings often play themselves out in a state of anxiety in which nouveau middle-class people try to hide their identity by conforming, never letting their guard down, fearing that "if they open their mouth they will 'say the wrong thing' and be thrown out of paradise" (Walkerdine, 1990, p. 47).

I live this double life and find it arduous and alienating. I have learned that becoming a member of the club is a little more complicated than it seems. The material and professional codes that accompany middle-class life are embraced by educators as universally good. By implication, there is a suggestion that the moral codes and lifestyles of other-than-middle-class life are inferior. Is teaching after all a grand exercise in civilizing Others? Is a way up and out the best educators have to offer? Up to what? Out of what?

My immersion in a variety of middle-class and professional communities has taught me that there is much that is problematic about middle-class values. The lines between right and wrong are too often obfuscated with fancy double-talk. To be accepted in middle-class society one must adhere to codes of conduct in which self-interest and careerism, hidden under rhetorics of politeness and civility, are more important than naming and acting on injustices. Naming racism, classism, or other forms of domination violates rules of civility and norms of collegiality. I question the assumption of the universal goodness of middle-class values. Middle-class discourses too often sustain unearned privilege, legitimate social injustice, and serve only to protect the interests of middle-class people. As James Loewen (1995) noted, the American middle-class has often supported regressive social movements (e.g., the war in Vietnam) that advance their economic and social interest, apparently oblivious to the terrible cost to poor and working-class people.

Resisting Classism in Schooling

One important thing teachers can do is become conscious of the inequity of class relations in U.S. society. The idea that our society is classless is a myth. Mechanisms of class discrimination and exploitation are constantly at work. These are intimately tied to the stratification of labor required for our capitalist economy. Our society demands that people be sorted. A primary function of schooling is to do just that. Once educators become conscious of their role in the production of class relations, they can then make class differences and underlying class exploitation the focus of critical inquiry in their classrooms. A good place to begin might be by sharing their own class backgrounds, and inviting their student to do likewise. Teachers may find it useful to explore the ambivalence and insecurities associated with their class positioning and the class transitions they are making. The Social Class Questionnaire in *Radical Teacher: Special Issues on Working-Class Studies* (1995, p. 46) offers a possible starting point.[2]

American Dream mythology is also worthy of critical exploration. Teachers should examine with students the degree to which this myth has permeated their worldview and their pedagogy. How palpable is American Dream thinking in their student's desires and aspirations? Teachers might profitably look at the presence of working-class lives and communities in their curriculum. Do the students' lives and worlds occupy a respected space in the classroom discourse? Are working class voices from literature and film honored in the curriculum? The Radical Teacher issue just cited offers a useful starting point for teachers invested in reevaluating their curriculum. The writings of Myles Horton and the late Paulo Freire (Freire, 1996; Horton, 1990; Horton & Freire, 1990) have been inspirational for me in my efforts to develop with my students a curriculum that is critically and respectfully anchored in students' lives and experiences.

Educators can challenge students to go beyond individualistic notions of success and failure and help them imagine forms of social organization that are not based on oppression and exploitation. What it comes down to is whether we accept class, race, gender, and other oppressions as inevitable or reject them as reprehensible. Do educators have a responsibility for nurturing and preserving visions of a more just and equitable world? Who but teachers and writers can nurture in the imaginations of future generations images of a pluralistic and inclusive democracy in which all of our peoples can claim a respected place? The role teachers play in preserving historical memory, nurturing hope, and stirring ideas in students is what makes teaching for democracy such an inspiring task and such an awesome responsibility.

A Cautionary Note

A flaw in the literature on poor and working class people, as Lynch and O'Neill (1994) note, is that it is written about but not by working-class people. Analyses such as the one presented here advance a cultural sensitivity argument suggesting that working-class people are marginalized by the failure of schooling to offer a hospitable and inclusive environment. While Lynch and O'Neill do not dispute the presence of prejudice between poor and working-class children and their teachers, they worry that this emphasis deflects attention from the main issue, the effects of grinding poverty of people's lives: "... what alienates working-class children from the system most is not necessarily the middle-class character of the curriculum or even the hidden curriculum per se, but the absence of financial resources to make the system work for themselves" (1994, p. 320). If they are correct, then arguments for more egalitarian and social democratic education are unlikely to have the kinds of ameliorative effects on the life chances of poor and working-class children that we would like. Perhaps a more fundamental social revolution is called for.

· 9 ·

RECREATING THE SOCIAL LINK BETWEEN CHILDREN AND THEIR HISTORIES: THE POWER OF STORY AS A DECOLONIZING STRATEGY

In every nursery there are ghosts. They are the visitors from the unremembered past of the parents, the uninvited guests at the christening. Under favorable circumstances, these unfriendly and unbidden guests are banished from the nursery and return to their subterranean dwelling place...This is not to say that ghosts cannot invent mischief from their burial places. Even in families where the love bonds are stable and strong, the intruders from the parental past may break through the magic circle in an unguarded moment, and a parent and his child may find themselves reenacting a moment or scene from another time with another set of characters.

—FRAIBERG ET AL., (1975, PP. 162–163)

This is how Selma Fraiberg opens her important discussion of cultural transmission of trauma, "Ghosts in the nursery." While Fraiberg was more concerned with immediate familial trauma, transmitted from parent to child, she also recognized the particular difficulty of families who appear to be possessed by ancestral ghosts "that take up residence and conduct the rehearsal of the family tragedy from a tattered script" (p. 163). Fraiberg noted that trauma that occurred three or more generations earlier and that has dropped completely out of conscious memory is the most difficult to treat. In this chapter I intend to explore the issue of ghostly presences in children's lives, and to explore the implications of engaging children in a pedagogy that seeks to reanimate ancestral memories with a view to engaging these children with more expansive and critical notions of their own subjective sense of being.

I frame this as a *decolonizing* approach to pedagogy in that it seeks to probe under inculcated knowledge and dispositions to reveal ancestral histories that may enable individual children to construct more expansive narratives of their being that take into account historical legacies of accomplishment and suffering and thereby enable children to choose to live their lives according to alternate scripts than the ones currently available to them. As I present the argument here it applies particularly to children from indigenous groups such as Native Americans and Aboriginal peoples, who have historically suffered trauma variously from displacements and migrations; physical and cultural genocides; systemic sexual abuse; and from the imposition of rational Enlightenment thought to replace indigenous ways of knowing, indigenous modes of feeling, and religious beliefs and healing rituals.[1] However, this argument can be made with respect to any group that has suffered trauma, and is particularly relevant to any ethnic and cultural groups that have experienced displacement, loss and trauma, either in the present world, or in their historical pasts.

My work is informed by a line of inquiry, mainly from Lacanian psychoanalysis, which has focused on the consequences for people whose capacity to repair trauma has been impaired by severance of social links. This has occurred for generations of indigenous families through forced geographic displacements, forcible placement of children in boarding schools, systematic elimination of ceremonial practices and indigenous rituals of healing, and a devaluing of indigenous narrative as a mode of cultural transmission. What is often characterized by dominant culture authorities as oppositional, pathological or deviant behavior may well be unconscious responses to culturally transmitted trauma, or the *lack* produced in people whose subjectivities have been progressively displaced by alien values and expectations. However, the argument applies to children from all groups who have histories of either collective historical trauma or familial trauma in their backgrounds.

Children who have had their experience of their histories foreclosed will live with *lack*, but are likely to be unaware of the causes of the absence within. Therefore, in addressing the needs of such children we need to figure out how to engage with the unconscious knowledge in their lives. Classrooms are filled with silent ghosts—silent spectral realms of unanchored anguish and lost possibility. Teachers need to be taught how to go beyond imparting inert, dominant culture cognitive knowledge, and should be prepared to engage children in emotionally and imaginatively liberatory pedagogy rooted in ancestral lore but widening to a future of healing and possibility.

I envisage a curriculum that will allow children to locate themselves critically within their own ancestral histories and memories. The curriculum that will emerge from such a venture is what I refer to as *small-h history*—a curriculum that implies a readiness to accept the wisdom of elders, and the power of myth, storytelling, folk art, performance, and other forms of knowing that bend, stretch, and even transcend *logos*—and particularly the institutionalized and bureaucratized *logos* of dominant culture schooling. For teachers to become guarantors for the *speakability* of children's unnamable experience, I suggest, they must be prepared to enter into a sympathetic conversation—a deep existential encounter—with children, individually and collectively (cf. Buber, 1971).

I propose using the kinds of understandings discussed here to articulate what I will call an *evocative* pedagogy for children. This is a pedagogy that by addressing the unconscious, the soul, and the spirit, has the capacity to unhook particular, culturally located children from the anomie of an amnesiac, universalist, globalized consumer society to begin to reconnect with the latent historical subjectivities deep within their own beings and in their communities of origin. This can lead to a way forward anchored in the historical and spiritual past and offers an alternative to a life haunted by an unnamable past.

Troubling Decolonizing Pedagogy

These idealistic statements about teaching need to be couched in a series of *caveats*, however. In the first place, the appalling legacy of residential schooling and subsequent official efforts at assimilationist schooling for indigenous communities (e.g., in Australia, Canada, United States) must be acknowledged. The damage done through use of schools as blunt instruments of assimilation and cultural annihilation, not to mention the breach of trust caused by systemic sexual abuse in all of these locales, mandate that in developing educational proposals for indigenous communities educators be mindful of this history, and take care to advance ideas that are non-hegemonic, sensitive to indigenous epistemologies, and open to discussion and adaptation by particular groups according to their needs.

Advancing the notion of a decolonizing pedagogy is problematic too. The term *decolonization* appears to imply that colonial values are somehow layered on top of colonized people's pre-existing values, and can be removed. However, as Ashis Nandy (1983) indicates in *The intimate enemy*, colonialism maintained its grip by interpellating the subjectivities of colonized peoples. In addition to being a structure of economic and political exploitation, colonialism succeeded in India, Nandy argues, in part by a "psychological invasion from the West" that began with "widespread internalization of Western values by many Indians" (p. 24). Meditating on the challenge of developing an authentic Indian historiography, for example, historian Dipesh Chakrabarty (1995) noted that it is impossible to write an authentically *Indian* history of India because all historiographic ways of seeing are infused with western ways of seeing and thinking. The field of postcolonial studies has been preoccupied with this conundrum (e.g., Ashcroft et al., 1995; Bhabha, 1994; Butler & Spivak, 2007; Hall 1996a, b; Morley & Chin, 1996). The challenge for educators, then, is to articulate pedagogies that can adapt complex understandings of pedagogy that neither valorize the latest Western understandings of what is good for indigenous children, nor valorize essentialized nostalgic notions of returning indigenous communities to some romanticized originary state of innocence and purity.

Considering the decolonizing project in the context of official schooling is even more fraught. Schools are the chief ideological instruments of governments, totalitarian or otherwise, and are therefore likely to be held on a tight ideological leash. Teachers are part of the establishment, and any subversive leanings that they might have are typically disciplined through extensive mandated curricular requirements and onerous regulation that appears to be increasingly global in reach. Is it possible for teachers to find gaps in the received curriculum that might enable children to do the kind of critical memorial exhumation that I have in mind? A more complex question still is how our ways of understanding liberation, hope, and possibility are themselves structured within westernized, Enlightenment notions of being. Is it possible for westernized academics, curriculum writers, and teachers to cast off what appears to be an inherently colonizing gaze?

Despite the pessimism such thinking evokes, I believe that while discourses may appear totalizing, counterdiscourses have the potential to make their presence felt. Disciplinary boundaries that appear fixed and solid are invariably porous and cracked, and it is in these cracks that counterdiscourses can be nourished. Like the tiny weed that eventually cracks a thick slab of concrete on an airport runway, these counter-discourses have the capacity to disseminate fractures through a received world view however apparently totalizing. I will argue below, however, that to be effective, such counterdiscourses need to emerge organically with community members (cf. Gramsci's notion of *organic intellectual*, 1971) and must be cultivated from the felt needs of particular groups rather than being handed down from on high.

It is these potentially porous, albeit invisible, borders that represent a prime opportunity for decolonizing interventions in schooling. My purpose is to discuss ways in which teachers, having become sensible to their own deeply embodied histories, and to the deeply embodied histories in each of their students, can use myth, ritual, and narrative, to engage children's minds, hearts, bodies, and souls in the reclamation of embedded memories. I will argue that these memories, currently unthought and unspoken, represent a psychic burden for children and communities. However, having become spoken, these memories have the potential to set individuals and communities free to live lives that are deeper and more linked to their histories, rather than the scripted, materially impoverished, consumer lives contemporary global material culture assigns to them. The capacity of Pai, the protagonist of the movie *Whale rider* (Caro, 2003), to commune with ancestral memory through her communication with whales is suggestive of the deeply embedded unconscious cultural knowledge that I have in mind. Finally, since a large proportion of my argument rests on psychological and psychoanalytic theory, it is necessary to acknowledge the shameful role psychology has played both in the development of racial classification schemes, in conceptualizing subjectivity as an autonomous, essentialized self, and in the conceptualization of nonwhite others as primitive (cf. Adams, 1996; Atkinson, 2002; Duran & Duran, 1995; Duran et al., 1998; Fine et al., 1996; Fournier & Crey, 1997; Guthrie, 2003; Lane, 1998; O'Loughlin, 2002a, b; Rezentes, 1996). Referring to psychoanalysis Derrida (1998) eloquently pointed out the acultural, ahistorical, and Eurocentric values at the heart of psychoanalytic theory and practice: "[T]here is practically no psychoanalysis in Asia, or in the South Seas. These are among those parts of 'the rest of the world' where psychoanalysis has never set foot, or in any case where it has never taken off its European shoes" (1998, p. 69).

For too long much of psychoanalysis has focused on individual change, and has valorized rationality, verbal ability, autonomy, individual experience, and indeed, the experience of being middle-class. Nevertheless, psychoanalysis has been blessed with schisms and splits that reveal its resistance to totalization and its continually resurgent transgressive potential (e.g., see Molino, 2004). For all its limitations, psychoanalysis gives us a vocabulary for speaking about loss and creativity through conceptualizing the unconscious, and it offers mechanisms for conceptualizing individual and collective responses to pain and suffering. Lacanian psychoanalysis, which I invoke here, is particularly relevant because of its focus on understanding the relationship between language and culture, the individual and the social, the external and the internal.

To be clear, my purpose here is not to argue that psychoanalysis, pedagogy, or *small-h history*, separately or together, provide a magic bullet for changing the lives of indigenous children. My hope is that opening up these issues will motivate teachers to engage children in journeys of self-exploration in order to expand their *mindfulness* (cf. Epstein, 2004) and political awareness (cf. Freire, 1969, 1972), and that it will also encourage teachers to begin engaging their students in organic investigations of the kind I suggest below so that new forms of curriculum making and learning might emerge that expand the liberatory possibilities of indigenous children's lives.

The remainder of the essay is in two parts. First, drawing on the work of two French Lacanian psychoanalysts, François Davoine and Jean-Max Gaudillière, I will explore ways in which suppressed memories are encased in our bodies and transmitted silently across generations, often with catastrophic consequences. These authors argue that such repressed memories need to be voiced, and they offer provocative thoughts about the characteristics which a therapist must possess in order to release such memories in people. Then, drawing on the writing of Trinh Minh-ha, I will explore the power of story-telling as a rubric for conceptualizing this kind of memory-based teaching process in pedagogical terms. I will conclude by offering some recommendations for how we might prepare teachers more effectively to grapple with the issues under discussion here.

As for the limitations of my point of view, let me state the obvious. To the degree that structures of oppression are built into the global capitalist economic system—the latest manifestation of colonialism—clothed in the garb of popular culture, consumer choice and liberal democracy, they need to be challenged by revolutionary political education of the kind Paulo Freire (1969, 1972), for example, championed. I know of no national education system that will willingly permit such a challenge to its hegemony. Nevertheless, I cannot see how success is possible unless we focus on decolonizing discursive aspects of the internalization of colonial ways of being, deconstructing structural inequalities, and challenging the insidious reach of global capitalist material culture and an accompanying discourse that equates free markets with freedom of choice for people in indigenous communities. I try to illustrate in a general way the outlines of an organic approach to childhood pedagogy that embodies these ideas, and I conclude by proposing a documentation project that will allow local teachers to begin to construct this kind of politically grounded memorial pedagogy organically with their students.

The Catastrophic Consequences
of Severing Social Links

Horrific television footage from Davis Inlet, Labrador, in early 1993 served as a dramatic wake-up call to Canadians about the hopeless lives endured by so many aboriginal children in the nation's North. The sight of seventeen Innu children huddled in a shack, high from sniffing gasoline fumes and crying out that they wanted to die was impossible to ignore.

Viewers may have been shocked by the self-destructiveness of gasoline addiction, but it soon became apparent the children's despair had an underlying cause. As hordes of media personnel descended on their remote community, the children said they could see no other way to escape the torture of the sexual abuse they were enduring than to die.

The adults of Davis Inlet, demoralized, dispossessed of their traditional land base and their spirituality, sexually victimized themselves in church-run schools, were preying without mercy on their own children. Canadians learned that virtually no child in Davis Inlet reached adolescence sexually unmolested. Many had been violently raped by drunken adults, mostly their own relatives, and assaulted by older children crazed on gas fumes. (Fournier & Crey, 1997, p. 115)

The cumulative trauma suffered by indigenous peoples in North America and in Australia has been well documented (Allen, 1998; Altman & Hinkson, 2007; Atkinson, 2002; Churchill, 1997, 2004; Crow Dog, 1991; Deloria & Lytle, 1983; Duran & Duran, 1995; Duran et al., 1998; Fournier and Crey, 1997; Gagné, 1998; Raphael, Swan & Martinek, 1998; Stannard, 1993; Zinn, 2005). This trauma originated with colonization, dispossession from ancestral lands; disruption of kinship ties; replacement of communal land ownership with individual title; and massacres and genocides. It was succeeded by focused attempts at assimilation that included forced removal to residential schools and to foster families designed to annihilate culture and sever familial ties. The residential school systems were also frequently sites of egregious sexual exploitation that left the imprisoned children with shattered trust, lack of cultural connection to forebears, considerable psychological trauma, and severely depleted capacity for parenting. Couple this with cultivated welfare dependency, structural poverty, and infrastructural neglect, and the presence of despair is hardly surprising in many indigenous communities in both regions.

In *Trauma Trails: Recreating song lines: The transgenerational effects of trauma in Indigenous Australia* (2002) Judy Atkinson lays out in great detail some of the central tenets of Aboriginal epistemology, including the key idea of "spiritual continuity between present and past" (p. 33). Studies in the area of white privilege (e.g., Fine et al., 1996; Frankenberg, 1993) suggest that white dominant postcolonial cultures are predominantly presentist and materialist in orientation—there is often total amnesia for prior ethnic heritage and collective cultural memory. Indigenous cultures are very different in that past is valued as an anchor for present and a harbinger for future. To understand the significance of the cultural excision of ancestral memory in Aboriginal people's lives it is essential, Atkinson argues, to grasp the importance of "The 'Time Before Morning' or 'The Dreamings', and the ancestral beings who were active in that past" (p. 33). Atkinson describes the consequences of the eradication of this continuity as follows:

> The willful denigration and destruction of Aboriginal ceremonial responsibilities and processes by the colonizers has therefore had profound transgenerational effects on the people of this land. Aboriginal people have been prevented from engaging in ceremonial processes for healing from trauma. The distressed feelings that accompany loss, death, and devastation remain as destructive forces within the land and the people. (p. 35)

Atkinson speaks of *lore* as the wisdom that passes down through generations and suggests that the trauma of colonization and the institutionalized bureaucratization of indigenous people's lives have led to the collapse of lore—a *lorelessness* (p. 45) that leaves indigenous people adrift without history, memory, or well-being. Drawing on Kai Erikson's (1976) writings, Atkinson argues that violation of the boundaries of family and place opens the door to the collapse of the social infrastructure, a collapse that then leads to alcohol consumption and domestic violence and to further deterioration of the social fabric. She cites the example of the occupants of the Grassy Narrows Reserve who were removed from their native lands in 1963 after an international papermaking company poisoned the lakes and rivers with methyl mercury. This dis-place-ment had profound consequences for the group:

> These now-poisoned waters had represented both the life support and spiritual identity of the people. Within a short period following relocation, sexual assault, child neglect and abuse, extreme alcohol abuse, petrol-sniffing and death through violence became epidemic within the community. Men beat women and abused children, women discarded dependent infants and abused children, and older children beat and raped younger children. Hierarchies of power abuse and misdirected pain and anger were expressed in community violence. Old people could remember "the time before"; in their shame at the "time present", they felt powerless to effectively intervene. In fact, they were often victims of violence themselves. Abuse became transgenerational. (pp. 54–55)

Atkinson outlines the cruelty, humiliation, degradation and dislocations that occurred under the auspices of the police, euphemistically named *protectors* of Aboriginal peoples. In a mirror-image of the U.S. and Canadian governments' approaches, the Australian government created conditions that sought to induce in Aboriginal peoples a state of powerlessness, dependence, cultural erosion, and humiliation that foreshortened their futures and led them towards paths of self-destruction which, when criminalized, led to further enmeshment in regimes of pathologization and incarceration by the federal and territorial governments. The dislocations of wounded people led to what Atkinson calls *trauma trails*—trails of disaster, pain, and dislocation that can be traced across time and people (p. 88). These trauma trails are invisible to most of the people who are suffering such great losses and this invisibility is what makes the suffering so profoundly damaging to individual and collective psyches and contributes to its continuance.

Psychoanalytic Understandings of the Social Link

In *History beyond trauma* Davoine and Gaudillière (2004) address the process by which trauma is transmitted intergenerationally. They begin with the unremarkable argument that if no cause for trauma can be found in immediate lived experience then we can suspect that the trauma is located in history. Davoine and Gaudillière do not say such events are located in the past, however, because they assume that events that were never encoded in memory are timeless, and are waiting to be named so that they can claim their rightful place in history. When we speak of reclaiming memories these are not necessarily literal memories. Traumatic memories are often embodied, and have never entered conscious memory at all.

Symptoms of psychological distress in our patients in the present can be traced to social origins in the past. "Sometimes," they note, "a fit of madness tells us more than all the news dispatches about the leftover facts that have no right to existence" (p. xxvii). The therapist's responsibility is to bring unconscious knowledge into the present through a process in which therapists become acutely attuned listeners who struggle "to make a story out of what has not been received by any form of speech" (p. xxviii). Whether we are speaking of individual suffering or seeking to understand the kind of collective pain depicted in the movie *Once were warriors* (Tamahori, 2003) and in the examples quoted earlier, Davoine and Gaudillière would argue that all of these are potentially symptoms of frozen trauma desperately seeking to be voiced. They note that if catastrophic symptoms can be acknowledged and named, the potential for creativity and healing exists (p. 27). But naming requires an acknowledgment of the silent, ghostly echoes of trauma that are carried within. In psychoanalysis this concept is discussed in many forms including Lacan's (1977) "return of the Real," Sullivan's (1968) "the dreadful not-me," Bion's (1961) "nameless dread," Abraham and Torok's (1994) "phantom," and Rashkin's (1992) "secrets." Aspects of the idea of ghostly presence are discussed in detail in Chapters 3 and 6 of this book.

From an analytic perspective, then, the question which the anguish of an individual or community raises is an archeological one pertaining to "where our patients have been before, and toward which they are, paradoxically, seeking to guide us." (Davoine & Gaudillière, p. 29). If, in a school context, students are angry, alienated, or merely silent, how might we enable them to enter history and speak the unspoken that has so profoundly shaped their individual and collective experiences? In what way might the dead of our ancestral and spectral pasts (cf. Blackman, 2001, 2002; Gordon, 1997; Venn, 2002) live on within all of us? Who in our societies is equipped and willing to take on the responsibility of serving as what Davoine and Gaudillière call a *guarantor* that from now on those ancestral experiences will be given voice? Is this a task only for therapeutic healers, or is there a role for teachers in this process?

Davoine and Gaudillière argue that dehistoricization of experience is particularly traumatic in that it causes people to lose the social link with their pasts and they suggest that we must assist such people in "regaining a foothold in history" (p. 47). Drawing on Wittgenstein, they employ the concept of petrification, arguing that people's bodies can be so numbed by trauma that, as Wittgenstein said, "I turn into stone and my pain goes on" (quoted in Davoine and Gaudillière, p. 49). The authors note that children are particularly susceptible to noticing the blank affect of petrified adults, and are likely to absorb that pain into themselves, "becoming," as they note, "the subject of the other's suffering" (p. 49). This is how trauma is transmitted intergenerationally both within families and in whole communities (cf. Kaplan, 1996a). As to the psychosocial effects of such a calamity on people, Davoine and Gaudillière are very clear:

> Our patients are perpetuating such a hell, one that continues on in the anesthesia of several generations…these descendants may manifest only an omnipresent shame, unalloyed misfortune, a sense of radical injustice, and a global sadness, all these being signs of an imminent catastrophe that they can neither name or dispel. (p. 50)

How might we address traumatic events that cannot be recounted because they were never recorded as past—events that are still "suspended like a present without time"? (p. 52). How does one re-vitalize an individual or community weighed down by events that, on a conscious level, they simply do not know that they know? The psychoanalytic answer is to assist the anguished person or community in turning these *unthought knowns* (Bollas, 1987) of their *foreclosed history* (Davoine and Gaudillière, p. 54) into narrative. This is not an easy task since the disturbing events have never been encoded in narrative memory. Psychoanalysts rely on their own unconscious to serve as a receptor for the patient's anguish, and, through free association the analyst gives voice to the trauma the patient cannot speak and thereby returns it to the patient in speakable form.

Bearing Witness to Trauma

Addressing trauma treatment, Davoine and Gaudillière draw lessons from the Salmon principles, a series of treatment principles articulated by Thomas Salmon (1917) to treat shell-shocked World War I soldiers. These four principles offer a means for engaging in sympathetic conversation with the unspoken parts of individual or collective unconscious that are likely to harbor trauma. As the authors remind us, the goal of these conversations is "to enable the patient to pass from the asphyxia of a lethal impasse to the respiration of words exchanged to name the unnamable" (p. 118).

The first principle is *proximity*: We must find within ourselves the capacity to approach the hidden experience of the traumatized person to absorb from the person the disguised emotion that will communicate "the forbidden link to their ancestors" (p. 135). It is by accepting the subject's experience, that invitation is given to non-existent parts of the subject to become present. As Davoine and Gaudillière note, the alive subjective presence of the therapist is vital, since those "who have been threatened with vitrification by the impact of the Real do not need to be turned into objects yet again" (p. 129; cf. also Apollon, Bergeron & Cantin, 2002). As Davoine and Gaudillière note, proximity creates what Winnicott (1989) refers to as a potential space, a safe place in which a person can allow unspoken or dead parts of themselves to come to be once more.

Davoine and Gaudillière emphasize that the therapist must be neither a passive observer nor an intrusive interlocutor. Rather, what is at issue is the *receptivity* of the professional listener, one who can, as Bailly suggests, speaking of traumatized children, "exchange one's own knowledge of catastrophes for the child's terrible knowledge, so that the child is not longer the only one holding it" (Bailly, quoted in Davoine and Gaudillière, p. 146). In responding to trauma we bear witness as the narrative unfolds (O'Loughlin, 2007b, c). We return to the narrator what is already theirs, but now in a manner that increases their capacity to own their own histories (p. 152). The situation with children is all the more poignant because of the probability of sensitive children assuming the psychic burdens of their families. In psychological jargon such children are often referred to as *parentified*. Davoine and Gaudillière describe the process this way: "As we have seen, a baby may be assigned the role of *therapôn*, keeper of the mind for its parents, the boundary of their irrationality, remaining welded to them by a bond that may prevent any attachment" (p. 157).

The second Salmon principle is *immediacy*. Trauma theory suggests that traumatic experiences are best dealt with immediately. Davoine and Gaudillière, noting the *timelessness* of unconscious material that has not been turned into narrative, point out that any time an attempt is made to communicate unconscious material we must strive to be immediately present to it. Irrespective of how often trauma attempts to make itself felt—for example through aggression, withdrawal, emotional outbursts—until trauma is truly named, each encounter should be considered a first encounter and treated with immediacy, as "an unknown that is imminent" (p. 171). Traumatized people may experience time as stopped and may feel that they are haunted by invisible ghosts. Their past is continually, albeit invisibly, present and they need our active assistance in re-entering present time.

Expectancy, the third of the Salmon principles expresses faith and hope. This refers to perhaps the most fundamental need of all people: the belief that somebody will see something of value in them. If a traumatized person comes to us expecting nothing, Davoine and Gaudillière suggest, our responsibility is to have expectations for them, and most important of all, to have a willingness to name the truth: "The abolition of pretense, unvarnished access to the truth of situations, and tearing the veil from the weakness of adults free up an energy block usually held back by repression" (p. 218). The authors also warn against the dangers of intellectual detachment, what is sometimes referred to as a *professional* attitude in a therapist, which keeps the traumatized person in a state of detachment which is antithetical to the deeply personal encounter required for healing.

The final Salmon principle, *simplicity*, refers to the authenticity of the existential encounter between therapist and trauma sufferer. Davoine and

Gaudillière pose the question rather elegantly: How is it possible to *meet* someone? The goal, they suggest, is to be receptive to "fossil messages" in the traumatized person's speech and to articulate "*social links* around these fossils" (p. 256) that allow people to repair the links with their histories.

Psychoanalysis deals in narrative, albeit narrative privileged by a Westernized set of assumptions. Atkinson (2002) invokes the Aboriginal concept of *Dadirri*, a restorative form of listening that creates something that might be considered equivalent to the healing circles described in Canadian First Nations contexts by Fournier and Crey (1997). What is distinctive about this approach, which Atkinson illustrates with copious examples of heart-breaking narratives of suffering, and hopeful paths toward healing, is an emphasis on *community* and *ancestral memory* that is for the most part absent from Western therapeutic regimens. Atkinson advocates using reflective discussion and "storytelling, drawing, writing, dancing and drama, and Aboriginal cultural tools for healing" (p. 238). Atkinson also underlines the importance of group process, in which people work collectively to make sense of their experiences (p. 248). However, in addition to the conventional strategies of group therapy, Atkinson emphasizes the importance of the socio-historical aspect of the work, that is, helping "participants locate their own trauma within the network of global colonisations and histories—seeking answers to questions about why colonisers needed to leave their own countries, to colonise and subordinate other groups" (p. 249). In the final section of this paper I will offer pedagogical recommendations that can be drawn from psychoanalytic practice and indigenous notions of narrative. First, I will explore some of the possibilities and limitations of narrative as a pedagogical device.

Troubling Narrative

It is hardly controversial to argue that our identities are inscribed in language, and are therefore inherently social (cf. Lacan, 1968; Bakhtin, 1981, 1986). As Couze Venn noted, "every self is a storied self. And every story is mingled with the stories of other selves" (2002, p. 57). Venn extols the power of story, arguing that a story is a "promissory narrative" that holds out hope of recovery from loss through the exhumation of history and the construction of emancipatory narratives. What could be simpler, then, than to invite young children to share their stories? There is relentless charm, for instance, in the storytelling in Vivian Paley's *The boy who would be a helicopter* (Paley & Coles, 1991). Yet, story is in many respects culture-bound, and it is possible to engage children in modes of storying that, despite our best intentions of opening up speech and possibility, serve instead to foreclose meaning—situations in which, to use Davoine and Gaudillière's words, "the thread of speech may be radically cut" (p. 71).

Consider, for example the experience of Jiana. In a study of sharing time in her U.S. first-grade classroom, teacher Karen Gallas talks about an attempt at sharing by this African American student. This is how Gallas and her students responded to Jiana's tall tale:

> In the second week of March, following a child's account of a trip to the zoo with her mother, Jiana got into the chair and launched into a narrative about how she went to the zoo with her mother; and the zookeeper came out and took the gorilla out on a leash for her mother to pet. That was simply too much of me. I blurted out, 'Jiana, this is a time for true stories'; but she was adamant that the event had occurred and tried to continue her story.

> No sooner were the words out of my mouth than all of the children in the group turned around and looked at me very hard and long. Time seemed to stop for me as I realized from the change in their expressions what I had done. They turned slowly back, mumbling about it not being true, how it couldn't be true. Jiana tried to maintain her story in the face of their questions…but within those few seconds her audience had turned away from her. (Gallas, 1992, p. 176)

Here we gain a glimpse of the overwhelming power of the teacher to set epistemological rules for what counts as story. Gallas's example makes clear that a teacher's silence about or ignorance of the epistemological structuring of the classroom environment does not make the classroom a neutral space. Instead, that silence privileges dominant ways of knowing and telling. The fact that it is unexamined makes challenging the status quo all the more difficult. Similar privileging systems no doubt operate throughout the genres of literature and text to which children are exposed in school.

A teacher who is aware of these privileging systems might set out to redress the balance by, for instance, privileging local genres of story-telling. Awareness of Geneva Smitherman's (1986) inquiry into African American vernacular, for instance, might prompt a teacher such as Gallas to understand the significance of fantastic stories in African American communities, and sanction that genre as an appropriate mode of expression. This may indeed be helpful, but it raises again the difficult question of whether a teacher with a privileged perspective can ever deprivilege that perspective enough to set up a genuinely accommodating space for the eruption of alternate ways of knowing and telling. In *Woman, native, other* Trinh Minh-ha (1989) addresses this issue. She critiques the ways in which the hegemonic westernized gaze has pierced the Others of our world. Trinh notes the hazards of writing that seeks out "the *real* native," and describes the dilemmas that this invitation to *planned authenticity* creates for the marginal person seeking to voice their story:

> We no longer wish to erase your difference. We demand, on the contrary, that you remember and assert it. At least to a certain extent. Every path I/i take is edged with thorns. On the one hand, i play into the Savior's hands by concentrating on authenticity, for my attention is numbed by it, and diverted from other important issues; on the other hand, i do feel the necessity to return to my so-called roots, since they are the foundation of my strength, the guiding arrow to which i constantly refer before heading for a new direction. (p. 89)

In seeking cultural authenticity, teachers hardly want to engage in hegemonic appropriations of authenticity. To the extent that they do, paradoxically, the result is to taint genuine authenticity so that paradoxically the *real* and *authentic* feels fake! As Native American Writer Vine Deloria Jr. noted with respect to authentic Indians, "Not even Indians can relate themselves to this type of creature who, to anthropologists, is the 'real' Indian" (quoted in Trinh, p. 94). Trinh points out that even with changes to make our language *sound* inclusive, western academics continue to define themselves as the reference point or norm against which all others are measured, and speaking specifically of women's identity, she points out—and this is remarkably echoed in Davoine and Gaudillière's later discussion of madness and the social link—that such Othering can make a person feel quite mad. The antidote to this madness, as Trinh sees it, is to recognize that in addition to the factual truths enshrined in westernized ways of knowing, there are also narrative truths that speak to the inherited wisdom of groups of people. This qualitative notion of understanding has much more to do with accumulated cultural truths, than with any enlightenment (Trinh calls it "endarkenment") form of objective knowing. This form of storytelling is the stuff of which community can be built.

Trinh suggests that grand narrative *large-H History* concerns itself with very different truths, than what I have called *small-h history*—a history that is concerned with the truths of fiction, magic and myth. Trinh is very clear that while our stories are us, they are also very much more:

> In this chain and continuum I am but one link. The story is me, neither me nor mine. It does not really belong to me, and while I feel greatly responsible for it, I also enjoy the irresponsibility of the pleasure obtained through the process of transferring. Pleasure in the copy, pleasure in the reproduction. No repetition can ever be identical, but my story carries with it their stories, their history, and our story repeats itself endlessly despite our persistence in denying it. (p. 122)

This constructive form of storytelling is, Trinh notes, anathema to *civilized* people who have no doubt about their ability to distinguish fact from fiction and who insist on a rigorous "apartheid" between the two (Trinh, p. 125). This is the kind of apartheid that Jiana experienced when she embarked on her tall tale. In Trinh's thinking story is a powerfully regenerative force: "So that living traditions can never congeal into fixed forms, so that life keeps on nurturing life, so that what is understood as the Past continues to provide the link to the present and the future" (Trinh, p. 149).

Evocative Pedagogy and Regenerative Curriculum

'Innocent' intentions have often justified what have later come to be seen as abhorrent institutional practices and outcomes, such as those employed to separate Indigenous children from their parents and communities 'for their own good.' Or 'for the greater good.' Each new set of strategies is said to be distinct from earlier ones and to have good prospects of success However, the consistent experience of failure suggests that deep structural processes are at work. (Hinkson, 2007, p. 287)

As John Hinkson's quote suggests, the road to disaster for indigenous peoples has been littered with well-meaning solutions. Cultural annihilation is almost inevitable in the clash between indigenous cultures and a globalized free-market culture, Hinkson suggests, because of the antithetical world-views on which each is premised. He argues that the Western notion of an autonomous self denies the role of context, culture, and history in the constitution of our subjectivities and leads to the formation of what he calls "distance societies" which "are composed of social relations that shift the balance away from knowledge of particular others" (p. 294). Thus, emphasis is placed on nuclear families and the regulation of interchanges through commerce (e.g., purchase of child care arrangements, landscaping and house cleaning services etc. for cash) at the expense of kinship systems, historical memory and rituals of cultural transmission. Hinkson argues that the blindness of dominant culture participants to the ideology underlying their views (e.g., in provision of education, health, welfare, retail services) produces pressure for assimilation and cultural annihilation for indigenous peoples that are traumatizing.

Reviewing the history of the Māori people in Aotearoa/New Zealand Mason Durie (1996) notes that "personal and tribal identity were inextricably linked to Papatuanuku—the mother earth—and alienation from land carried with it a severe psychological toll…" (p. 2). Durie goes on to explain how eradication of Mäori language and Mäori healing rituals, as well as paternalistic and assimilative policies eroded the wellbeing of the Mäori people. Aotearoa/New Zealand has changed considerably, Durie notes, to the extent that it is now possible to gain access to traditional healing rituals on an equal basis with conventional medical services. Jenny Ritchie (in press) notes that Aotearoa/New Zealand has made progress in developing culturally appropriate early childhood education programs for Mäori children. All of this occurred, as a result of the Treaty of Waitangi, an accord that has created considerable impetus for nonpaternalistic relations between Mäori people and their dominant culture compatriots. In Jonathan Lear's (2006) terms, one might say that the Mäori people have managed a more successful adaptation to new possibilities and hope in the face of potential annihilation. Despite ongoing difficulties facing Mäori people (cf. Durie, 2003; Walker, 2004), they are exceptional among indigenous peoples in this respect.

In his discussion of the suffering of Aboriginal peoples in Australia, Gregory Phillips (2007) makes the case for an approach to social policy that is premised on healing. Rather than viewing drug addiction, gasoline sniffing, sexual abuse, and domestic violence as isolated pathologies, he properly suggests that we recognize them as *symptoms* of embedded trauma: "If a people have been told for generations that they are worthless, and if they have seen people being constantly abused or dying, they often believe these messages, internalize them, and become traumatized or psychically numbed" (p. 144). His work, with its emphasis on building caring communities, and focusing on cultural renewal, and the work of Judy Atkinson at Gnibi—the College of Indigenous Australian Peoples Southern Cross University (Atkinson, 2007—see also www.scu.edu.au/gnibi/) both point to the importance of approaches to service delivery in health, family services, law enforcement, and education that acknowledge the lacunae left by persistent and pervasive social trauma, and argue for culturally grounded approaches to wellbeing and renewal.

If societies continue to *train* teachers generically in dominant culture epistemologies and worldviews, education for indigenous children will continue to perpetuate the kind of traumatizing cultural hopelessness that the earlier quote from Hinkson suggested (see also Chapter 10). There is no generic recipe for indigenous education. To be successful as revolutionary and hopeful pedagogy, teacher preparation and classroom education must be locally grown. In a world in which accountability standards are defined nationally—and perhaps even globally—in terms of the individual and the market, local pedagogies cannot exist within official schooling. The challenge in creating the pedagogy

I propose below lies not in the logistics of implementation, but is a matter of sovereignty: Who ultimately gets to control education for indigenous peoples? Or, perhaps it could be phrased more honestly: Shall we continue to perpetuate a dominant culture pedagogy that provides indigenous peoples with the terrible choice, as Gregory Phillips notes, between instant cultural death and what he calls "the living death of assimilation"? Or could we perhaps furnish sufficient resources and sufficient local control that indigenous peoples can take charge of articulating their destinies?

Keystones of an Evocative Pedagogy

My approach begins with the assumptions that each indigenous child has a culturally constituted unconscious and is thereby a bearer of the collective history of their people. Trauma in the unconscious may be unspeakable because of the severance of social links through devices such as residential schooling, fosterage, language prohibition and cultural genocide. This severance may continue to occur in the present or may be located in history. Teachers of indigenous children need to be thoroughly familiar with the history and customs of the groups with whom they work—and ideally they should be members of those groups—and they should also be trained, as Judy Atkinson is doing at Gnibi College, in understanding the workings of intergenerationally transmitted trauma so that they know how to recognize and address trauma symptoms.

Psychoanalysts have long recognized that a powerful agent of change in therapy is the presence of the analyst as witness and receiver of unconscious knowledge. Teachers, too, ought to be prepared to receive such knowledge, and should understand how to evoke the unconscious in children through their own evocative presences. A teacher with a passion for myth, storytelling, drama, memory, and the wisdom of elders will draw these evocative knowledges into the classroom, and will elicit evocative responses from students that allow students to experience their own inner knowledges as namable and addressable.

In developing specific pedagogical approaches to embody this process, the Salmon principles, discussed earlier, are of particular relevance. *Proximity* refers to the importance of the subjective presence of another person to allow a child to feel recognized. As Max Van Manen (1986) so succinctly stated, "every child needs to be seen" (pp. 20–23). This suggests that the classroom become a place for close existential encounters, a community, a place in which each child can find a sense of identity and self-respect, and a fundamental recognition of their own worth that allows them to take pride in their ethnic, cultural and class origins. Irrespective of the humaneness or caring of the environment, however, this cannot be accomplished if the classroom and school are not community resources that invite in community stakeholders to assist *their* children in constructing hopeful and proud identities. Sadly, this dimension is all too often lacking in schools for disenfranchised children as, for example, the works of Anyon (1997), Books (1998), Churchill (2004), Fine (1991), Polakow (2000), and Quint (1994), demonstrate in U.S. contexts, and as I illustrate in the case study detailed in Chapter 11.

Immediacy refers to the continuing presentness of unconscious material and underlines the need to prepare teachers to recognize and respond to signifiers from the unconscious. Atkinson's work at Gnibi is the only explicit example of which I am aware of an explicit attempt to address this outside of psychoanalytic training, though of course there has been some work pointing to the power of psychoanalytic ideas for teachers (e.g., Boldt & Salvio, 2006; Field et al., 1989; Jersild, 1955). *Expectancy* refers to the notion that teachers should have boundless notions of possibility for children, and should always be prepared to be frank with them, while *simplicity* attempts to articulate the nature of the existential encounter so that a teacher can engage in the kind of unconscious communication that is the essence of the psychoanalytic relationship (cf. Rogers, 2006). This requires the kind of intensive professional preparation typically lacking in teacher preparation programs. And, above all, as the discussion in Chapter 11 illustrates, it demands a deep capacity for respect.

To the extent that teacher education programs have depth, it is invariably in the area of delivery of received curriculum, and the facilitation of cognitive outcomes. A focus on the unconscious requires a considerable reassessment of the goals and intent of teacher education. It is worth noting here that while there are profound intellectual components to an imaginative pedagogy of the kind I envisage the mundanely cognitive is not privileged. Instead, important weight is given to ancestral memory, current emotion, the cultural and historical context of children's lives, and the power of epistemologies and narrative modes that transcend delimited Western notions of *logos*, the kinds of reductionist learning that can be boiled down to answers on multiple choice tests.

Regenerative Curriculum

If severance of the social link comes from the foreclosure of history, then a major focus of curriculum ought to be on the regeneration of those links by assisting children in experiencing their latent historical subjectivities and in claiming a specific indigenous identity (cf. Lear, 2006). Reanimation of ancestral memories, and reconnection to latent pasts can be facilitated by drama, performance, participation in rituals, viewing of films, reading novels, poetry and myths, and by experiencing and retelling folklore. Recalling Judy Atkinson's discussion of *lorelessness* in the lives of many indigenous children, the challenge is to engage children in narrative possibilities that allow for the construction of new lore. This is not the kind of reanimation of fossil knowledge that leaves children severed from an estranged past. Rather, working organically with the children and with their elders, this is an opportunity to recreate a history that allows for pride, possibility, and a hopeful future. This is the process of constructing a narrative of one's own subjectivity that I discuss in Chapter 3 in the context of my own childhood.

Speaking in terms of narrative, this kind of teaching privileges the active construction of narrative. However, the epistemological and identificatory possibilities of narrative are enhanced by introducing children to multiple modes of narrating, privileging particularly narrative modes that embody the ancestral lore, rituals, and worldviews that particular indigenous children have inherited. Curriculum, in this conceptualization, is an organic process that gets constructed with children and with community stakeholders for the children of that particular community. Teachers might then consider themselves as documentarians of the collective unconscious of the community; documentarians of existing lore; and documentarians of the processes and products involved in constructing new forms of lore with children and community members. The work of Myles Horton and Paulo (Freire, 1969, 1972; Horton & Freire, 1990) and Eliot Wigginton's oral history (e.g., Wigginton, 1972) offer pointers to what might be possible in this area. More important, writings that explore indigenous notions of narrative and epistemology provide crucial insights in this regard, and engaging with this tradition is a future direction of my work in this area (e.g., Archibald, 2008; Fixico, 2003; Hulan & Eigenbrod, 2008; T. King, 2003; McConaghy, 2000; McKegney, 2007).

Conclusion

Dominant culture ideology, with its ethos of distance from the self, individualism, and achievement conceptualized as success in the market, is the antithesis of the kind of pedagogy under discussion here. The approach advocated here is inherently political in that it is postulated on the notion of a counterdiscourse that allows each child a possibility to imagine a life otherwise. It is unclear to me if conventionally trained teachers can ever adopt this kind of revolutionary pedagogy. Recall, that in choosing activist agents for the citizenship education initiative in the U.S., Myles Horton (1990) chose beauty parlor operators rather than conventional teachers. They were economically independent and therefore free of institutional allegiances and they were exceptionally well-bonded with their communities. Horton wanted people who were *of* the people and could talk *with* the people, not those, such as teachers, who were all too well trained to lecture *at* the people. If indigenous education is to be anything other than a mockery of the hopes of indigenous people we need to stop foisting our poorest teachers and an assimilationist curriculum on such communities, and instead work to assist them in developing indigenously appropriate curriculum and pedagogy that will allow them to achieve their aspirations with our assistance. To adopt such a stance, of course, requires a fundamental commitment to the capacity of indigenous peoples to chart their own futures. This is a far cry from what typically passes for *multicultural education* in U.S. society.

· 1 0 ·

SEVEN PRINCIPLES UNDERLYING
SOCIALLY JUST AND ETHNICALLY
INCLUSIVE TEACHER PREPARATION

Societies establish schools to educate a workforce, to control access to occupations through credentialing systems, and to serve the interests of dominant classes (Bourdieu & Passeron, 1977; Nasaw, 1981). Because teacher educators occupy a strategic location in this process, they are expected to comply with regional and national accrediting standards and state regulations. Other pressures toward conservatism come from aspiring teachers, who often desire to reproduce their own experiences of schooling, as well as from local schools that seek to hire teachers who fit into the system. The prospect of producing socially active teachers is frustrated, too, by the lack of control teacher education programs have over the field experiences beginning teachers receive. Schools control practical training as well as the job market. As a result, students end up balancing the utopian hopes and ideals we project onto them with the harsh realities of tracking, segregation, explicit racism, and inequitable distribution of resources that are characteristic of public education in the U.S. today.

This situation makes it difficult to address issues of ethnic difference in teacher education programs. From the earliest days of the Indian Conquest through the establishment of slavery to current xenophobic responses to immigrants from certain regions of the world, the racial fissures identified by W. E. B. Du Bois (1903/1990) as "the problem of the color line" continue to reside at the heart of the debate over difference in the U.S. Those of us concerned with social justice, equity, and access cling to the utopian hope that, by making new teachers conscious of the historical legacies of their own ethnic formation and the insidious workings of institutional racism in our society, we may spark their consciousness so that they will join the struggle for a more just and equitable world.

My purpose is to explore ways in which teacher educators who are committed to addressing issues of equity and justice might move "from awareness to action" (Lawrence & Tatum, 1997, p. 333). While I am in no doubt as to the benefit of individual efforts to develop antiracist pedagogies, the challenge is to move beyond individual effort to develop a collective culture in our teacher education programs that values equity and social justice. The following principles are derived from my own experiences struggling with these issues in teacher education.

Principle #1: Place Social Justice and Equality on the Official Institutional Agenda

When NCATE accreditation came up for renewal at my previous institution, it seemed an unlikely vehicle for social change. Over the course of two accreditation visits, however, faculty in our programs were required to come together to articulate an institutional mission. The conversations helped raise faculty consciousness, and by the time of our most recent accreditation, faculty who shared concerns about social justice and inclusion were vocal in pushing for an explicit acknowledgment of their concerns. Institutional mission statements offer an opportunity to get a foot in the door. When a commitment to diversity and social justice is officially acknowledged, it provides authority for the inclusion of a similar commitment in departmental mission statements. These statements can then be invoked to blunt resistance and to leverage program changes that move academic departments toward enacting principles of social justice and inclusion.

Principle #2: To Recruit and Retain Faculty of Diverse Ethnic Origins, it is Necessary to Adopt a Proactive Stance with Regard to Issues of Race and Social Justice

Addressing issues of difference in teacher education must include a commitment to the recruitment and retention of diverse faculty. While most institutions pay lip service to this idea, recruitment and retention will be difficult without significant changes in our understanding of what commitment to diversity means. As Reyes noted from her interviews with Chicana scholars in academia, for scholars of color there is "tremendous pressure to assimilate and emulate Eurocentric models of scholarship in order to be successful" (1997, p. 30). When ethnically diverse scholars are hired, too often they discover that they are expected to assimilate to a Eurocentric standard or that they have been hired with the presumption that they will be the standard bearer for diversity issues, serving as the racial conscience of the faculty. This kind of tokenism excuses faculty from self-examination. It is demeaning and demoralizing to scholars of color. Reyes proposes that "if universities are to retain these women, they must affirm genuine diversity, even the kind that challenges the dominant paradigm. They must legitimate and respect ethnic identity, and its expression in their work. They must recognize the negative effects of racism, sexism, and white privilege on women of color and create safe places for public discussion of these issues in the academy" (p. 31). Teacher educators must also be prepared to begin doing their own critical work around issues of difference before they begin seeking diverse faculty. Teacher educators should take the bold step of rethinking issues of difference and thereby create an inviting climate in which diverse scholars can contribute to this work.

Principle #3: To Recruit and Retain Student Teachers of Diverse Ethnic Origins, it is Necessary to Adopt a Proactive Stance with Regard to Issues of Race and Social Justice

The absence of teachers of color is a significant concern for our society. Long Island, for instance, contains a population that is 11.4% African American, 9.3% Latino, and 3.8% Asian American. Yet only 3% of the teachers are African American, 2% are Latino, and 0.33% are Asian American (Evans, 1998). While there are many reasons for the absence of teachers of color in our schools (S. King, 1993), the generic quality of many of our teacher preparation programs cannot be ignored. Teacher education appears to be predicated on a universalizing assumption: One pedagogy fits all. We prepare our teachers generically, and we expect them to teach their students generically. As George Counts (1932/1969) noted and Delpit (1995) reiterated, generic pedagogies promulgated in teacher education programs privilege the interests of white middle class children and their families.

Despite extensive scholarship on culturally relevant pedagogy (e.g., Delpit, 1995; Hilliard, 1995; Hollins, 1996; Ladson-Billings, 1994; Walshe, 1996), we have made little progress in constructing culturally inclusive teacher preparation programs. Students of color tell me that they are seeking programs that value difference and are committed to the educational potential of their communities. If we believe that the interests of specific communities are served by having members of those communities in the teaching profession, then we must create contextualized teacher education that addresses the needs of specific groups and communities. If we can do so in consultation with members of diverse communities, we will be successful in recruiting and retaining ethnically diverse student teachers.

Principle #4: Forge Connections with Diverse Communities to Construct Contextually Appropriate Teacher Education

We need to abandon the notion of generic teacher preparation and opt instead for partnership models in which we co-construct contextually sensitive teacher education programs with interested groups (e.g., public schools, adult literacy groups, grassroots organizations, churches, social service agencies). We should take the initiative in setting up discussions with local groups with a view to developing programs that are responsive to the needs of the communities our teachers serve. In view of the chasm between public schools and universities, on the one hand, and the even greater chasm between educational elites (i.e., public schools and universities combined) and poor communities, and communities of color in many areas, this task will not be easy. If teacher education is to exert any leadership in educational reform or social change, however, this step is essential.

Principle #5: Make a Commitment to Explore the Meaning of Whiteness in Teacher Education and Schooling

> Who teaches white teachers about the meaning of race? What do they need to know? How well prepared are white teachers to understand their own "whiteness" and the meaning it has when interacting with students and parents of color? How cognizant are they of their own racial socialization and how it may influence their perceptions of the performance potential of all their students? (Lawrence & Tatum, 1997, p. 333)

Lawerence and Tatum name a truth that is gaining increasing recognition in discourses about difference: Before we venture to change others, we must change ourselves. Before white teachers can undertake the task of bringing an antiracist stance to white students and before they can engage students of diverse ethnic backgrounds, they must become conscious of their own ethnic formation and the manner in which, by virtue of their insertion in white supremacist discourses, they benefit daily from being white. As Frankenberg noted, "Finding the way home, then, entails finding the way out—out of the master's house" (1996, p. 3). Winant explains the complexity of whiteness in the U.S. as a struggle by liberal whites to advocate for equality and social justice while simultaneously maintaining a system of which they are the primary beneficiaries: "The contemporary crisis of whiteness—its dualistic allegiance to privilege and equality, to color consciousness and color-blindness, to formally equal justice and to substantive social justice—can be discerned in the contradictory character of white identity today" (1996, p. 199). Breaking this silence involves confronting white student teachers with their complicitness in the social construction of their own racial identity and economic status through construction of inferior racial others. Frankenberg poignantly describes what it felt like for her when she finally "witnessed" her own whiteness:

> What went on for me, what stunned me, often, into an outer silence and inner turmoil might, once again, be easiest to begin naming as a process of remapping. The ways my world was put together, and the way Estee's was made, were different in a way that literally shattered the logics and certainties in which I had formerly, and unthinkingly, been ensconced. (1996, p. 12)

Assisting student teachers in uncovering their own ethnic histories, the relationships between their ethnicities and patterns of colonial domination, and the workings of contemporary white privilege in the economic and social realm is a complex undertaking. It goes without saying that it cannot occur unless the teacher educators who undertake this work with students have begun this journey for themselves.

Principle #6: Prepare Teachers for Specific Ethnic Contexts by Extending their Knowledge and Changing their Attitudes

While most teacher education programs nod toward multiculturalism, few if any programs systematically address issues of difference. To do so, we need to address student attitudes, provide knowledge about the history of diverse groups, and focus on culturally relevant pedagogy. Changing attitudes is perhaps the most complex. Assuming most students are white and have grown up unconscious of the institutional racism in which they participate, a series of carefully sequenced workshops on unlearning racial oppression is essential. Students who have taken my summer institute on autobiography and racial identity have shown themselves capable of significant attitude shifts in a single week. The long-term benefit of such workshops is questionable, however, unless the content of workshops is systematically interwoven with regular course content.

With respect to the knowledge we teach, much of the generic information imparted in teaching methods course might be replaced by specific information on diverse groups and an exploration of the politics, sociology, and linguistic bases of culturally relevant pedagogy. Students are often woefully ignorant of the historical origins of diverse groups and of the role education has played in privileging the life chances of some groups at the expense of others. I currently teach a course in family and community literacy that surveys the cultural characteristics of the main ethnic groups in the U.S. Courses like this one offer a useful starting point. People who plan to teach in specific communities, however, need much more specific cultural knowledge about those specific communities to be successful. Rather than generic teacher preparation, we might do well to offer contextualized programs that prepare students for the communities in which they intend to work. For students who intend to work in white communities, a thorough grounding in the history of the civil rights struggles in the U.S. as well as opportunities to unlearn white privilege is essential.

Principle #7: Develop Antiracist Practicum and Field Experience Sites

In responding to pressure from accreditation agencies to prepare students for diversity, teacher education programs often attempt to diversify field placements. The results can be disastrous. In segregated communities like those that abound on Long Island, often this means shifting students from all white schools to schools populated entirely by students of color for some of their placements. In the absence of a systematic curriculum that addresses the politics of ethnic and class difference, there is a real danger that such an approach will serve to reinforce negative stereotypes of communities of color. This situation is exacerbated if faculty give students the message that these placements are inferior but that they must put up with them to meet their diversity requirement. Furthermore, if the implicit ideology of the teacher education program is that best practice is white middle class pedagogy, then it becomes impossible for student teachers to find virtue in poor school communities. Observing teachers with limited resources teaching poor children who lack middle class cultural capital, student teachers are susceptible to adopting a pathological perspective on class and ethnic difference.

Too often, also, we are cowardly about acknowledging the presence in our society of what Anyon (1997) calls "ghetto schools"—schools for children of color that embody the worst forms of racial oppression. By placing our student teachers in such schools without speaking out against such brutal practices and without enabling our students to name and analyze these practices, we send a very powerful message that poor children of color deserve such treatment. If we are to take seriously our responsibility to educate our students to work with diverse populations, we need to be willing to work collaboratively with community groups and open-minded public school officials to help develop models of culturally appropriate pedagogy that will serve to enhance the educational services they deliver. We also must provide our student teachers with opportunities to practice socially just, respectful, and culturally relevant pedagogy.

· 1 1 ·

THE CHILD AS SUBJECT OF LITERACY[1]

When children enter school they come with complex histories as family and community members. And in our responses to the children, we help shape their understanding of what it means to be an educated person in our society. If our classrooms are not places of sociocultural breadth and depth, we risk sending messages of alienation, messages that say that educated people are not rooted in their own histories, in strong relationships with people that matter.

—(DYSON, 1993, P. 230)

The Children's Farewell

Paul's letter[2] came on May 20, 1995 in one of our university business reply envelopes. Others arrived during the following weeks. His letter had no signature but he had written a return address and "From Paul to Brennen" on the outside. The letter was accompanied by a drawing of a dragon (Fig. 2):

Dear Mr. Brennen you are the best of all and may you put in the mail a smale X-man.

Lorenzo's letter arrived May 31. It was written in his own hand but showed some signs of external assistance:

Dear Reading Professionals,
I am sending you this letter
because I want to know when
I will see you again.
I like your reading and
being around you. Take good
care of your self and write
back soon.
Sincerely,
Lorenzo.

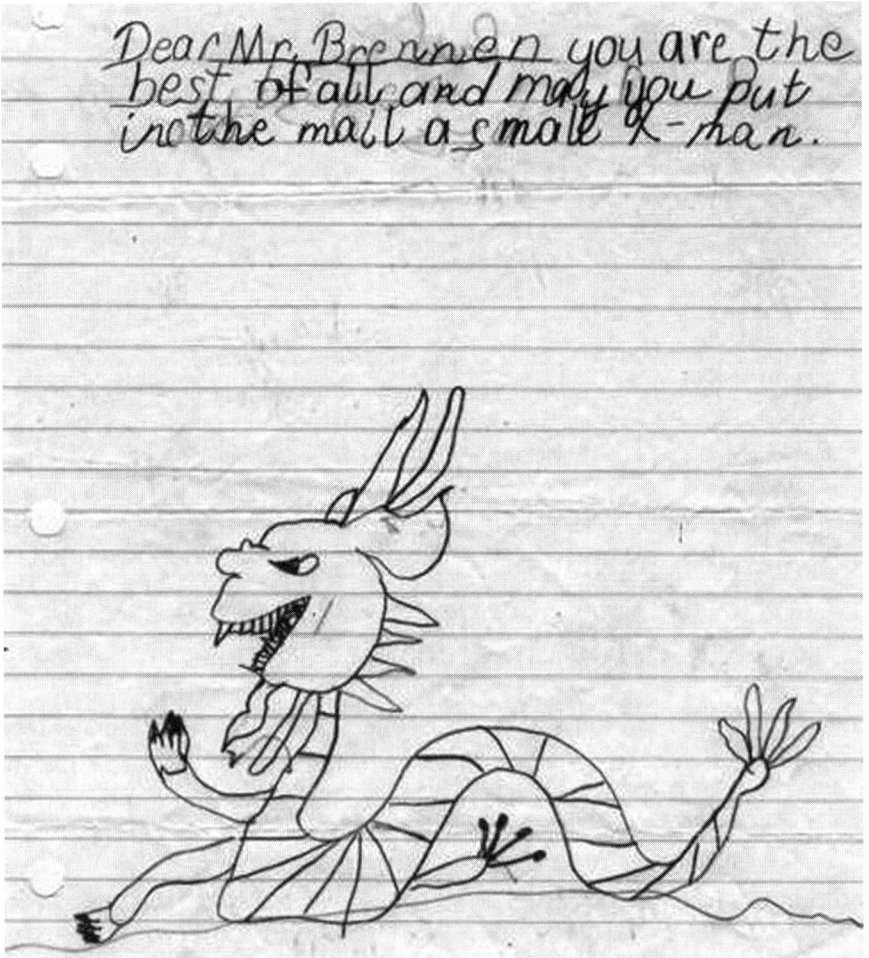

Fig. 2. Paul's letter

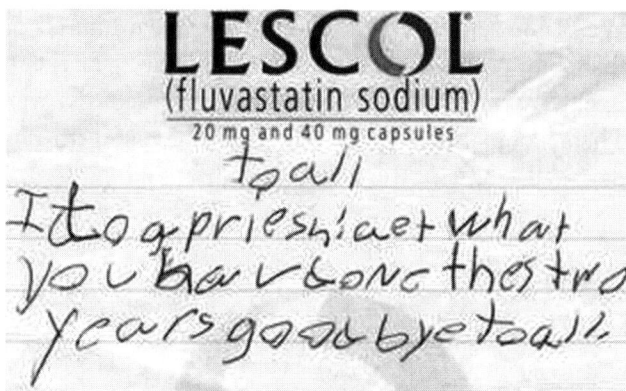

Fig. 3. Franklin's letter

Arriving around the same time, Franklin's note was brief (Fig. 3), written on a page pulled from a pharmacist's pad advertising some medication:

> toall
> I do aprieshaet what
> you havdone thes two
> year goodbye to all.
> by
> Franklin

Our trusty friend Danny wrote too, his slanting script written across the blue page in inch tall orange letters, and as always, accompanied by a superhero illustration:

> Dear M.r Michael I miss you
> coming to read to us
> I hope I see you
> next year because
> I love your books
> your friend. Danny

Mischievous Lameke's scrupulously folded letter was perhaps a greater surprise:

> by, lameke
> dear marta I miss you I wish you could
> stay
> me and DeltonDannymiss you to.
> and thank you for the paper
> Dogzilla is a good book
> The end

Edwin's picture of himself arrived later. He had drawn himself on a sheet of paper with a ballpoint pen, accented with the highlighting marker that was one of our parting gifts. Written across the top in highlighted text were the words "I am sad." The accompanying letter, written in the emergent handwriting of this first-grader, no doubt with the help of an adult, said:

> by Edwin
> Dear Brennen
> I miss you
> than kyou
> for all the fun we
> had in mss. _____'s
> class. I hope you
> come again soon
> to see me and my class
> I miss you

What could induce such compelling communications from children?

First Impressions: The Children in the School

The poignancy of the letters of these six-, seven-, and eight-year-olds is underlined and perhaps explained by the painful contexts in which they were expected to live out their school lives. Our field notes were replete with heart-wrenching examples:

From Michael's journal:

> While Ms. X is bad, my worst experiences have been with Ms. Y. I visited twice and she was extremely shrill and oppressive. I had a terrible headache from the tension after half an hour. Anyway I'd been observing Jamal and as I left Ms. Y yelled out: "He should be behind bars. Those kids in the back should be behind bars—all of them should be behind bars." She turned directly to me and yelled, "Don't you agree?" She put me in an absolutely intolerable position. [Field notes, Michael, 10/'94]

And again...

> I went to Ms. X's class. Now that the visit by district officials was over she'd taken apart all of the learning centers that I'd helped her build. The room was in the usual state of chaos and disorder, and she was in the middle trying to "teach". I went around to those who weren't working and asked them why they weren't busy. Finally I took four girls

down to the back of the room and picked out books for them. They were eager to read to me and I stayed listening to them the whole morning. I just ignored what Ms. X was trying to do. At lunch time she was making one of her ill-conceived efforts at shaping them into a line. By now, my four students were at the board with me doodling and having some fun. Ms. X, at the front of the line, led her students into the hallway just as another teacher's class was passing. Seeing her mistake she yelled at her students to stop. In the chaos they didn't hear her so she physically pushed the front children back into the room, screaming all the while. Of course, this caused a domino effect of children bumping into each other. Julius, the volatile one, got bumped by somebody and retaliated by throwing chairs. Others started to fight back. I went over, got him to stop, and had him begin to pick the chairs up when Ms. X lost it. She took what she decided were the "good ones," to lunch and just left the others there. They were all climbing the walls by now. I was trying to figure out what to do when Ms. Y across the hall, strode into the class, seething with rage. She screamed at them at the top of her lungs and gave them a dreadful dressing down. Ms. X then returned and took them to lunch. She was beside herself with rage. I didn't have the heart to go back there in the afternoon. [Field notes, Michael, 4/'95]

Marta recalled her first impressions of the school:

I always asked Michael about his visits to Little Oaks.[3] He often shared his feelings about his work with the teachers, their responses to his suggestions, his progress and his frustrations when he thought his efforts were futile. I think it was the children that kept him going back. Whenever Michael talked about the abusive behavior, the corruption, or the dismal conditions of the school, he easily broke into stories about the children's energy, their enthusiasm, their potential. What I experienced that winter day that I visited the school has stayed with me. The disorderly area surrounding the school indicated hope and renewal as condominiums were in the midst of construction. The external structure of the beige, rectangular building was more inviting than other urban schools I had seen. Michael and I walked through the hallways, our arms filled with stories to read. The excitement Michael's presence produced for the children was electric. As they shouted, "Hello Pink Panther! Hello Mr. Michael!" I knew he had become more than a welcomed guest. As the boys and girls saw him they were immediately transformed with new felt emotions which illuminated the severity of the bare hallways. Their happy faces and expressions of joy cut through the dispiriting sounds of disciplining booming around us. Some children even dared to poke their heads out of their classrooms as I walked by to say hello; as I peeked in I saw more bare walls, disinterested students and apathetic teachers seated behind their desks. The children knew that Michael's arrival meant a break from monotony and austere seating arrangements. Their eagerness to have 'Mr. Michael' read to them could not be contained. I read to several classes that afternoon. The children loved to hear stories. They could not get enough. In the bilingual and ESL classes Michael and I took turns reading bilingual stories. The Latino children expressed amazement when they learned I spoke Spanish. I felt such a connection with them; they touched me in a place I had long since forgotten. [Field notes, Marta, 11/'94]

And later, in Marta's journal:

> From the first day she stood out for me. Taller and heavier than the other children, her eyes were tinged with sadness and her expression was too serious for her seven years. She sported a beautiful dark braid, resembling a horse tail in length, bulk and shine. After several visits to her classroom, I began to notice that she always wore the same clothes; a midnight blue bib, crisscrossing in the back, connected to a calf-length skirt. The contrast of the white long-sleeved cotton blouse worn underneath gave the child an even more staid appearance. I quickly learned Alicia's name because it was etched onto her teacher's tongue, leaving her lips with force for any misdemeanor. I was stunned by her acceptance of her teacher's yelling. She remained stoic. She seemed accustomed to the outbursts. At our second visit to the classroom she approached me, eager to share something about herself. "My mother is taking me to a holiday party at her work on Friday," she told me proudly. She inquired if I spoke Spanish. When I responded, "Si" her staid look immediately changed, accompanied with excitement and eagerness to talk. "Where are you from? Yo soy de Puerto Rico!" she declared. I became friendly, speaking in Spanish, as she shared things about her life, in stolen moments amidst the chaos of the classroom. On several occasions Alicia was sweeping the floor when I came in for our sessions. "This one is not cut out for anything else," I was informed by the teacher in a loud voice. "She can't do the work." Alicia, head down, continued sweeping around our feet. "This is her vocation, and she's good. She could be my maid when she's old enough." [Field notes, Marta, 1/'95]

I could tell many such stories. Jamal lost all of the buttons on his shirt while being "disciplined" by the principal on the way to the lunch room one day. By the time I arrived to Ms. Z's class of third-graders at 10:00 on another day half of them had already received one thousand lines to write as punishment for speaking to each other in class. Nothing we said or did could ease their despondency or resentfulness at this servitude. One day when I entered Ms. Z's room a substitute was standing helplessly at the front of the room. More than half a dozen students were playing tag or fighting on the stairway at the end of the hall. Some of the remaining students in the class were climbing on the tables. Many looked quite scared in this anarchic situation. We rounded them up to read and talk awhile, and they begged us to stay for the day and be their teacher.

While the children grew to love our stories and begged to borrow our books some teachers did their best to discourage us from trusting the students enough to loan them our books. The library, a beautifully decorated facility, had received a grant, and spent $15, 000 on the latest in "multicultural" books, CD-ROMs etc., yet practically every classroom in the building was devoid of books. The library was mainly used for teacher meetings. The librarian said the children messed the place up too much. A reading resource room in the school was lined with library bound editions of classics of children's literature, many of them fifteen, even twenty years olds. Most were in mint condition and showed no sign of ever having been handled by a child. In a building in which eighty nine professional and paraprofessional staff served less than seven hundred children, there were many classes with thirty, even thirty five children. Seven of the highest paid professionals in the school had full-time administrative responsibilities and never worked directly with children: among these were the principal, the special education coordinator, the attendance coordinator, the disciplinarian, euphemistically titled "learning strategies specialist," and two staff developers whose sole supposed responsibility was teacher mentoring.

On my first visit to the school the principal's description of Little Oaks left me wondering what role there might be for me:

> When I first met the principal of Little Oaks he painted a very rosy picture of the school. He spoke about the division of the school into three mini-schools, the thematic emphasis on multiculturalism, the presence of a school band and, rooms full of computers, and a school-wide emphasis on meaningful learning. [Quarterly summary of activities, Michael, 6/'93]

But my impressions as we began visiting classrooms and speaking with teachers and students was very different:

> The first thing that struck me as I made my rounds of the classrooms was how false the principal's picture of the school was. From my observations it is clear to me that many of the teachers are custodial in their approach to children. There is a lot of time devoted to the reiterating and enforcement of rules. Paradoxically, apparently because of pervasive low expectations and low morale among the staff, disciplinary breaches are extremely common. In many classes children are extremely distractible and aggressive. Fights frequently break out in the halls, and children often wander the halls banging on classroom doors. Some staff discipline through screaming and intimidation and there are whispers of children receiving corporal punishment. From my observations the staff as a whole seems very poorly informed about student-centered and process-oriented forms of pedagogy. I have seen practically no evidence of thematic teaching, culturally relevant curriculum, use of literature, writing process, math manipulatives etc. As a matter of fact there isn't even a lot of traditional didactic teaching in many classes. My impression is of worksheets and busy work, but little of academic engagement by teachers or students. I doubt that very many teachers teach science or social studies! Not one child in a fifth grade class with which I worked was capable of defining the word *democracy*, nor could anybody name the current president of the United States. Students seem astoundingly ignorant of routine geographical and historical information, and discussions of current events are a rarity in all of the classrooms I visited. From the work on display I suspect that the academic work being covered by

teachers is a couple of years below what one would expect at any given grade level. My gut feeling is of a barren curriculum, bored and distracted students, and teachers with low expectations who make few demands on their students. [Quarterly summary of activities, Michael, 6/'93]

The story of the children and their resilience in living out their school lives under these oppressive conditions is situated at the vortex of a much more complex narrative of school and society.

The Official School story: The Pedagogy of Poverty Up Close

The school was caught in a series of vises, each of which exerted its own limitations on action. Little Oaks served a community of color: sixty-five percent of the children were Latino, and the remaining students were African American. The poverty index of the school, as indicated by eligibility for free school meals, was one hundred percent. Twenty two percent of the students were identified as having limited proficiency in English at the point of entry to school. The school had a mobility index in excess of thirty percent indicating that more than one third of the school population arrived and departed every year. This was in part due to family dislocations associated with poverty and family crises and the presence of a significant number of homeless shelters in the area. It was also due to dissatisfaction among parents who shuttled their children from school to school in search of better educational options.

Achievement levels, as measured by standardized tests, had shown a steady decline for many years and had recently bottomed out with less than a quarter of the children on any grade level attaining the fiftieth percentile on the State reading test. The constant mobility of students in and out of the school confounds the interpretation of these results, yet one fact is indisputable: this school had been doing a markedly poor job of providing academic preparation for students in basic literacy and numeracy.

Predictably, the publication of test scores and school rankings based on these scores put considerable pressure on the school district and the school. Unfortunately, the result has been a series of contradictory policy initiatives and edicts. The district had published a Comprehensive School Plan that embraced progressive, process-oriented pedagogy wholeheartedly. Buzz words such as the following leap from the pages of the Plan: *meaningful; active learning; transactional rather than transmission learning; thematic; integrated instruction; collaborative;*

group instruction; *authentic assessment; print-rich; whole language; writing process; authentic literature; writing and publishing; hands-on; primary source material; race, ethnicity and gender sensitive instruction.* Despite this rhetoric, a consistent message from the school and district office was that all that really mattered was test scores. Teachers were under pressure to devote the *entire school day* for the first half of the year to fill-in-the-blank test preparation.

Schools in this district, like schools in many poor urban communities, are caught in a vicious cycle of alienating curriculum, declining academic expectations, and desperate pressure to gain elevated test scores at all costs. Failure of schools such as Little Oaks to improve despite all this pressure has led to plummeting morale among faculty. It has reinforced a corrosive belief among some teachers in this and similar schools that what are often referred to as *these children* cannot learn.

Despite the adoption of the progressive comprehensive plan described above, no effort had been made to implement it and the teachers fully understood that the rhetoric was both cynical and hollow. All of the teachers in the school had also been put through intensive training in an extensive self-esteem curriculum package but this was not implemented either. The principal had pinned all of his hopes on technology. By the end of 1995, with funding from political sources, the school had expended a substantial sum of money in develop three fully equipped computer labs which were solely devoted to skill-and-drill instruction in reading and math skills.

As achievement in the school continued to slide the refrain from the school administration and teachers was that the State and district carried a big stick but did nothing material to assist the school. There was more than a grain of truth in this. District and State evaluators came in at critical times to assess achievement and then disappeared until the next evaluation cycle. The school personnel's cynicism, while justified, was nevertheless devastating to the educational mission of the school.

The Pedagogy of Poverty: A Metanarrative for Urban Schools in Poor Communities

The scandalously low level of achievement and the oppression of poor children of color in Little Oaks is hardly remarkable. This is a commonplace illustration of what Haberman (1991) dubbed the *pedagogy of poverty,* and what Janice Hale (1994) described as *incarceration education.* The pedagogy of poverty has been—and continues to be—characteristic of the schooling of too many poor children in urban communities. Many discussions of the deleterious effects of racist and inequitable schooling have appeared throughout the years,[4] yet such schooling continues to be the norm for children our society has accepted as marginal and perhaps disposable. In *Lives on the edge*, Valerie Polakow summarized the deleterious effects of such pedagogy:

> In the majority of preschool and elementary school classrooms described in this book there was a pervasive ethos of containment and regulation—drilling children to produce the correct responses, regulating their imagination, presenting them with tasks to be completed rather than learning encounters. Teachers, with the exception of three sensitive ones, saw obedience and compliance to the routinized tasks as indicating success. The classrooms were, for the most part, rigidly segregated by gender and ability groupings, and out-of-order children often young black boys in poverty, rapidly becoming classroom deviants. Even when they exhibited giftedness, as did young George with his poetry, they were not seen as gifted by those who had already condemned them as impaired. (1993, p. 150)

Michelle Fine (1987), drawing on a case study of a low-income urban school, argues that such schools "establish themselves as fortresses against low-income communities" (p. 158). Echoing Freire's arguments in *Pedagogy of the Oppressed* (1972), Fine suggests that schools in poor communities actively conspire to prevent students and parents from naming and thereby critiquing and possibly acting to change the nature of their schools or communities:

> Silencing, I would guess, more intimately informs low-income, public schooling than relatively privileged situations. To question from above holds intellectual promise; to question from below forebodes danger... Silencing sustains the belief in schooling as the mechanism of social mobility, with contradictory evidence barred. And silencing diverts critique away from the economic, social, and educational institutions which organize class, race, and gender hierarchies. But the silencing process bears not only ideological or cosmetic consequences. These very demands permeate classroom life so primitively as to make irrelevant the lived experiences, passions, concerns, communities, and biographies of low-income minority students. In the process the very voices of students and their communities that public education claims to nurture, shut down. (1987, p. 158)

Yet it is possible to get so taken in with the monolithic nature of the pedagogy of poverty as to not recognize the pockets of possibility and resistance that exist in all human interactions. Jean Anyon (1995), for example, presents a devastating portrait of an oppressive, racist school in a community not unlike Little Oaks. She describes "a lived professional culture of many teachers and the administrators in this school... [that] had deteriorated into a dehumanizing and abusive stance towards the student population, whose families lack the clout to ensure better treatment" (p. 69). Following a graphic description of the appalling pedagogical practices in the school, Anyon draws on Wilson's arguments from *The truly disadvantaged* (1987) to suggest that urban poverty is intimately linked to a decline in the economic infrastructure of poor urban communities. I am sympathetic to her claim that "educational reforms cannot compensate for the ravages of society" (p. 88). However, I think that Anyon overstates the powerlessness of people in poor urban communities. It is necessary to recognize the sense of agency and possibility that, Rigoberta Menchu (1984), Anchee Min (1994), Malcolm X (1965) and others have exemplified in their struggles against oppression. I am more sympathetic to Fine's characterization of urban schools as fortresses of official silencing and her recognition that underneath the official silence much potential for subversion exists.

In our study we fumbled our way to understanding how to nurture the capacities of the children to find the cracks in their official school world as we moved from attempts at conventional "progressive" approaches to literacy toward a more genuinely grounded and emancipatory approach. We owe much to the children who taught us how to do this.

Our literacy stance

My initial intention was to engage the teachers in staff development activities. However, due to low morale and fatigue from the saturation of the school with outside evaluators and experts, the teachers were not interested. A few grudgingly agreed to some experimental instructional activity in their classes, but for the most part they took our presence as an opportunity to take a break or catch up on paper work. Brennen, a current graduate student, and Marta, a former graduate student, joined me in the literacy project described here. We worked in the school from October 1994 through June 1995, attending usually one full day per week, and spending approximately one hour per week in each of the five classrooms. Brennen, Marta, and I took full responsibility for one class each and we shared responsibility for the remaining two classes. Brennen was attending my graduate education class for part of this time, and we were reading Anne Haas Dyson's *Social worlds of children learning to write in an urban primary school* (1993), and Valerie Polakow's *Lives on the edge: Single mothers and their children in other America* (1993), among other works. These works, and the discussion of our literacy project in class, together with visits by some class members to Little Oaks, were formative in developing our understanding of the work we were doing. I was unable to attend the school for an extended period in January-February due to surgery, an absence that proved important in relation to the story I tell here.

At the outset, our thinking about literacy instruction was closely anchored to process oriented approaches such as those commonly identified by the terms *whole language* and *writing process*.[5] The initial impetus for the project came from our reading of Hayes, Bahruth, and Kessler's *Literacy con cariño* (1991). This work, embodying a typical process-oriented approach, was of particular interest because of the authors' success in engaging a population of Mexican American children of migrant farm workers in Southwest Texas in meaningful literacy activities. I was hopeful that we could similarly engage the children of Little Oaks.

As the year progressed our understanding of what we were about grew clearer. We began to experience the socioculturally situated nature of learning, and the way in which children negotiate the permeable boundaries between their "unofficial worlds" at home and the "official worlds" of schooling. We observed the "social work" Dyson (1993) says is entailed in learning, emphasizing the importance of creating discursive structures in classrooms that allow children to begin the process of composing themselves through their literacy activities. Dyson notes that Harold and Connie Rosen posed the essential questions of schooling this way:

> "What does this place say to me?" [the children] ask and look for the answer in every intonation of the institution. In finding the answer they also discover what it is possible for them to say. (Quoted in Dyson, 1993, p. 30)

In time we were to convey very different messages to the children than the official messages the school conveyed and we had to deal with the ensuing tensions and ethical implications.[6]

Storied Lives: A Conventional Beginning

We decided to make reading and storytelling the center of our relationship with the children. In the bilingual class we used many bilingual Spanish/English stories and worked with the children in both languages. The children were quite unaccustomed to being read to and this became an enormous source of pleasure for the children. It is a mark of the lack of nurturance in the school, and the rarity of storytelling in the children's school lives that our modest story reading efforts were celebrated so much by the children. We brought in a wide variety of books, beginning with culturally diverse folktales. Over the year we added poetry, fantasy, and adventure. Later, after the children began vociferously complaining that they had grown tired of our never ending supply of folktales, comics and cartoons such as those in Groening's (1987) *School is Hell,* and other popular culture sources were added to the mix. The children begged to borrow our books and it became a mark of prestige for children to be seen reading them. Despite dire warnings from teachers not to loan our books to children, no book was lost or damaged.

We viewed reading as a conversation starter (cf. Paley, 2004a) as well as an opportunity to build relationships with the children. If, as I suggest in Chapter 3, subjectivity is constructed through narrative, then deeply personal conversation (cf. Buber, 1971, also Chapter 9 of this volume) and the diverse identificatory opportunities provided by narratives from books, films, and poetry are vital to the development of an expansive subjectivity in children. Initially trapped within a middle-class whole language view of literacy we were quite unprepared for the children's desire to participate performatively and transgressively in our storytelling. We wanted the children to be *receptive* to our reading and we often struggled mightily to gain their attention. The children often went wild. Raucous laughter, exaggerated fear, teasing, impersonating characters from the stories, anticipating plot, reading aloud with us, and making fun of us and of each other were all part of their repertoires. It took us a while to recognize and value the powerful theatric and storytelling genres embodied in their transgressive responses. Jamal's talent at enacting, performing, and appropriating a story Michael was reading on one occasion, was captured by Marta:

> After the first few visits I knew what to expect when entering the classroom. No matter what the activity, it was impossible to be immune to Jamal's energy. His prescribed seating assignment alongside the teacher's desk did not deter him. He made himself visible; abruptly standing to greet us with an exaggerated wave of his arms while yelling, "They're heeeeeeeeeerrree!" He was everywhere, seizing opportunities for action by looking for or creating classroom adventures. From our first meeting I liked him. As Michael attempted to read *Lon Po Po* to the class, Jamal sat right next to him, high up on his knees to preview the illustrations, and insisted on interrupting by commenting on the characters and making jokes. Michael pleaded with him to be quiet and finally Jamal surrendered. Well, only for a moment; again he found the spotlight. Addressing his audience using his hands, upper body and electrifying expressions, he stretched as much as he possibly could on those little knees and skillfully acted out Michael's words, demonstrating fierceness and fright, to my delight. [Field notes, Marta, 10/'95]

We learned to be flexible and whenever the children's needs dictated that we go in other directions we did so:

> I didn't get much writing done in Ms. Y's class, but what did happen was just as powerful. I had decided to split the class and let the children choose with whom to work. Brennen brought in an autobiographical book he had made, and all the boys immediately gravitated to him. I had poems to share and the girls decided to stay with me. After reading *Good Times* by Lucille Clifton, an African American writer, Shelli began to talk about her mother, a topic mentioned in the poem. I learned of her parents break-up, her mama's new and irritable husband. Other little girls began to share stories of their parents and home, and they began to ask me about my life, "Do you have a husband? Are you married? Why not? How old are you?" Even Monique, who had been especially quiet during most of our visits, spoke of her anger for her stepfather. I spent the time sitting together on the reading rug, engaging in real talk. [Marta, field notes, 11/'95]

Composing Lives I—Windows into Children's Lives

We began with autobiographical writing because, again like Hayes et al. (1991), we were convinced that our success with the children would hinge upon our ability to engage them in affirming personal relationships with us. We had not yet established the kinds of relationships with children that would yield the types of writing that Kohl (1967), for example, describes, and that we experienced later. Nevertheless, these early letters were informative and some actively invited dialogue and thus offered the kinds of conversational opportunities we were seeking. We wrote replies to all letters and helped the students read our responses. The children were electrified by our responses. It is as if, in Max Van Manen's (1986) terms, they had finally been *seen* in school:

> *I like to do work reading and playing*
> *and whtch TV to all the times*
> *Some time I play with me games I like*
> *Gameboy*
> *My favorite game is Dorter marol I love*
> *That game it fun and my favorite tv show*
> *is Ghost Wirter I like*
> *I play it a lot the End my name is Liliana*
> [Grade 3]

> *I have a snak and fishs*
> *I play*
> [Gloria, Grade 2]

Once I saw
a little cat
going with me
with a little
tall she look
like my cat
I like my cat
and a little dog
come it was good
to cats I like
my cat and a dog
the end
[Monique, Grade 2]

Some of the children framed their responses as letters, addressing us personally:

Dear Marta
I like my sisters
and my brothers I
have a snale and a
Igyana I play with
my brothers and sisters
[Gloria, Grade 2]

Dear Michael I had fun time writeing story
and . . . my mother is going to have a babby and
I go to boy scouts every Thursday.
[Darwin, Grade 2]

to m.r Michael
my name is Julius
like to play game
and have 6 people in my
hose and I have a nephew
and a brother and a sister and like
to see tv
[Julius, Grade 3]

We wrote individual letters in reply, responding to their stories and inviting further dialogue[7]:

I had for Chrismas is a comquost and a   *Dear Annette*
barbies house and a can with   *Your letter is really nice. How many*
mickie mouse and a dog had   *babies did your dog have? What did*

babes on Christmas
[Annette, Grade 3]

you do with the puppies? Write soon
and tell me more about yourself.
Michael

I had a cat but is was m sister
and I like the cat I allway had fun
but it went with my sister new house
but he having fun
[Shawn, Grade 3]

I bet you miss your cat. Do you have
any pets at your house now? Write
soon and tell me more about your
family
Michael

Dear Michael
I like to watcth [TV—rebus] and
I like Do you have a
Girlfried
[Marisa, Grade 3]

Dear Marisa,
I have a wife and a son, 12 years old
and a daughter, 9 years old. Her
name is Jennifer. Write back and tell
me more about yourself and your
family.
Michael

Composing Lives II: Subjectivity and Formal Narrative

We were interested in reading-writing connections and we devoted a lot of effort in the early days to brainstorming "interesting" and "meaningful" writing tasks. Often, for example, we asked the children to write on themes related to the stories we read. We framed the tasks in ways that encouraged divergent thinking and connection with their own lives. Although signs of personal ownership appeared in these writings, they differ markedly from the more deeply personal and dialogical writing we received later.

The children seemed to greatly enjoy Ed Young's book, *Lon Po Po* (1989). They were quick to point out the similarities and differences between it and the traditional Red Riding Hood tale. I initiated the writing task with a discussion of a fantasy Marta had shared with them about a wolf that was loose in the City. Afterwards I asked the children to compose their own stories. Some children produced school-like retellings of which Yvonne's story was typical:

> *There was a wolf and he like to walk down the street*
> *and he like to eat children because he was so hurrg one*
> *day he knon on a girl door and the girl said who is it*
> *and the big bad wolf said it's grandma and the little girl*
> *told her mother it's grandma so the little girl mother open*
> *the door and the wolf jamp up and ate the little girl*

up and then ete the mother up and then he saw some
peanuts and ate them all up and went out
side and all the people was scear and then he ate the people word
The End
[Yvonne, Grade 2]

Some children made allusions to Marta's "dream," but appropriated it in their own unique ways:

I had a dream that a wolf was following
me and I was scared My mother was
in the house and then I screamed and my
mother herd me and she came out and
she was the wolf running and she ran
after him and she hurt her seid and my mother
name is Wanda. Wolf is dead now
[Sandy, Grade 2]

The story of my dream and is there an
Alagader under my bed
I had a dream about there an Alagader
under my bed. Tha when I got up he
was walking bake of me. The end.
[José, Grade 2]

Others offered emotionally engaging performative responses that opened windows into their lives:

I will cach The Wolf
with a cacher and shoot him
with a gun. And sale him.
[Willie, Grade 2]

Onec there was a big bad wolf.
and he eat children when he
is hunry. One day he walked in the
street and he eat a little baby and the
mother was crying and wolf threw the
mother in the gabash and the children
ran away
[Shelli, Grade 2]

We introduced legends by reading *Rainbow Crow* (VanLaan, 1989) and *The legend of the bluebonnet* (DePaola, 1983). After reading the stories we discussed the concept of legends. We invited the children to choose something enigmatic from their own experience and compose a legend about it. Because only two days remained until Christmas, many of the children's legends focused on that theme, though Gloria incorporated *Rainbow Crow* directly into hers:

> *one day Santa Cam*
> *to give all of*
> *children toys but*
> *a Crow cam in*
> *Santa Sleigh the*
> *Crow cam in al*
> *color. The Crow bit*
> *all of the toys*
> *Santa did not*
> *have now moor toys*
> *for the children*
> *Santa Cards the*
> *Crow and Santa*
> *let the Crow go*
> *away but Santa Sad to*
> *the Crow you can not eat*
> *the toys.*
> [Gloria, Grade 2]

> *Reindeers fly because*
> *Santa Claus put magic in*
> *The reinders and that's*
> *Why the reindeers could*
> *Fly and I wich I*
> *Could fly*
> [Sandy, Grade 2]

Some children ignored the topic and used the opportunity to communicate some of their own anxieties:

> *Legend "Santa can't fly"*
> *I love to be*
> *friends. I don't*
> *like to Fig.ht*
> *and I don't like*
> *to yeld*
> *I just like to*
> *play with them*
> *The end*
> [Jose, grade 2]

We also used the Native American tale, *Whale in the sky* (Siberell, 1982) to stimulate writing. In the story there is a good deal of conflict between the animals until Thunderbird intervenes to restore order. We left the writing activity open-ended. Although we never invited the children to retell the stories, many of the children chose to do so. This seemed to come quite naturally to them, perhaps because this is one of the most common academic demands that is made on children in schools. Many of their retellings were quite comprehensive:

> The Whatle and Thunderbird got
> Together and came to be
> Friends. Then They saw Turtle.
> and they saw shark
> and because. Now Thunderbird
> and Shark got Together
> and the shark never eat
> a Fish aging
> > The End
> [Takia, Grade 2]

> The Whatle eat fish that what he get
> For eating the fish. The eagle was mad at the
> Whale. Because he ate the fish.
> He was a ugly Whale Because he ate the fish
> The ugly one who ate the fish was so
> The one who ate tehe fish is a ugly whale.
> The eagle came to see what happen he
> Shad be pardes.
> Because he ate the fish
> The eagle was very mad because he
> Ate the fish
> Ate the fish was ugle
> And the fish was gone
> > The end
> [Yolanda, Grade 2]

After reading *The Great Kapok Tree* (Cherry, 1990) we invited the children to write, purposely leaving the assignment open-ended. Some children apparently taking no risk at all, responded by attempting to copy the text exactly. However, Shelli's retelling, voiced poetically, is notable for its accuracy and beauty. Her writing challenges any imputation of "illiteracy" to children such as those with whom we worked:

> One day a man told a nutha
> Man to cut down the tree with an ax

I tried to but then he feled a sleep
Then a snak came down and I said
Jame you can't cut down the tree we
Live in it Then a bird came down and
Said Jame you can't cut down this tree
It need Air if you cut down
This tree you I will not live.
And you want too Then a frog came down
And Said don't cut down this Tree
I like this tree because I live
It then a lion came and said jame
You know all the animals live in This
Tree so don't cut it or I will have
You for dinner Then a —boy came
And said Jame wake up
And look all over with your New
Eyes then Jame pick up the ax
And he looked at the Animals and
Dropt he Ax and leaf.
[Shelli, Grade 2]

Ron extended the boundaries of the story, expanding it to include popular culture and social relations:

the monkey and the turtle
dare was to friends. Dare nemas wr
courtney and Ron. and Tay
like to play all day but dare was
some body how did'in like to play
the duck Howard he like to teas
Courtney and Ron to tay
[Ron, Grade 2]

Composing Lives III: How are You Feeling?

When I was recuperating from surgery Brennen and Marta stopped by each week to brief me. As they showed me the children's work, I began to sense a certain repetitive, school-like, quality in the work. We were unclear how to break this mold. But then the children led the way. When I returned to the school after my surgery, responding to a deluge of questions, I decided to share details of the experience with the children and causally invited them to write to catch me up on what had been going on. This request proved the catalyst for an outpouring of feelings and purposeful writing that did not cease for the rest of the year, and even continued after we had left the school as the letters that opened this chapter reveal. Some children exhibited touching concern for my health, or curiosity about my surgery. Mostly, though, the letters reveal the powerfully evocative pull of our work on the unconscious of many of the children, and illustrate the importance of *love* and *depth* in teaching, as the illustrations in Figs. 4 & 5 and the following letters indicate:

> *Diar Michael. How do you feel to*
> *Day. You friends are waitint to*
> *You. Koam bak. Michael how*
> *Old are you.*
> [Jose, Grade 2]

> *Dear Michael*
> *I hope you is find*
> *I hope you feel good.*
> *My name is Yolanda.*
> *How are you both dpong.*
> *Marta. Micha, Brennen, and Martha.*
> *I hope you feel good Martha.*
> *Dear Michael: Did it hart hwne they take out your yeye.*
> *Im doing fin haw you doing in school. Why they touke*
> *Out your eye and chang.*
> [Pedro, Grade 2]

> *Dear Michael*
> *How are you Michael.*
> *I love your story.*
> *Michael I feel for you .*
> *because I feel that much.*
> [Sheena, Grade 2]

Ron, by no means the most studious child in the class, was absent the day Michael invited the children to write him, but he lost no time putting pen to paper when he returned to school:

> *Dear Mecgo (Michael)*
> *I missed the last tiem win the othra*
> *Children wota the litssr.*
> *I like the boos you read Da rae*
> *Fun and xsiting*
> [Ron, Grade 2]

Fig. 4. Michael as superhero

Fig. 5. Michael reading to class

Zina decided to inform Michael about Marta's and Brennen's accomplishments during his absence:

> *Dear Michael:*
> *I had fun with Brennen he taut me loust of*
> *Things I keep on asking him thing I hand*
> *Run sounding out loust of things and marta*
> *Was working with the boys and Brennen*
> *Was working with the girls and they*
> *Was screaming but I was thinking about the last story you told us*
> *About the* (here she drew a big picture of a whale).
> [Zina, Grade 2]

Jamal, who has extremely limited formal literacy skills and rarely engaged in academic tasks for the teacher, managed to get his ideas across too:

> *Dear Michael:*
> *My varet show is Power Rengers and*
> *Super Humans and I read Nobiah's Well.*
> *How are you feeling alte the operation.*
> [Jamal, Grade 2]

Many of the children used their letters to open up conversations with us. Our replies, indicating that we took their letters seriously, helped build close bonds. Many children were enthralled with our letters and wrote repeatedly to us. Their letters exemplify the kind of "social work" that Dyson describes when children are using literacy to negotiate their space in the community. Although the children defied many of the conventions of formal literacy, this proved no obstacle to their ability to ask their questions and communicate their feelings. For instance, here are some exchanges revolving around Michael's surgery. Consider first this beautiful compassionate response from Alicia, the girl whom her teacher believed would make a good housemaid one day:

> *Dear Michael*
> *You are betr now*
> *You are a good friend*
> *You talk funny*
> *I like story You are the best*
> *Friend*
> *I even met you*
> [Alicia, Grade 2]

> *Dear Alicia*
> *Thank you for your letter*
> *you are my friend too*
> *Write back and tell me more*
> Michael

> *Dear Michael,*
> *Thanks for the letter?*
> *That was beautiful*
> *You are big?*
> *I love you Michael*
> *You my firends*
> *I went to my*
> *sister home*
> *my friends. Michael*
> *is good To me.*
> [Alicia, Grade 2]

George expressed similar sentiments:

> *Michael how do you fee*   *Dear George,*
> *Do you feel orit Im George*   *I am fine now, thank you. It*
> *I hop you feel orrit rit*   *was nice of you to ask.*
> *And I hop you feel good.*   *What do you do on the weekend?*
> *[George, Grade 2]*   *Do you watch T.V.?*
>   *Write back soon.*
>   *—Michael*

Dave and his friend Delton took the time to express their feelings in writing to Marta and Jennifer, a student who was visiting:

> *Dear Marta I will miss you*   *Dear Marta and Jennifer*
> *reading*   *I will miss both of you*
> *rs much me and Delton*   *and I wish that you*
> *miss you so much Marta*   *will stay with us*
> *pleas come back to us Marta*   *and Jennifer but*
> *and your friends read to us again* *both of you read*
> *[Dave, Grade 2]*   *beautiful too. And*
>   *your beautiful Marta*
>   *and Jennifer.*
>   *and I hope both of you*
>   *have a good weekend.*
>   *[Delton, Grade 2]*

Others expressed similar sentiments:

> *There Mack (Dear Mike)*
> *I have list of fun in side of*
> *my nice school.*
> *you are the Bas artist in this school*
> *mack and I help my momy clean The*
> *ho house.*
> *I do List of fun when I all*
> *are toger in a line.*
> *and I love to write Latters.*
> *about everyThing I Love wrteing*
> *The end.*
> *[Andrew, Grade 3]*

> *MarRta yo t a mu*   *Marta I love you*
> *Yotamu a t MaRta*   *I love you Marta*
> *Marta you t amuestoria*   *Marta I love your stories*
> *Yo amu estoria yo amuestoria*   *I love stories I love stories*

Marta titi   *Aunt Marta (endearing form)*
Marta tia   *Aunt Marta*
[Sonja, Bilingual Grade 2]   [Our translation]

In an effort to help the children write stories from their lives and to see the imaginative possibilities of their worlds, Brennen shared two homemade books with the children. The first was an autobiographical story about a childhood adventure. The second book was incomplete; the story was set in and around the school and used many of the children as characters. Brennen presented the second book in this incomplete form and enlisted the help of the children to finish the story. These story-making activities were quite exciting for the children and inspired many to create their own stories. Some children wrote to Brennen about these experiences:

Dear Brennen   *Dear Brennen*
I like all of your story that you read   *I am glad you like my*
I like your story about your wife and you   *story cause I like yours*
Did you finish the story about the wof but Ms.   *To maybe next time you*
___ head off?and make a heart.   *Come can show me the*
[Danita, Grade 2]   *book you write storys so nice*
                                        Ps. Please bring the book
                                        [Nakiba, Grade 2]

Everybody seemed to be asking questions, to be reaching out for connections and identifications:

Me and my Father watch Power Ragners
My father watch it because
I watch it I like it
It is fun to watch now do you
Like power rangers tel me where yes or no
[Daryle, Grade 3]

I like to play with my   *Dear Beverly*
Dog.   *Thank you for your lovely letter.*
I like to the park   *What is your dog's name?*
I like to go to my friends   *I have 2 children. Brian is 12, and*
House   *Jennifer is 9. I have 3 sisters and one.*
More   *brother.*
I like to go to my aunt   *They live in Ireland. Write soon and tell me*
House Michael do you got kids *about yourself.*
Do you got a sister or brother   —Michael
Do you got a aunt
[Beverly, Grade 3]

I am a nice good girl. I know you.
Are to Micheal. I love your friends (Marta and Brennen)
I am a little happy to see you
I am so happy to see you Dear
Michael thank you for your letter Do you friends
Have a brother or sister? Warite soon Micheal
[Toni, Grade 2]

Dera Mr. Michael
Do you have cheilrng do you bre thme
To school I like to meat thme
[Maria, Grade 3]

Der Brennen
You forgot my Birthday
Please answer back
[Elena, Grade 2]

Dear Brennen
I like you as a Best specail
Friend and I love all you stories
You raed to us and I love your
New friend I was hoping
For you to come tody
I am happy you came cause
With out you it won t be all
That fun
——Love Shelli
[Grade 2]

Dear Marta
I was hoping for you to
Come but a new friend of
Mine came but you
Will always be my best specil friend
Love Shelli
[Grade 2]

Dear Brennen
Do you have
A wife wahts he name.
[Takia, Grade 2]

Dear Marta: How are you Doing. I missing is so
Can you come next Friday. Because I got a lot to
Tell you so peace and have a good Day and so come
Next Friday. From you fiend Yolanda and you other.
Can you write back to me.
[Yolanda, Grade 2]

Composing Lives IV:
The Expression of Desire

We brought in writing materials and shared them freely with the children. Brightly colored drawing paper was a novelty, as was the notion that a child might get more than a single sheet of paper from an adult. The teachers attempted to stop us from dispensing extra paper to the children, and intervened whenever the children helped themselves to paper. All of this was not lost on the children, who became astute navigators of the shifting social boundaries of the classroom between ourselves—the first-name people—and the official teachers. At one point I had promised to supply fluorescent markers to the children and when they did not arrive in a timely fashion, letters soon began to appear. Likewise when I failed to read the last part of *Rainbow crow* due to time constraints, and failed to follow through on my promise to bring the book in the following week, some children picked up their pencils to express in writing what a chorus of voices had proclaimed when I had returned. Some children offered pointed reminders of my responsibility to live up to my commitments:

> *May 5, 1995*
> *Dear Mr. Micarl,*
> *On Friday's you don't come*
> *You sade give us color markers and color*
> *Pens. To read us rainbow crow*
> *Why are do you not come on*
> *Fridays . I wish you come to*
> *Our classroom. Coimes stip with*
> *You all storys. He allways like*
> *My drawing everytie he like*
> *Everybody drawing a lots of drawing*
> *Please read my letter Mr. Micarl*
> *I hope it he come here to*
> *Our classroom I miss you*
> *Mr. Micarl it you come back to this school . Everybody*
> *Be happy becaue Mr. Micarl*
> *I miss you badle Please*
> *Mr. Micarl come back to us*
> *Because. I miss you*
> *You friend,*
> *Scott*
> [Grade 3]

Worrying about my forgetfulness, Scott followed up with another letter:

> Dear Mr. Michal,
> Please bring the markers and pens
> Today or on Wednesday you said
> You to read to the class The
> Story Rainbow Crow to finish
> Up of Rainbow Corw
> I want you to bring magic markers
> And magic pens. And read funny poems
> Your friend,
> Scott
> [Grade 3]

Walter wrote the following:

> May 5, 1995
> Dear Mr. Michael,
> I want come here a lot of time
> And I miss you Read poems to us
> I will like you to come every Friday
> And read to us and make us make
> Picture for you and will give
> You a picture of me in kindergarten
> Class I want you to keep ok Mr. Michael
> I will like you to see the picture
> Of me and you Mr. Michael
> Dray me a picture for me on the
> Wirter paper.
> [Walter, Grade 3]

Danny was one of many children who expressed increasing anxiety as our departure date grew near:

> Dear Mr. Michael
> I are having fun in our class room
> With and only read so please come
> And visit us again before June 28, 1995
> Because I want to here more
> Books in this class room
> Because all the books
> In here are boring
> P.S. pleas herry up
> From Danny
> [Grade 3]

Others expressed their feelings as follows:

Querida Marta Gracias	*Dear Marta Thank you*
Por todo las iyodsaquethe	*for all your help*
Alodaste no quiera	*you have given I don't want*
Que te valla queda	*you to go stay*
Pa donde vas teveo	*Where are you going See you*
[Alfonso, Bilingual Grade 2]	[Our translation]

Marta replied:

Hola! De quien es esta carta?	*Hi Alfonso!*
Nos encanta leer para Uds.	*I love to read to all of you.*
No volvemos porque Tenemos que regresar	*I am no longer returning*
a la Universidad para leer Muchos	*Because I must return to*
libros y escribir ensayos. Te vamos a hechar	*the university and read many*
de menos.	*Books and write papers. I*
Con carino,	*will miss you.*
Marta	*With affection,*
	[Our translation]

Quierda Marta tea mo	*Dear Marta I love you*
Mucho con mucho carino y	*very much and with much affection and*
Yo creo que te boy a	*and I think I am going to*
Regular algo y tu ere la	*give you something and you are the*
Mas faborita amiga y	*best friends*
Si you te boy areglar	*and if I give you*
Algo tu me regala algo	*something you give me something*
Igusl que yo X besos	*the same as me*
[Diana, Bilingual Grade 2]	*I love you for over*
	[Our translation]

Querida Marta I love you	*thank you for helping us*
Querido Bren I love you	*and everything I did read the books*
Gracias por ayudarnos	*and play*
Y todos isimos leer los libros y	*and I all say you are*
Jugar	*the best*
Y to dicimos que ti ere	[Our Translation]
Lo mejor	
[Mauricio, Bilingual Grade 2]	

Dear Marta	*Dear Marta*
I will miss you very very very very	*I miss you.*
Much.	*I'm not going to forget you.*

I will miss your reading
I will miss your buatiful fast and
Your reading fast so so so so
So so so so so so so so
Much I love you Marta
From Kahmiyah
To Marta
[Grade 2]

I like how you Read and
you readfast. Good by
Love
from Ronielle
[Grade 2]

By Lameke
Dear Marta and I wish you can
Stay and I will miss you and dogzilla
It is my best book.
The end
[Lameke, Grade 2]

Dear Lameke
I wish I could stay with you too but
I have to go back to the colleges to write and
Read. Do you realize school is about
over for you. Just one more month to go!
How do you feel about that?
Take good care and write soon.
Dogzilla says, "HELLO—AAARRRFF!!"
Marta

Composing Lives V—The Official and Unofficial Lives of Children

The forgoing letters capture some dimensions of the children's capacities to weave their lives into their literacy activities. In the short time frame of our weekly visits this kind of connection-making became a main focus for many children. Some children took the opportunity to widen the conversation further by drawing more directly on their life experiences. Nakiba's story about poverty and hunger provides a moving illustration of the kind blurring of boundaries between official and unofficial school worlds in which children engage when given a suitable invitation.

Nakiba's story

As one of the most visibly gregarious children in Ms. Y's class, connecting with Nakiba came easily for us because of her eagerness to share. She not only demonstrated her confident and uninhibited nature orally, interacting with us, her classmates, and her teacher, but also through her writing. Nakiba wrote a story entitled *How People are Poor*. This story, written in three parts, recounts a boy's journey in search of food for his mother.

Part one	Part two	Part Three
How people are poor		
One day a little boy	and he was	The next moreing
And his mother was	back from before night	the little boy and his
Huggry so the mother	Time his mom	mom were hungry
Told the boy to find	was so happy That	and The lady
Food she said—harry	he was Back with food	had more soup leaft
Harry before mighnig.		so They went to eat
And when he was		now so The did
Boy		ummm said–The
Walking he saw a		That was good.
Old laday she said		can I have more?
Why are you all alone		yes son.
I am looking for food		Then when he was
Said the boy O!		done he looked
Said The old lad		at his mom
I will give you some		and said
Soup and if you need		you are the
More come to me.		Best and give
		His mom
		A hug.

Stories: Shakanda, Monique, Sheena and Annette

Just as Lensmire (1994) experienced in his work with children, with permission to express personal feelings, some children used their writings to express their feelings about each other. Shakanda, Monique, and Sheena, for example, used their writing to negotiate interpersonal conflicts and peer groups status, a topic that, as Lensmire (1994) notes, raises complex ethical dilemmas for teachers: What if free speech becomes hateful speech? Shakanda expressed her and Monique's feelings about Alicia:

> By Shakanda and Monique
> I het Alicia I wat to
> Kill Alicia because
> She is fat and stoppbit
> And ugly and she had
> No friends I well het Alicia
> The end
> [Shakanda, Grade 2]

Sheena's anxieties about her social positioning in the group also surfaced:

> By Sheena
> Legend Friends

I don't know how to be friends with Yolanda
And Nakiba. And Alicia to. And I want to
Throw a cake at they chocolate cake.
And that's not it but am gine kill they.
Because they are mean to me and I hate
They are fat Alicia is fat Nakiba and Yolanda
Are sckine. What happened
[Sheena, Grade 2]

Annette's writings illustrated better than most the ethical dilemmas that face a teacher who gives children permission to examine and talk about their worlds. On a number of occasions we brought in cartoons to encourage the children to break the boundaries presented by traditional writing tasks and styles. Annette used this opportunity to develop a five-panel graphic story. The first panel contains nothing but the words "I heat (hate) you" in large letters (Fig. 6). In the second panel Annette depicts a mother and daughter. The mother has a terrified look on her face. The daughter, with a gun pointed at the mother's stomach, and, with a trace of a smile on her face, utters the words "HEAT (hate) my mom." In the background, "BOME" (boom) appears in large letters, suggesting that the gun has discharged (Fig. 7). The third panel contains three characters. One lying prone on the ground, is presumably dead. Again, one is wielding a gun, while the third, with her hands in the air, pleads for her life: "Please don't kil me to like you did her (Fig. 8)." The fourth panel appears to be a continuation of this theme. The gun bearer appears to be smiling; the gun is discharging all over the place, BOME! BOME! BOME! And the other two characters lie prone on the ground (Fig. 9). The fifth panel appears to depict a domestic scene, again with the dominant character visibly discharging a gun at one of the other characters (Fig. 10).

Unfortunately we failed to respond to Annette's work. It was completed late in the year, and lay in her folder unnoticed until we began to sort through the material

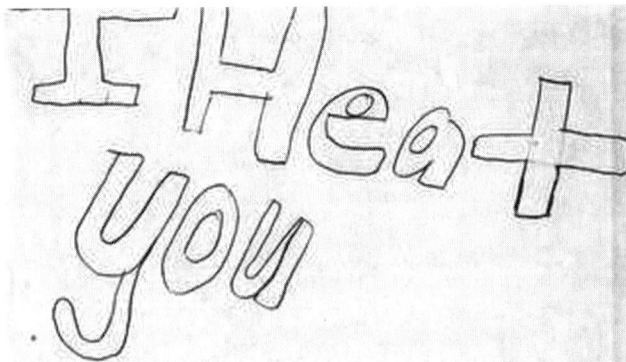

Fig. 6. Annette. Panel 1

Fig. 7. Annette. Panel 2

Fig. 8. Annette. Panel 3

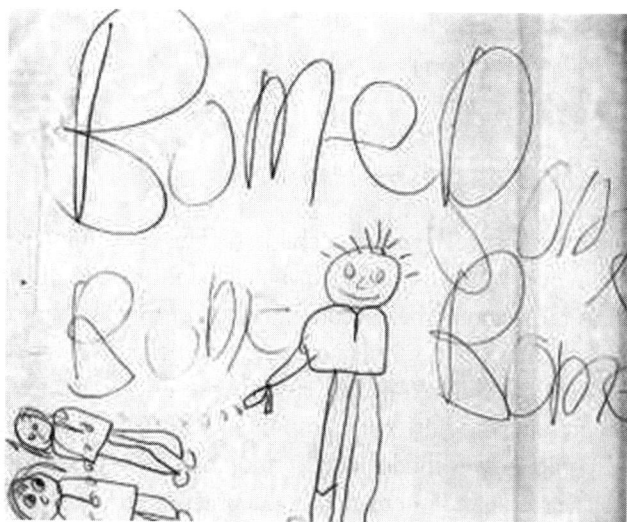

Fig. 9. Annette. Panel 4

Fig. 10. Annette. Panel 5

Fig. 11. Marlon's pogo stick fantasy

after we completed our work with the children. These writings provoked a very heated debate in our graduate class, with some student teachers maintaining that writings such as these should be censored, and others, including us, arguing that Annette was using these texts for her own social purposes. We were in agreement, however, that granting children permission to write in their own voices needs to be theorized carefully, a point that Lensmire (1994) has emphasized. With my subsequent experience as a child therapist and analyst (see Chapters 2 & 5) and my interest in the social and intergenerational origins of trauma (see Chapter 9) I would read and respond to these writings with much more *depth* today.

Fun

Of course, not everything the children pulled in from their lives was painful or serious. The children used drawing and cartooning to express humor as Marlon's pogo stick fantasy (Fig. 11) and Julius's take off on a Calvin and Hobbes cartoon illustrate (Fig. 12).

The story written by Winston is worthy of note too. Winston wrote a three page minimalist story containing three powerful illustrations and all of five words. In the first panel (Fig. 13) the figure with the horrified expression in its face is depicted as screaming "Oh No!" as a large "thing" bears down on it; in the second panel the "thing" appears more blurry, the character is prone on the ground, and the cryptic words, "he's dead" sum up the situation (Fig. 14); in the third panel an equally cryptic "bye!" sums up the thing's departure, an image reinforced by the change of direction in it's foot (Fig. 15). The economy of Winston's storytelling is quite extraordinary.

Fig. 12. Calvin & Hobbes by Julius

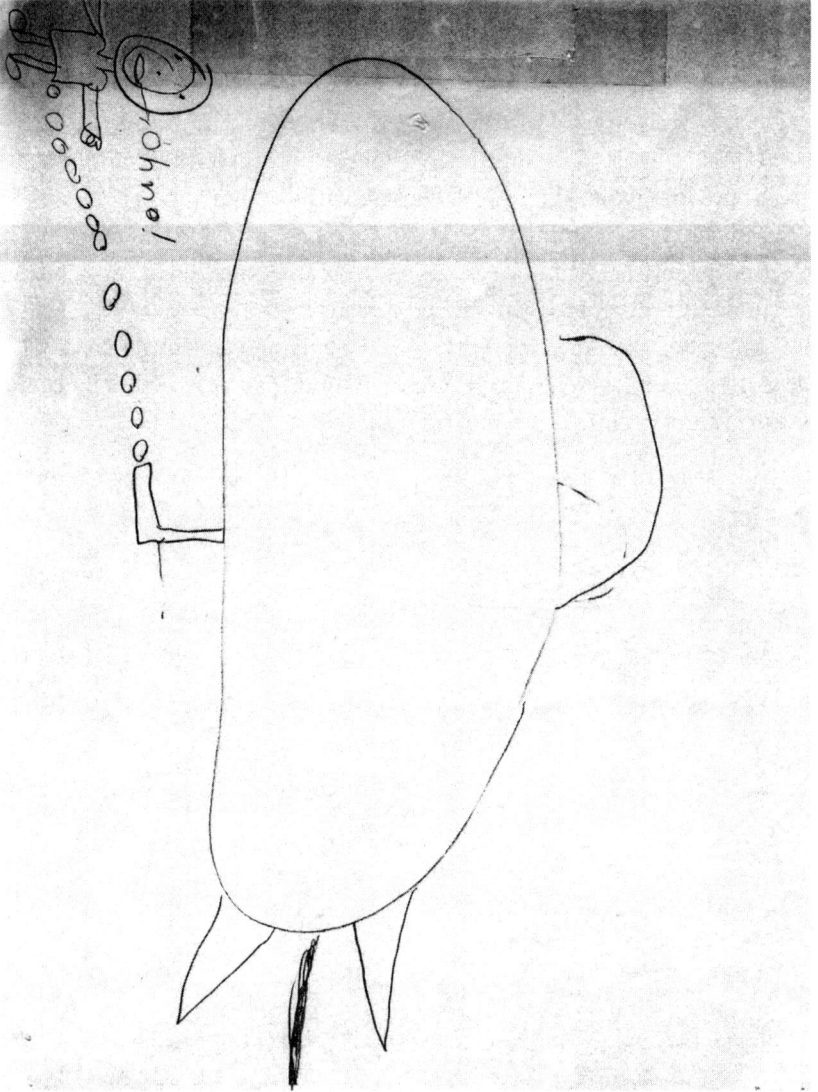

Fig. 13. Winston. Panel 1

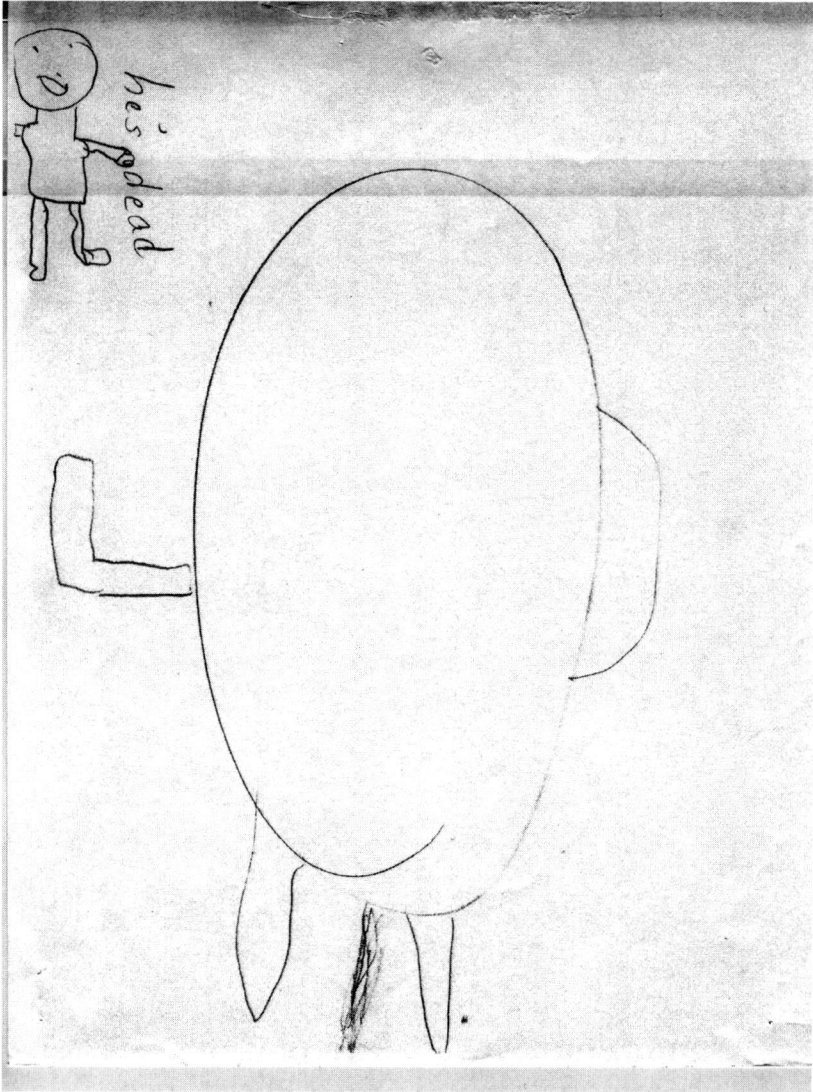

Fig. 14. Winston. Panel 2

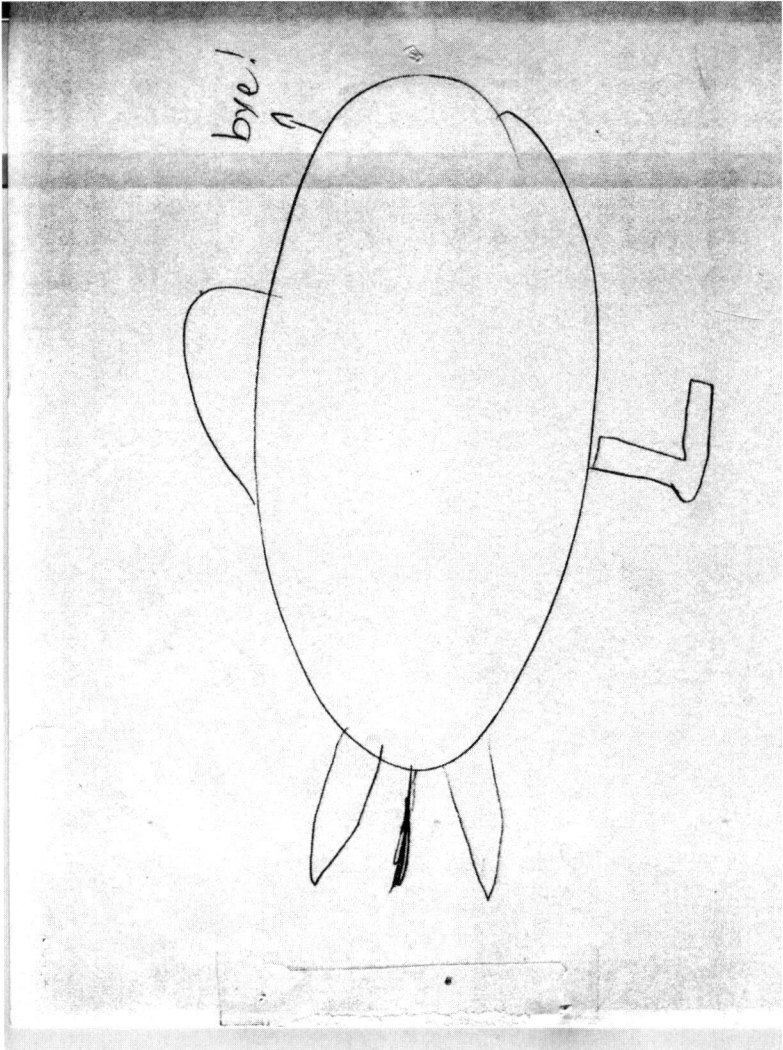

Fig. 15. Winston. Panel 3

Composing Lives VI: School is Hell—Sly commentary and Overt Resistance

Literacy instruction is about much more than creating opportunities for pleasant social interaction and imaginative engagement with reading and writing.[8] Nowhere is the political imperative of schooling clearer than in schools such as Little Oaks, in which silencing is pervasive and often brutal. As Fine (1987) noted, this silencing serves the political purpose of denying children and their families opportunities to critique the sociopolitical and economic structures of schooling, including the role schools play in perpetuating economic and social inequality, racial injustice, gender oppression, and so on. After engaging with the children and all of their wonderful possibilities in the preceding sections, it is painful to come back again to the brutal oppression of their daily school lives. Nevertheless, return we must, because it is through our observations of their differing strategies for coping with this oppression that we began to develop avenues for exploring with them possibilities for naming and hence critiquing their experience. The children were making astute judgments about the oppression they experienced. All we could do was legitimize the naming of those experiences in school contexts. This, however, was a radical threat to the silent oppression of the school, an act in which all of the adults in the school were complicit, and one to which we, too, at times, became a party.

Victor, Jamal and Elijah

Children developed different ways of dealing with Ms. Y's abuse. Some gave it right back to her, and resisted openly. These were the children whom she disliked the most. Victor was among them:

> She marched over to where he was standing and grabbed his arm firmly. He pulled away and commanded "Don't you touch me!' She began to pull him toward the classroom door and he resisted while continuing to yell at her to get her hands off him. She pulled more and he lay down. She grabbed him by the leg and started dragging him out of the room. With his free leg, Victor kicked at her hand to loosen her grip. He lost, but only because she was bigger. [Field notes, Brennen, 2/'95]

Open resisters like Victor are often forced to leave school and are summarily shipped off to special education programs. This was Victor's fate just a few weeks after the above incident. Jamal adopted the same strategy, to the point that he was perceived by his teacher as uncontrollable.

> I witnessed the price Jamal paid for his fearlessness, for his imagination. His role in our activities was usually short-lived. In-your-face shrieks from his teacher descended on him like torrential rain, instantly turning his excitement into surging anger. [Field notes, Marta, 2/'95]

Other children were too fearful to resist. Many of the teachers nurtured the powerlessness the children felt by employing a strategy of divide and conquer. Rarely was the teacher's wrath directed to the class as a whole. Rather, individuals were singled out for public humiliation and the rest of the class was silenced by fear and intimidation. The abuse by teachers was not named. It pervaded the room and colored all relationships, yet it was never discussed.

> The children set about preparing to work. Some returned to their desks, some continued to question Marta. I went to the desk of Elijah, a little boy who was new to the class. Before the class had come together as a group, I had been helping him compose a letter to Michael. The other children had previously written to Michael during the time he was out recovering from surgery. His replies to them were distributed at the beginning of today's class. The children were very excited to receive their personalized correspondence. Elijah was anxious to participate and have what the others had...suddenly Ms. Y interrupted the proceedings with another one of her violent verbal assaults. I had grown used to them at this point, but poor Elijah was terrified by her screaming. I watched him as his body and his eyes became frozen with fear. Elijah didn't know what to do. I put my arm on his shoulder and I continued. [Field notes, Brennen, 2/'95]

The emotional and physical abuse that the children had to endure on a daily basis can hardly be exaggerated. Ms. Y, and some of the other teachers we observed, regularly employed fear and intimidation as a means of controlling bodies and silencing voices. Many of the children in Ms. Y's class had grown accustomed to this sort of treatment. They had accepted it as part of their school experience. Little Elijah however had not been here long enough to develop strategies for coping with the persistent abuse.

Nakiba

> Earlier in the period Ms. Y had maliciously aggravated Nakiba into a tantrum. I could not tell what the particular occasion for the abuse had been as the tirade was taking place in semi-isolation up behind the teacher's desk. I do know that by the time the audibility of their discussion had reached attention grabbing decibility, Nakiba was crying and throwing papers on the ground in frustration. Ms. Y silenced her with a deafening roar, sent her to her seat, and told her that she was not allowed to join us for group time. I thought that it was unusual that Nakiba had gotten in trouble. She is one of the brightest kids. She is smallish and introverted. She reads and writes very well, often helping the other children with their writing. I approached Nakiba after this episode and spoke to her privately. I told her that I did not agree with what her teacher had done. I told her that she had done nothing wrong and that I wanted her to join us in the back. She did not speak; she sobbed quietly... This episode with Nakiba was the first occasion that I shared with the children (privately) our contempt for the behavior of their teachers. Previously my reaction to the abuse I witnessed had been to ignore it. Of course, this was impossible to do while it was happening; but I would pause as the teacher yelled, then pick up where I had left off when she finished. Love was completely foreign to her dealings with the children. Their relationship was forged on the basis of authority and apathy. She regularly talked derogatorily about the children

in front of them. As our work with the children progressed, I became increasingly bothered by just standing by. Often I had been so outraged by the behavior that I had been on the verge of publicly intervening and defending the student. I had refrained from these types of acts because I thought such acts of public humiliation may cause her to be even more severe with the children when I was not present. Besides, I thought, such an intervention would jeopardize our work with the children. Ms. Y would resent our presence even more than she already does, and would go to greater lengths to undermine us. I too had been silenced...Nakiba joined us near the end of sharing time. I had been reading and listening to love letters. She wanted to share a piece of writing from her notebook, but she did not want to read it. The children coaxed her to present; some offered to read it for her. Finally she allowed Victor to give it a try. He had trouble reading, and was soon relieved of his duty. From what I could see and hear her story was about her affections for Ms. Y!! The first two lines read, "Ms. Y is my favrit teacher. She is a good artist." I couldn't believe it. I wasn't sure if Nakiba had written this as she sat at her desk after the attack, or if it had been written some time before. No matter when it was written, Nakiba felt the need to share it now. After more encouragement, Nakiba finally took the chair and read her tribute to the Good Ms. Y. the remainder of the note was as glowing and affectionate as the opening lines. [Field notes, Brennen, 2/'95]

Nakiba's story shows a child's desperate attempt to get back in the good graces of her teacher, to make public amends. Yet, just after this Nakiba passed a note surreptitiously to Marta as Brennen prepared to depart for the day. In this note, addressed to Michael, still absent for medical reasons, Nakiba made her feelings for her teacher very clear:

> Dere Mike
> I heat my teanch
> But I do
> Like you
> Why don't you come
> No more. Nakiba
> [Grade 2]

Thus, while adopting a public stance of obedience and docility, Nakiba was still able to express her true feelings. Within the classroom she was forced to publicly live as subjugated, but there is strength in Nakiba's spirit that will not be broken and she makes use of the confidential and safe nature of our relationship to let this be known.

Soon after the Nakiba incident, our resistance to the silencing that we were experiencing in the face of the abuse of the children had occasion to appear in a different form. We encouraged the children to begin discussing, openly, their struggles in school. We used cartoons from Matt Groenings's *School is hell* (1987) to provide the children with texts that enabled them to name and examine their school experiences. We held group discussions about "getting in trouble" in school. We, too, were beginning to find our own voices!

Is School Hell?

Our presence in the classrooms disrupted the existing social boundaries and soon the children began to respond to us in ways that they never could respond to the adults in their school lives. We created with them an atmosphere of joy in which they could temporarily slough off the constraints of their school lives. The children were acutely aware of the disciplinary regime of the school. The almost total change in their demeanor as we entered their lives each week indicated that they were adept at switching roles as the boundaries of their social worlds changed.

The effect of *School is hell* on the children was electrifying. It was evident from the raucous manner in which they responded to the cartoons; the zest with which they approached the task of making their own cartoons; and the furtive manner in which they grouped in corners of the room to explore the texts, that they relished the subversive potential of the work and the permission it gave them to name their own experiences. The resulting texts provide windows into some children's constructions of their schooled lives, as well as into the pedagogical potential of popular culture genres such as cartoons and comics as a means of exploiting the emancipatory possibilities of literacy (cf. Dyson, 1997, 2003).

We read and discussed portions of Groening's text over a number of weeks. A few children took our blank cartoons sheets and attempted to reproduce elements of Groening's cartoons. Angelina's effort (Fig. 16) contains some literal copying though there are also some elements of boundary crossing and of her own personal voice.

Fig. 16. Angelina's cartoon

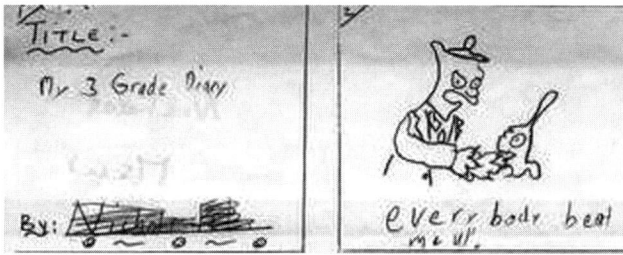

Fig. 17. Winston's cartoon

Other children took more poetic license with the task, and appropriated the cartoon genre to capture some of their own very personal feelings about school. Winston, expressing a commonplace of many children's experience in these classrooms, adapted a Groening title, calling his piece (Fig. 17) "my 3 Grade Diary." He then traced Groening's pictures of a teacher and student, and added his own personal text: "everybody beat me up."

The five following cartoons recall Jameel's work from Dyson's (1993) study, in the multivocality of the texts, the crossing of boundaries, and the blurring of genres, all in the service of a very explicit social purpose. Danny's cartoon, entitled "School is hell" embodies an interesting combination of elements from Groening's work, mixed with his own words and images and superhero drawings. The character in the first panel says "School is hell," and when I asked Danny to elaborate he said: "evil (Panel 1 character), the punk of the school, he beat up all these kids (characters in panel three appropriated from Groening)." A similar theme appears in Daryl's work, though he appropriated far fewer elements from Groening and more from the world of superheroes. His cartoon, entitled, "My day in Hill (i.e., Hell)," contained no words, but Daryl explained that the character in the first panel was "The evilest kid in my school, Strong Jackson." The remaining three panels depict, respectively, his car, his weapon, and his phone and gadget.

Cartoons by Marlon (Fig. 18), and Elijah (Fig. 19) depart significantly from Groening's cynically humorous depictions of school oppression. The images are explicitly violent, in Marlon's and Elijah's cases. Marlon drew from superhero images in popular culture, entitling his cartoon "I don't like school." Elijah labeled his cartoon "John the killer," and presented a picture of a character shooting another character, with the stark legend, "John had killed."

Damon's cartoon (Fig. 20) represents a wonderful blend of cartoon genre, science fiction, and his life in school. Instead of using one of our cartoon blanks,

Fig. 18. Marlon's cartoon

Fig. 19. Elijah's cartoon

Fig. 20. Damon's Alien cartoon

Damon created his own cartoon panels, the first of which depicts a spaceship, with the legend: "Then alen came after me," and "so I escape." Panel two depicts a spaceship, with two speech bubbles, bearing the legends, "so I lafe," and "School is hell." The spaceship appears on its own in the third panel.

A number of children developed multi-panel cartoons that emulated Groening's style, but carried their own distinct messages portrayed in an eclectic range of voices and images. Walter, for example, presented a rare positive perspective on school, depicting himself and a smiling Ms. Z. Margarita, entitling her cartoon "Butthead," used the genre to recount her version of every child's story of being picked on in school. Kim's cartoon (Fig. 21) presents the reality more starkly. In the first panel a girl is depicted screaming for help while a boy waves a stick menacingly. In the second panel Kim draws a speech bubble with an image inside, and the message "Help I am in troub(le?)" written on the outside. At the top of the panel appears a commentary: "I hate boy and He hiead her bad time." In the third panel the girl is again seen screaming for help, this time appealing to the principal: "pricpl He is killing me." In the fourth panel no images appear, merely the words: "I need a plan to killd him."

Annette, Julius, and Maria used cartooning to present a biting commentary on classroom life. In the first panel of her cartoon Annette depicted a large teacher and a number of small children (Fig. 22). The teacher, with an agitated look on her face, says: "Stop yelling." Underneath the cartoon Annette began a running commentary. In the first panel this reads: "Stop yelling, it is really hell." In the second panel Annette drew a student sitting at a desk, with the general comment, "to Day is realy Hell." In the running commentary underneath she noted, "today my teacher made me do social studies." Annette was not finished with her commentary however. At the bottom of the page in huge letters was written the legend: "I haet Hell Days and today is one."

Julius began his cartoon (Fig. 23) with a direct appropriation of the male teacher Figure from Groening's work, stating, "School is bad." He also included an authorial comment, "Feb 22 1995 is my birthday and it was." In the second

Fig. 21. Kim's cartoon

Fig. 22. Annette's cartoon

Fig. 23. Julius's cartoon

panel, he switched to a depiction of his current classroom teacher, complete with an apple on her sweater. She is clearly identified by the caption, and out of her mouth come the words: "Bad—this class is bad." The third panel, presumably depicts Julius himself, with the comment, "This is on (no) fun."

Maria (Fig. 24) decided to depict the same teacher, and captured a recent incident in which, by the children's account, the teacher had burst into tears when they refused to line up for her. Maria appropriated the title panel almost directly from Groening. In the second panel she drew a picture of her teacher, obviously weeping, with the caption: "my teacher was crying." In the third panel of this unfinished story she drew a picture of the children in the class, with the legend, "the class was going to line up."

Fig. 24. Maria's cartoon

Derrick, an astute observer of the classroom scene, gets the last word:

> Ms. Q have a loud voice and she yell at us And sometime
> I YELL BACK I do something wrong and sometime she need
> Asperys (aspirin) supe And she be all wright.
> [Derrick, Grade 2]

Conclusion

This study demonstrates to our satisfaction the boundless capacities of the children with whom we worked to build effective human relations with us and with each other, and to compose a space for themselves in their school worlds through powerful literacy activities. The children demonstrate some resilience in the face of oppression, and the study shows the capacity of the children to negotiate the complex shifting boundaries of school authority as we came and went from their lives. The children also, demonstrated that the scandalous lack of effective literacy instruction in their classrooms was no obstacle to their ability to use their imaginations, and to draw upon multiple discourses from home, school, and popular culture, to engage in meaningful oral, performative, and written communication. It saddens us, however, that work such as this and Dyson's studies (e.g., 1993, 1997, 2003) are necessary to demonstrate that poor children of color in urban schools have these capacities. Should that not be a given in our thinking about all children? Why is it not a commonplace of instruction that all children are affirmed for who they are? What does it say about our society that we cannot guarantee all children, at the very minimum, that school will be a safe haven and a place of respect in which they can get on with the work of composing their selves and exploring their potentials?

I am haunted by the children's voices. I hear the beauty, the potential, the yearning for affirmation and connection. I warm to the beauty of their expressions of love. I marvel at the imaginativeness of their boundary crossings. I delight in their raucous sense of humor, astute reading of their situations, playful humor, and carnivalesque caricatures of the oppression they experience. Then reality smashes down with a hammer blow. They are disrespected. Hurt. Demeaned. They are not loved. They are not taught. They will leave this school stigmatized as "functionally illiterate" in society's eyes. Will the world accept the beauty of their thoughts if in their writings they continue to be oblivious to conventions of syntax and style? What will happen when one day they face reality and are told that they are "illiterate"? What happens if sustained abuse continues to turn their wondrous beauty to bitterness and rage? What moral responsibility do all of us bear for this tragic situation that condemns these children to a level of functional literacy that hobbles their imaginations, denies their identities, and prevents them from naming the cruel injustices they have to live with on a daily basis?

Sadly, at the end of our work, I feel the pain Herb Kohl (1967) recounts at the conclusion of 36 Children—pain that our small contribution to these children's lives cannot be sufficient to ensure the flowering of their potential, nor sufficient to protect them from the continuing oppression in their daily school lives. The fact that this kind of schooling is reserved for children of the poor only heightens my anguish at the social divide that our formal education system is perpetuating.

Work such as this is laden with ethical dilemmas. The choice of not doing anything is unacceptable to me. However, by entering the system, I necessarily became a part of it, and hence complicit in some measure. I struggled constantly with the challenge of maintaining my affiliation with the school so that I might have access to the children. I struggled with how to speak out against the oppressive practices I observed. I struggled with the ethical implications of bringing hope and possibility to the children, when, ultimately, I was unable to help them gain the kind of power that would allow them to challenge the oppression they lived. Was the net effect of our intervention that we made the children more sensitive and responsive, and hence more vulnerable to the brutalities the school inflicted on them? Can we console ourselves that we opened up possibilities for the children and gave them what Lear (2006) calls radical hope, or is Jean Anyon (1997) correct, after all, when she suggests that, absent structural change, inequality and oppression will continue to persist? Literacy instruction is a complex ethical and moral venture in our society. There are no easy answers.

This study certainly gives the lie to the myth of childhood innocence so ably deconstructed by Jacqueline Rose in The case of Peter Pan (1992). As this study illustrates, these children are not infantilized. Instead, they come to experience from very early on the harshness, cynicism, and brutality of the compulsory education that has been ordered up to keep them in their place at the lowest echelons of society. Rose points out how supposedly liberal and child-centered children's literature shapes the unconscious subjectivity of children in concordance with very particular colonialist modes of being. How much more must this be true for children who are compelled to receive their education in the crucible of a system that engenders fear, anxiety, inferiority, and shame, and that further renders opaque and therefore unspeakable the very means by which this is accomplished? Is this not precisely a recipe for the kind of intergenerational social trauma and annihilation of individual and collective subjectivity that I addressed in Chapter 9? I can only imagine what scars ten additional years of this kind of education inflicted on these children's psyches. Patrick Chamoiseau's memoir *School days* (1997) offers some clues, but the pedagogy of poverty certainly cries out for further psychoanalytic investigation of the deep emotional and traumatic consequences that it engenders for those unlucky enough to encounter oppression in its crudest forms.

Postscript

This work did not begin as a research study. We set out to make a contribution to the children's lives. We kept journals as best we could, only because that is part of our normal reflexive pedagogical practice. We took copies of the children's writings to try to assess our success in engaging them in the kinds of literacy activities we described above, and to help us plan where to go next. We decided to tell this story only when it became apparent to us that there was a compelling story to be told. We never placed our desire to tell this story above our desire to make a difference in the children's lives. Faced with a choice between writing field notes and writing responses to the children's writings, we always chose the latter. We were not disinterested outsiders. Theoretically, our research has been informed by Patti Lather's (1986, 1991) thoughts on research as praxis, and Margaret Le Compte's (1993) discussion of the ethical responsibilities of researchers to the people whose lives they study. I tell the story here in hopes that it will give us and others courage to take the risks that speaking truth to power entails.

The children described here are now adults, and soon, too, their children will be received by the schools...to what end?

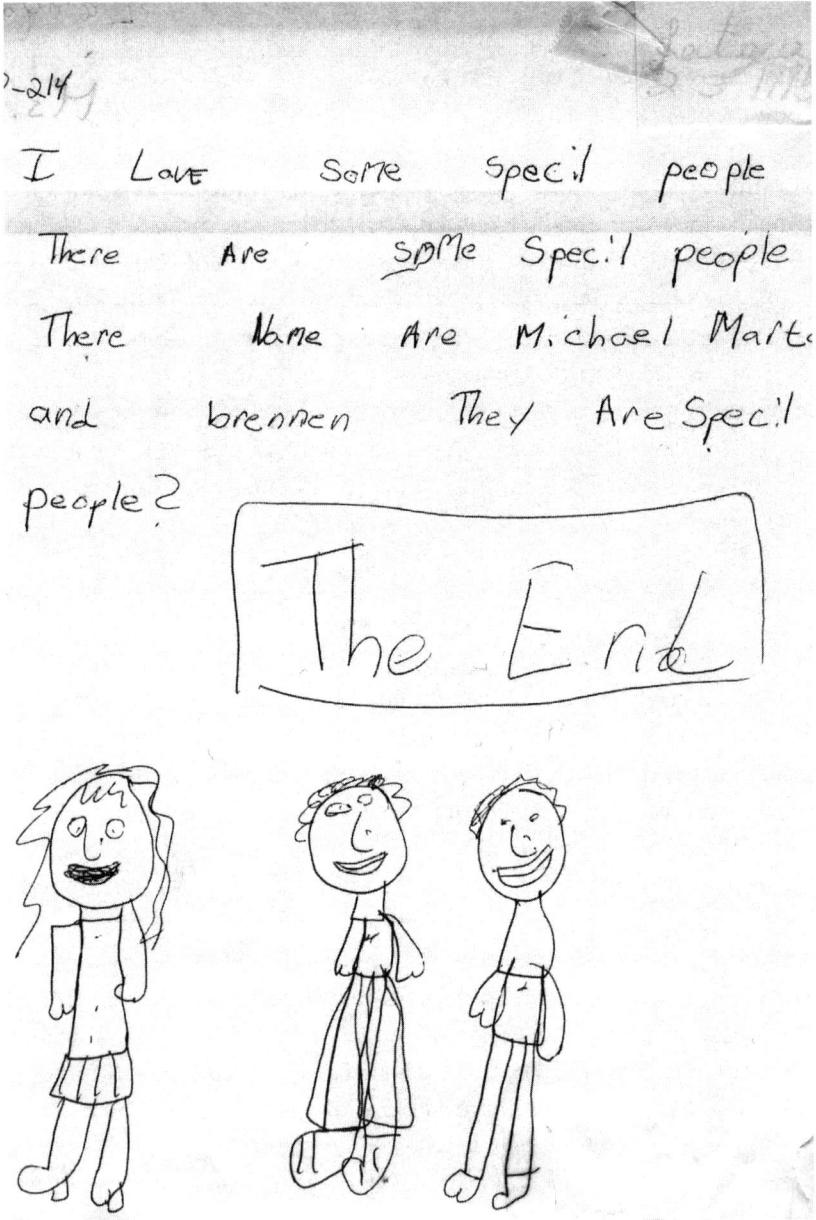

?-214

I Love   Some   Specil   people

There   Are   some   Specil   people

There   Name   Are   Michael   Mart

and   brennen   They   Are Specil

people?

The End

Fig. 25. The end

· 1 2 ·

FACING MYSELF: THE STRUGGLE
FOR AUTHENTIC PEDAGOGY

All the way through school, and even into college, I was taught not to trust my instincts. I was taught that head rules over heart, knowledge rules over emotion, experts have answers. Nobody ever pulled me aside and advised me to follow my heart, trust my instincts, value my own judgments and opinions, and make sense of the world from my perspective. When I became a classroom teacher I had trouble connecting with my inner self. After many years of detached and impersonal schooling the authoritarian cloak fit all too comfortably. Unconsciously I drew on my own experience of school as a model for my way of being in the classroom. I was not all that I might be as a nurturing, caring teacher. It had never entered my head that teaching might be about the transformative possibilities of human conversations.

In graduate school in the 1980's the message from most of my professors, once again, was to deny myself and my roots. Use the passive voice when writing, I was told. Avoid personal language and anecdotes. Don't use the Irish spellings of English words because they are distracting to the readers who are used to American English. Be scientific! Be rational! Don't be emotional! Don't be angry! Don't show your passions! Be detached...Be invisible...My journey beyond those crippling messages has been slow and tortuous, a teetering walk between my desire to offer caring and enabling experiences to my students, and a sometimes paralyzing fear of self-disclosure and loss of control.

My journey has not been exclusively intellectual. I read Paulo Freire's *Pedagogy of the Oppressed* (1972) for the first time close to 20 years ago, and since then I have been committed in principle to notions of democratic and empowering education. Moving from theory to critical praxis proved difficult, and I found Freire's abstract writing wanting. I have, in essence, had to come face to face with myself. I have had to confront the ambivalences inherent in my autobiography. I grew up in a working class family in rural Ireland. Just as Valerie Walkerdine recounts so poignantly in *Schoolgirl Fictions* (1990), for me, too, teaching represented a chance to "get out," to "move up." Was it then my job as a teacher to teach other people's children how to get out and move up too? Just like Walkerdine, I, too, worried that people would find out that I am "only a teacher" (p. 83), and I experienced first-hand, as all teachers do, the ambivalence that many societies harbor towards teachers. A Ph.D. in development psychology from Teachers College brought me into the academy where I found that I did not fit very well. Just as I was seeking to recover my roots I entered an academic community where everyone appeared to masquerade as upper-class: Was I the only professor of working-class origin? Why was it taboo to speak your mind? Why did people seem uncomfortable when I raised issues of poverty, equity, and racial justice? Why were there no student voices included in our curricular and planning meetings? Valerie Walkerdine's choice of the term "coming out" to describe her naming of her working-class origins is testimony to the silent and silencing power of the academy within which many of us work.[1]

Understanding my autobiography is key to understanding my teaching. In teaching I necessarily teach myself. How else but through engaging my life story can my students or I make sense of my deep belief of the possibility of education as a vehicle of personal transformation and social change? How else can my students or I understand the dialectic tension between equipping students to access the "culture of power," as Lisa Delpit (1988) terms it, and validating children's socially and culturally constituted identities so that they feel affirmed, except through understanding the erasure I suffered at the hands of teachers and texts? How else can I step out of the dehumanizing cage provided for me by university apparatuses of regulation and surveillance, except through being available to students so that I can bring my life stories into conversation with theirs, and with the life stories of others we may encounter, so that we can mutually enrich each other's understanding of human possibility? Like the Cowardly Lion in the Wizard of Oz, I have been in search of courage—the courage to be existentially present to my students. I want to be honest, and I want to enable my students, too, to gain the courage to engage with the ambivalences that their entry into the opportunities provided by higher education, juxtaposed with their life histories, promises to provide.

When I started teaching education courses about ten years ago I considered myself a rather fast learner. Within two years I had abandoned textbooks in favor of trade books, I had given up lecturing, for the most part, and I had begun to experiment with a variety of progressive-looking assignments such as journal entries and informal writings. Most important, I had become conscious of the need for students to find their voices, and my classes provided a wide range of opportunities for students to engage in small-group and large-group discussions. My students were generally happy, and I was happy too. I got compliments often enough to feel that I was engaging in transformative teaching. And perhaps I was. However, there always seemed to be a few pesky students who "resisted" my progressive approaches. It always amuses me how we, liberal pedagogues, deride traditional teachers for their impositional teaching methods. Yet, when students resist *our* grand plans for them, we rationalize their dissent as resistance, and thereby delegitimize it! The students are at fault, not ourselves. Sociologist Basil Bernstein reminds us in *The Structure of Pedagogic Discourse* (1990) that the velvet gloves of progressive pedagogies, with their invisible rules of discourse, are not necessarily less repressive than the iron fists of traditional visibly authoritarian pedagogies.[2] On the contrary, Bernstein argues, by presenting a benevolent face to students while failing to change the underlying rules of pedagogic discourse, progressive pedagogies may be potentially *more* disempowering for students because they mask the workings of oppression and hence make it harder for students to name and usurp it.

I fell into this trap in my early attempts at developing a more empowering pedagogy. There can be no empowerment unless the teacher acknowledges the power relationships that are inherent in *all* formal teaching contexts and actively renegotiates as much of that power as possible with students. In my earlier years I took Paulo Freire at his word and thought that by sheer dint of goodwill I could create a relation of equity in which my students and I were on the same plane. I thought that my assurances to students would be sufficient to reassure them that they were on an equal footing with me. I always found discussions of grading, for example, irksome and embarrassing. The more fixated students were on grading criteria, the more purposely vague my answers became. I believed that by providing specific grading criteria I was focusing them on product rather than process. My attitude could be summed up as, "Trust me. If you are sincere and do the work you will have nothing to worry about. This is about learning, not grades." Students, for the most part, went along with cheery bravado, though I have to admit that occasionally a disgruntled student complained to me that others who had done well in my class had been known to boast that they knew how to play my game. This caused me some niggling worry, but I rationalized it away as the words of cynics. You cannot protect yourself from an occasional cynic, after all, can you?

Carol finally cured me. Carol was a graduate student in what was easily the most difficult and frustrating class that I have ever taught. I experienced that class as difficult and frustrating because the students refused to go along with my bland assurances that everything would be all right. Astute at reading the power relations of the university, these mature and worldly wise students decided not to confront me. After some early unsuccessful probing to get me to lay out clear and specific criteria for the class, they took refuge in a concerted strategy of passive resistance. Convinced that they were trying to maneuver me into a traditional didactic role so that they could become passive consumers of knowledge, I refused to give them the specific directives they sought. We soon reached a stalemate in the classroom. I claimed ultimate victory, however, when, just as students had anticipated, I retreated to my office once the class was over and graded their performance.

Although many of the students corresponded with me through their journals, Carol expressed most clearly the hypocrisy of my position. In an entry headed with the word "TRUST" in inch-tall letters, she wrote: "Michael said to trust him, but he looked a lot like Nixon when he said 'I am not a crook.'" Carol went on to explain to me that, my assurances to the contrary; they *knew* how the university worked, grades did matter and as long as they mattered, students would be driven primarily by grade-related concerns. They simply could not trust me. Carol was telling me that grade anxiety is not pathology within students but a product of inequitable power relations within the system. My failure to acknowledge this had negated my well-intentioned efforts at developing a collaborative pedagogy in the class. Her remarks made it clear that I had failed my students. They also raised the terrifying specter that despite overt signs of happiness in my classes generally, I might be failing all of my other students too. What if all of my students were merely playing my game? Even if they were sincere, what harmful message was I sending? Was my success a delusion? It was the wrenching anxiety that this prospect produced, coupled with Carol's memorable tutelage, that finally forced me to face myself.

Seven years later I have grown more honest. I know that everything that occurs in my classroom is governed by institutional power relations, as well as by choices I make long before I meet my students. There are many aspects of existing reality I cannot change. However, I now try to make as many of these power relations as possible explicit to my students and hence available for naming and negotiation. Instead of feel-good assurances and vague grading criteria, for example, I now provide detailed, explicit, and negotiable rationales. I also suggest assignments in a wide range of modalities (e.g., oral presentations, formal and informal writings, collaborative and individual activities, performance pieces) and I encourage students to experiment with different modalities and to choose those that best allow them to express their learnings. All students present some form of self-evaluation essay or portfolio toward the end of the semester, and its scope and content is negotiated in relation to their contribution to other assignments during the semester. Finally, we hold one-on-one grading conferences in which we exchange views on how the class was taught, and in what ways they and I have experienced growth. I make a pledge to my students that there will be no surprises when the final grades are announced. This pledge keeps me honest. I have had to develop the courage to look students in the eye and give them an honest appraisal of their work. I can no longer take refuge in my office and exercise my power in private. My new teaching philosophy does not lead to equitable relations with my students. Given, race, class, gender, age, and educational differences between my students and I, not to mention the institutional obligations of my role as professor and their roles as students, a truly equitable relationship is a chimera. We can, however, begin to work together to explore some of the limits and possibilities of our situation.

My understanding of other aspects of my teaching has also changed as a result of these insights. Early on, for instance, I rushed to embrace journal writing. Then came autobiographical sharing and the writing of life histories. My early attempts to use these approaches were insufficiently sensitive to the ethical dilemmas such work poses. Given the power relations of schooling and the institutional authority of the teacher, however well hidden, any invitation to students to share their lives is vulnerable to being interpreted as a demand for self-revelation. Such requests pose grave dangers of invasion of privacy, and risk placing the teacher in the role of voyeur. I now take time to explore with my students the ethical implications of all requests for private information, whether written or oral, public or private. We explore the privacy issues and the meaning of informed consent, and I take care to detach this kind of introspective work from any kind of evaluation mechanisms. In addition I have found that autobiographical work that is not mutual is inherently exploitative. If I hold the belief that autobiographical explorations and sharing are intrinsically beneficial for my students, then I must hold myself to the same disclosure risks with them that I expect them to take with me. Genuine mutuality is prerequisite to such work.

These concerns have not diminished my belief in the value of the transformative possibilities that emerge from sharing our life stories. I have found Robert Coles' (1989) *The call of Stories* enormously helpful in enabling me to think through the power of such sharing. For too long I think I was in a hurry. Influenced by the discourses of critical pedagogy and my own impatience for social change, I tried to rush my students into gaining the kinds of critical insights I believed were good for them. I wanted my students to intellectualize issues and develop critical reasoning skills. Now, however, I am much more conscious of the narrative structure of human experience. I believe that autobiographical work is a crucial first step in grounding curriculum in students' lives and experiences. By telling our stories we become conscious of the storied nature of our lives, and, as Freire taught us, once we can name our experience the possibility of changing it appears. Through mutual engagement with our life stories we come to name those aspects of cultural socialization we hold in common, as well as to recognize how the unique aspects of our sociocultural and autobiographical experiences have shaped our worldviews. The possibilities for widening these conversations are greatly increased, as Robert Coles teaches us, by engagement with diverse life stories through exploration of diverse fiction, poetry, movies, guest speakers, community action projects, and so on. In my work I refer to this widening as a movement from a grounded pedagogy to pedagogy of multiple discourses.[3]

All of the foregoing is subsumed within a broad notion of political literacy that assumes that my role is to provide opportunities for students to name their world and explore other imaginable worlds, so that they might act to change their worlds. Just as surely as those of us who are teachers mediate culture and knowledges for our students, so too can we provide opportunities for the usurpation of the status quo and the legitimation of dissent and moral possibility. I realize, however, that the pathway to that destination must begin with autobiography and human connection.

Most of all, I have learned to be honest. I have lost patience with professors who, from the safety of their tenured positions in academia, exhort their students to stand up to entrenched power structures. If I cannot find the courage within myself to stand up for what I believe, and to share my struggles as openly as I can so that others may question themselves, I really see no point in teaching. I am grateful to the students and colleagues who have helped me understand this lesson.

NOTES

1 Troubling Childhood

1. See David Nasaw, *Schooled to order* (1981), for an apposite example in the context of the history of public schooling in the U.S.
2. The name Abdul is a pseudonym.
3. See the various papers from the 1990s by Michael O'Loughlin cited in the reference list.
4. See citations in reference list by the authors mentioned here for representative samples of their writings.

2 In Search of the Lost Language of Childhood

1. In addition to Laub's account see also the videotaped testimony of Menachem S, available from the Fortunoff Video Archive at Yale University: www.library.yale.edu/testimonies [Reference tape no. 8063].
2. For detailed discussion of the deleterious effects of such schools see Chapter 11.
3. See Breggin (2001) for a detailed critique of the effects of such medications on children.

4. For samples of the Tavistock work see for example Alvarez (1992); Alvarez and Edwards (2001); Alvarez and Reid (1999); Briggs (2002); Rhode and Klauber (2004); Rustin et al. (1997); Tustin (1990, 1992).

5. To view my own attempts to address these issues in my courses, readers are invited to email me at oloughli@adelphi.edu for copies of course syllabi for my courses in Child Development, Classroom Management, Psychoanalytic Theory, and The Emotional Lives of Children.

6. Field, Cohler, and Wool (1989) and Youell (2006) are welcome exceptions to this trend.

7. All names of child patients and family members have been changed, and details of their lives have been altered in order to ensure anonymity.

8. See the case study of the family described in Chapter 2 of Luepnitz (2003) for similar issues.

3 The Curious Subject of the Child

1. See Mark Epstein, (2004), *Thoughts without a thinker: A Buddhist perspective on psychotherapy*, and Chapter 5 below for further discussion.

2. For further theoretical discussion of phantomic aspects of trauma from psychoanalytic perspectives see Davoine and Gaudillière, (2004), *History beyond trauma; Esther* Rashkin, (1992), *Family secrets and the psychoanalysis of narrative;* and Abraham and Torok (1994), *The shell and the kernel*. For an overview see Michael O'Loughlin (2008) *Radical hope or death by a thousand cuts?* and the discussion in Chapter 9 below.

3. See Sennett and Cobb (1993), *The hidden injuries of class;* Dews and Law (1995), *This fine place so far from home: Voices of academics from the working class;* and Ryan and Sackrey (1984), *Strangers in paradise: Academics from the working class* for further evidence of the complex nature of this class transition for some people.

4. "Thick" = unintelligent, dull.

5. See detailed discussion in O'Loughlin, *Radical hope or death by a thousand cuts?*

6. See Eva Hoffman (1990), *Lost in translation: A life in a new language,* for a compelling example of the author's capacity to construct new subjective possibilities despite the wrenching difficulties she faced immigrating from Cracow to Vancouver as a child. See also the essays in Andre Aciman (1999), *Letters of transit.*

7. See Michael O'Loughlin (In press, a), *Strangers to ourselves: The decolonizing potential of the displacement, loss, and "homelessness" of migrant experiences,* and see also Chapter 7 below.

8. For a portrayal of black deference see Langston Hughes (1987), *I, too,* and Toni Morrison's (1971), portrayal of Pecola's mother in her role as housekeeper to white folks in *The bluest eye.*

9. For a discussion of hauntology see Avery Gordon (1997), *Ghostly matters: haunting and the sociological imagination;* Lisa Blackman (2001), *Hearing voices: Embodiment and experience;* and Couze Venn (2002), *Refiguring subjectivity after modernity.*

10. See Cathy Caruth (1995), *Trauma: Explorations in memory;* Yael Danieli (1998), *International handbook of intergenerational trauma transmission;* Felman and Laub (1992), *Testimony: Crises of witness in literature, psychoanalysis, and history;* Louise Kaplan (1996b), *Images of absence, Voices of silence.*

11. See Tamahori's film *Once were warriors* for illustration, and O'Loughlin, *Radical hope or death by a thousand cuts?* for further discussion.
12. See "Introduction" in Kinealy (2006), *This great calamity* for discussion of how questions like this are finally coming into the open Ireland after close to a century of revisionism in which Irish historians systematically suppressed such discussion.
13. For depiction of the abusive conditions in Irish orphanages see Peter Mullan's (2004) film *The Magdalene Sisters* and Aisling Walsh's (2003) film *Song for a raggy boy*. For scholarly discussion see Raftery and O'Sullivan (1999), *Suffer the little children: The inside story of Ireland's industrial schools*, and Frances Finnegan (2001), *Do penance or perish: Magdalen asylums in Ireland*. For personal accounts see, for example, Peter Tyrrel (2006), *Founded in fear* and Kathy O'Beirne (2006), *Kathy's story: The true story of a childhood hell inside Ireland's Magdalen laundries*.
14. See David Nasaw (1981), *Schooled to order: A social history of public schooling in the United States* and Jay MacLeod (1995), *Ain't no makin' it: Aspirations and attainment in a low-income neighborhood* for discussion of the limiting effects of school discourses. See Barry Richards (1984), *Capitalism and infancy: Essays on psychoanalysis and politics* and Philip Cushman (1995), *Constructing the self, constructing America: A cultural history of psychotherapy* for discussion of the effects of contemporary capitalism on the self. For larger discussion of the totalizing effects of social systems on subjectivity see Jacques Donzelot (1997), *The policing of families* and Erving Goffman (1961), *Asylums: Essays on the social situation of mental patients and other inmates*.
15. For an introduction to Lacanian thought see Apollon, Bergeron, and Cantin (2002), *After Lacan*; Bruce Fink (1995), *The Lacanian subject: Between language and jouissance*; Bruce Fink (1997), *Lacanian Psychoanalysis: Theory and technique*; Danny Nobus (1998), *Key concepts of Lacanian Psychoanalysis*.

5 On Knowing and Desiring Children: The Significance of the Unthought Known

1. All names of child patients and family members have been changed, and details of their lives have been altered in order to ensure anonymity.
2. For further details see Chapter 2.

7 Strangers to Ourselves: On the Displacement, Loss, and "Homelessness" of Migrant Experiences

1. For the severe consequences of this for contemporary Australian Aboriginal communities see Michael O'Loughlin (2008), *Radical Hope or Death by a Thousand Cuts? The future for Indigenous Australians* and Jon Altman and Melinda Hinkson (2007), *Coercive reconciliation: stabilize, normalize and exit aboriginal Australia*. For a similar discussion in a North American context see Ward Churchill's (2004) aptly titled *Kill the Indian, save the man*.

2. Aboriginal actor David Gulpilil who plays Moodoo in *Rabbit proof fence* offers another variation on the *inscrutable native* in Rolf de Heer's (2002) film *The Tracker*.

3. In *Imaginary maps* (1995), Mashaweta Devi, commenting on oppression of Native American peoples in the U.S. notes: "Only in the names of places the Native American legacy survives. Otherwise entire tribes have been butchered. Their land has been taken away ... But I say to my American readers, see what has been done to them, you will understand what has been done to the Indian tribals [i.e., in India]. Everywhere it is the same story" (1995, p. xi).

4. See, for example, Frances Finnegan (2001), *Do penance or perish: Magdalen asylums in Ireland*; Mary Raftery and Eoin O'Sullivan (1999), *Suffer the little children: The inside story of Ireland's industrial schools*; Patrick Galvin (2002), *The raggy boy trilogy*.

5. See Michael O'Loughlin (2007b), *Spectral memory and trauma: Speaking with the ghost* and Chapter 9 of this volume for an overview of this literature.

6. See, for example, the depiction of anti-Irish nativist sentiment in Martin Scorsese's (2003) film *The gangs of New York*.

7. See O'Loughlin (2002b), *A decolonizing pedagogy: Introducing undergraduate students to the psychology of hatred and genocide and the nature of historical memory* for further discussion.

8. Referring to psychoanalysis, Jacques Derrida notes that "there is practically no psychoanalysis in Africa, white or black, just as there is practically no psychoanalysis in Asia or in the South Seas. These are among those parts of 'the rest of the world' where psychoanalysis has never set foot, or in any case where it has never taken off its European shoes ... African psychoanalysis was European, structurally defined in the profoundest way by the colonial state apparatus" (1998, p. 69).

9. See Paula Gunn Allen's *Off the reservation* (1998) for a critique of U.S. universities from the perspective of a Native American woman who finally left her academic post because of the predicament of marginality.

10. See Chapter 4 of this volume and Rose (1993) for further discussion. Psychoanalytic inquiry into the origins of autistic and schizophrenic states in children, conducted at the Tavistock Clinic, London, includes inquiry into the effects of the trauma of initial separation (cf. Alvarez, 1992; Tustin, 1992) as a contributing factor in the development of those conditions.

8 Helping Poor and Working-Class Children Make Something of Themselves: The Contradictions and Possibilities of Teaching for Equity and Democracy

1. See Chapter 11 for details of this work.

2. Available from *Radical Teacher*, P.O. Box 102, Kendall Square Post Office, Cambridge, MA 02142. See *www.radicalteacher.org* for information on how to access the *Radical Teacher* archive.

9 Recreating the Social Link between Children and their Histories: The Power of Story as a Decolonizing Strategy

1. For detailed discussion of the issues surrounding the lives and aspirations of indigenous peoples, using the case of contemporary Indigenous Australian peoples as a case in point, see Michael O'Loughlin (2008), *Radical Hope or Death by a Thousand Cuts?* and Michael O'Loughlin (In press, b), *An analysis of collective trauma among Indigenous Australians and a suggestion for intervention.*

11 The Child as Subject of Literacy

1. I am most grateful to Brennen Bierwiler and Marta Serra for the invaluable contributions they made to this project, particularly through their principled and loving work with the children. The work described here took place between September 1994 and June 1995.
2. Names of all child participants have been changed to protect their identities.
3. Little Oaks, the name assigned to the school, like all names used in this paper except our own, is a pseudonym.
4. See for example, Jean Anyon (1997), *Ghetto schooling*; Sue Books (1998), *Invisible children in the society and its schools*; Derrick Bell (1992), *Faces at the bottom of the well*; Lisa Delpit (1995), *Other people's children*; W.E.B. DuBois (1903/1990), *The souls of black folk*; Michelle Fine (1991), *Framing dropouts;* Janice Hale (1994), *Unbank the fire: Visions for the educations of African American children*; Asa Hilliard III (1995), *The maroon within us: Selected essays on African American Community socialization*; John Holt (1964), *How children fail*; Herbert Kohl (1967), *36 Children*; Herbert Kohl (1994), *I won't learn from you*; Jonathon Kozol (1967), *Death at an early age*; Susan Urmston Phillips (1983), *The invisible culture*; Carter Woodson (1933/1990), *The miseducation of the Negro.*
5. See, for example, Calkins (1986) and Graves (1983).
6. For discussion of our evolving understanding of critical and grounded notions of literacy, and the relationship between culture and thought, and literacy and social change see O'Loughlin (1995c). Bakhtin's writings (1981, 1986), and Dyson's interpretation of Bakhtin have been influential in my thinking, as have papers by Dressman (1993) and Lensmire (1994), and the works cited in O'Loughlin (1995b).
7. Most of the replies here and in the following are from Michael's correspondence. Due to an error many of Brennen's and Marta's replies were not copied.
8. For a critical discussion of the emancipatory possibilities of literacy instruction see O'Loughlin (1995c).

12 Facing Myself: The Struggle
for Authentic Pedagogy

1. For additional discussion of race, class, and identity from autobiographical perspectives see Dews and Law (1995) and Thompson and Tyagi (1996).
2. See Elizabeth Ellsworth (1989), *Why doesn't this feel empowering? Working through the repressive myths of critical pedagogy.*
3. For details see O'Loughlin (2002b).

REFERENCES

Abraham, N. & Torok, M. (1994). *The shell and the kernel*. Chicago: University of Chicago Press.

Aciman, A. (Ed.). (1999). *Letters of transit*. New York: New Press.

Adams, M.V. (1996). *The multicultural imagination: Race, color and the unconscious*. New York and London: Routledge.

Ainsworth, M., Blehar, M., Waters, M. & Wall, S. (1978). *Patterns of attachment*. Hillsdale: Erlbaum.

Alford, C. (1989). *Melanie Klein and critical social theory*. New Haven: Yale University Press.

Allen P. G. (1998). *Off the reservation: Reflections on boundary-busting, border crossing, loose canons*. Boston: Beacon Press.

Althusser, L. (1971a). Ideology and ideological state apparatuses (Notes towards an Investigation), in *Lenin and Philosophy and Other Essays*. New York: Monthly Review Press.

Althusser, L. (1971b). *Lenin and philosophy and other essays*. New York: Monthly Review Press.

Altman, J. & Hinkson, M. (2007) *Coercive reconciliation: Stabilise, normalise and exit aboriginal Australia*. North Carlton, Australia: Arena Publications.

Alvarez, A. (1992). *Live company: Psychoanalytic psychotherapy with autistic, borderline, deprived and abused children*. New York: Routledge.

Alvarez, A. & Edwards, J. (2001). *Being alive: Building on the work of Anne Alvarez*. New York: Routledge.

Alvarez, A. & Reid, S. (Eds.). (1999). *Autism and personality: Findings from the Tavistock Autism Workshop*. New York: Routledge.

American Psychiatric Association. (2000). *Diagnostic and Statistical Manual of Mental Disorders, Fourth Edition, DSM-IV-TR.* Arlington, VA: American Psychiatric Association.

Amery, J. (1998). *At the mind's limit: Contemplations by a survivor on Auschwitz and its realities.* Bloomington: Indiana University Press.

Anderson, B. (Ed.). (2006). *Imagined communities: Reflections on the origins and spread of nationalism.* London: Verso.

Anyon, J. (1997). *Ghetto schooling: A political economy of urban educational reform.* New York: Teachers College Press.

Anyon, J. (1995). Race and social class and educational reform in an inner-city school. *Teachers College Record, 97,* 69–94.

Anzieu, D. (1990). *Psychic envelopes.* London: Karnac.

Apollon, W., Bergeron, D., & Cantin, L. (2002). *After Lacan: Clinical practice and the subject of the unconscious.* Albany, NY: SUNY Press.

Archibald, J. (Q'um Q'um Xiiem). (2008). *Indigenous storywork: Educating the heart, mind, body, spirit.* Vancouver: UBC Press.

Ashcroft, B., Griffiths, G. & Tiffin, H. (Eds.). (1995). *The Post-colonial studies reader.* New York: Routledge.

Atkinson, J. (2007). Indigenous approaches to child abuse. In J. Altman & M. Hinkson (Eds.), *Coercive reconciliation: Stablise, normalise, exit Aboriginal Australia.* North Carlton, Australia: Arena Publications Association.

Atkinson, J. (2002). *Trauma Trails: Recreating song lines: The transgenerational effects of trauma in Indigenous Australia.* North Melbourne, Australia: Spinifex Press.

Augé, M. (1995). *Non-places: Introduction to an anthropology of supermodernity.* London: Verso.

Bakhtin, M.M. (1986). *Speech genres and other late essays.* Austin: University of Texas Press.

Bakhtin, M.M. (1981). *The dialogic imagination.* Austin: University of Texas Press.

Baldwin, J. (1998). White Man's Guilt. In D. Roediger (Ed.), *Black on white: Black writers on what it means to be white,* pp. 320–325. New York: Schocken (Originally published in 1963).

Barnes, D. (1992). *From communication to curriculum.* Portsmouth, NH: Boynton/Cook.

Barrie, J.M. (1902). *The little white bird.* London: Hodder & Stoughton.

Barthes, R. (1981). *Camera lucida: Reflections on photography.* [R. Howard, trans.]. New York: Hill and Wang.

Bell, D. (1992). *Faces at the Bottom of the well: The permanence of racism.* New York: Basic Books.

Berliner, A. [Director]. (1997). *Ma vie en rose.* Sony Pictures.

Bernstein, B. (2000). *Pedagogy, symbolic control, and identity.* Lanham, MD: Rowman and Littlefield.

Bernstein, B. (1990). *The structuring of pedagogic discourse.* London: Routledge.

Bettelheim, B. (1989). *The uses of enchantment: The meaning and importance of fairy tales.* New York: Vintage.

Bhabha, H. (1994). *The location of culture.* New York: Routledge.

Bion, W. (1993). *Second thoughts: Selected papers on psychoanalysis.* Northvale, NJ: Aronson.

Bion, W. (1989). *Learning from experience.* London: Karnac.

Bion, W. (1961). *Experiences in groups.* London: Tavistock/Routledge.

Birksted-Breen, D. (2003). Time and the après coup. *International Journal of Psychoanalysis, 84,* 1501–1515.

Blackman, L. (2002). A psychophysics of the imagination. In V. Walkerdine (Ed.), *Challenging subjects: Critical psychology for a new millennium.* New York: Palgrave.

Blackman, L. (2001). *Hearing voices: Embodiment and experience*. London: Free Association Press.

Boldt, G. & Salvio, P. (Eds.). (2006). *Love's return: Psychoanalytic essays on childhood teaching and learning*. New York: Routledge.

Bollas, C. (1987). *The shadow of the object: Psychoanalysis of the unthought known*. New York: Columbia University Press.

Books, S. (Ed.). (1998). *Invisible children in the society and its schools*. Hillsdale, NJ: Erlbaum.

Bourdieu, P. & Passeron, J. (1977). *Reproduction in education, society, and culture*. Newbury Park, CA: Sage.

Bowlby, J. (1988). *Attachment and loss*. New York: Basic Books.

Bowlby, J. (1982). *A secure base: Parent–child attachment and healthy human development*. New York: Basic Books.

Bradley, B. (1989). *Visions of infancy: A critical introduction to child psychology*. Cambridge: Polity Press.

Brantlinger, E. (1985). Low-income parents' perception of favoritism in the schools. *Urban education, 20*, 82–102.

Breggin, P. (2001). *Talking back to Ritalin: What doctors aren't telling you about stimulants and ADHD*. New York: DaCapo Press.

Brenkman, J. (1999). Introduction. In M. Mannoni (Ed.), *Separation and creativity: Refinding the lost language of childhood*. New York: Other Press.

Briggs, A. (Ed.). (2002). *Surviving space: Papers on infant observation*. London: Karnac.

Britzman, D. (2007). Little Hans, Fritz, and Ludo: On the curious history of gender in the psychoanalytic archive. *Studies in Gender and Sexuality, 7*, (2), 113–140.

Britzman, D. (2006). *Novel education: Psychoanalytic studies of learning and not learning*. New York: Peter Lang.

Britzman, D. (2003). *After-education: Anna Freud, Melanie Klein and psychoanalytic histories of learning*. Albany, NY: SUNY Press.

Britzman, D. (1998). *Lost subjects, contested objects: Toward a psychoanalytic inquiry of learning*. Albany, NY: SUNY Press.

Buber, M. (1971). *I and thou*. New York: Free Press.

Burman, E. (1994). *Deconstructing developmental psychology*. London: Routledge.

Butler, J. (1997). *The Psychic Life of Power*. New York: Routledge.

Butler, J. & Spivak, G. (2007). *Who sings the nation-state? Language, politics, belonging*. Kolkata: Seagull Books.

Calkins, L. (1986). *The art of teaching writing*. Portsmouth, NH: Heinemann.

Caro, N. [Director]. (2003). *Whale rider*. [DVD]. Sony Pictures.

Caruth, C. (Ed.). (1995). *Trauma: Explorations in memory*. Baltimore: The John Hopkins University Press.

Castañeda, C. (2002). *Figurations: Child, bodies, worlds*. Durham, NC: Duke University Press.

Chakrabarty, D. (2000). *Provincializing Europe*. Princeton, NJ: Princeton University Press.

Chakrabarty, D. (1995). Postcoloniality and the artifice of history. In B. Ashcroft, G. Griffiths, & H. Tiffin (Eds.), *The Post-colonial studies reader*. New York: Routledge.

Chambers, I. & Curti, L. (Eds.). (1996). *The Post-colonial question*. New York: Routledge.

Chamoiseau, P. (1997). *School days*. Lincoln: University of Nebraska Press.

Charles, M. (2003) The intergenerational transmission of unresolved mourning: Personal, familial, and cultural factors. *Samiksa: Journal of the Indian Psychoanalytic Society, 54*, 65–80.

Chaterjee, P. (1993). *The nation and its fragments: Colonial and postcolonial histories*. Princeton, NJ: Princeton University Press.

Cherry, L. (1990). *The great kapok tree: A tale of the Amazon rain forest*. New York: The Trumpet Club.

Churchill, W. (2004). *Kill the Indian, save the man*. San Francisco: City Lights Books.

Churchill, W. (1997). *A little matter of genocide: Struggle for the land and Indians R us*. San Francisco: City Lights Books.

Cisneros, S. (1991). *Women hollering creek and other stories*. New York: Vintage.

Clare, A. (1991). The mad Irish? In C. Keane (Ed.), *Mental health in Ireland*. Dublin: Gill & Macmillan and RTE.

Coats, K. (2004). *Looking glasses and neverlands: Lacan, desire, and subjectivity in children's literature*. Iowa City: University of Iowa Press.

Coles, R. (1989). *The call of stories: Teaching and the moral imagination*. Boston: Houghton-Mifflin.

Counts, G. (1932/1969). *Dare the schools build a new social order?* New York: Arno Press & The New York Times.

Crow Dog, M. (1991). *Lakota woman*. New York: Harper Perennial.

Cummins, J. (2001). *Language, power and pedagogy: Bilingual children in the crossfire*. Philadelphia: Multilingual Matters.

Cushman, P. (1995). *Constructing the self, constructing America*. Reading, MA: Addison-Wesley.

Daldry, S. [Director]. (2001). *Billy Elliot*. Universal Studios.

Danieli, Y. (Ed.). (1998). *International handbook of intergenerational trauma transmission*. New York: Plenum.

Danon-Boileau, L. (2001). *The silent child: Bringing language to children who cannot speak*. New York: Oxford.

Davoine, F. & Gaudillière, J. (2004). *History beyond trauma*. New York: Other Press.

DeHart, G., Sroufe, L. & Cooper, R. (2000). *Child development, its nature and course*. New York: McGraw Hill.

de Heer, R. [Director]. (2002). *The tracker*. [DVD]. ArtMattan Productions.

Deloria, V. & Lytle, M. (1983). *American Indians, American justice*. Austin: University of Texas Press.

Delpit, L. (2006). *Other people's children: Cultural conflict in the classroom* (Updated edition). New York: New Press.

Delpit, L. (1995). *Other people's children*. New York: New Press.

Delpit, L. (1988). The silenced dialogue: Power and pedagogy in educating other people's children. *Harvard Educational Review, 58*, 280–298.

deMause, L. (1974). The evolution of childhood. In L. deMause (Ed.), *The history of childhood*. New York: Harper.

De Paola, T. (1983). *The legend of the bluebonnet: An old tale of Texas*. New York: Putnam.

Derrida, J. (1998). Geopsychoanalysis: "...and the rest of the world." In C. Lane (Ed.), *The psychoanalysis of race*. New York: Columbia University Press.

Derrida, J. (1994). *Specters of Marx: The state of the debt, the work of mourning, and the new international*. New York: Routledge.

Devi, M. (1995). *Imaginary maps*. [G. Spivak, Trans.] New York: Routledge.

Dews, C.L.B. & Law C.L. (Eds.). (1995). *This fine place so far from home: Voices of academics from the working class*. Philadelphia: Temple University Press.

Dickens, C. (1854/1994). *Hard times*. New York: Penguin Popular Classics.

Doillon, J. (1999). [Director]. *Ponette*. Fox-Lorber.

Dolto, G. (1999). *Françoise Dolto, c'est la parole qui fait vivre: Une theorie corporelle du langage*. Paris: Gallimard.

Donzelot, J. (1979). *The policing of families*. New York: Pantheon.

Dressman, M. (1993). Lionizing lone wolves: The cultural romantics of literacy workshops. *Curriculum Inquiry, 23,* 245–263.

DuBois, W.E.B. (1903/1990). *The souls of black folks*. New York: Vintage. [Originally published, 1903.]

Duran, E., Duran, B., Yellow Horse Brave Heart, M., & Yellow Horse-Davis, S. (1998). Healing the American Indian soul wound. In Y. Danieli (Ed.), *International handbook of multigenerational legacies of trauma*. New York: Plenum Press.

Duran, E. & Duran, B. (1995). *Native American post-colonial psychology*. Albany: SUNY Press.

Durie, M. (2003). *Launching Moari futures*. Wellington, NZ: Huia Publishers.

Durie, M. (1996). *Identity, conflict, and the search for nationhood*. College address presented at the Royal Australian New Zealand College of Physicians Congress. Retrieved on 1/21/08 from http//:www.teiho.org/Identity/IdentityanaddressbyMasonDurie.aspx

During, S. (Ed.) (1993). *The cultural studies reader*. New York: Routledge.

Dyson, A.H. (2003). *The brothers and sisters learn to write: Popular literacies in childhood, school and cultures*. New York: Teachers College Press.

Dyson, A.H. (1997). *Writing superheroes: Contemporary childhood, popular culture and classroom literacy*. New York: Teachers College Press.

Dyson, A.H. (1993). *The social worlds of children learning to write in an urban primary school*. New York: Teachers College Press.

Eagelton, T. (2002). *The gatekeeper*. London: Penguin.

Ellsworth , E. (1989), Why doesn't this feel empowering? Working through the repressive myths of critical pedagogy. *Harvard Educational, Review, 59,* (3), 297–324.

Epstein, M. (2004). *Thoughts without a thinker: A Buddhist perspective on psychotherapy*. New York: Basic Books.

Erickson, F. (2004). *Talk and social theory: Ecologies of speaking and listening in everyday life*. Cambridge: Polity Press.

Erikson, K. (1976). *Everything in its path*. New York: Simon & Schuster.

Erikson, E.H. (1963). *Childhood and society*. New York: Norton.

Evans, M.C. (1998, February 1). Wanted diversity: In LI schools, dwindling supply of lack teachers. *Newsday*, A3+.

Fanon, F. (1967). *Black skin, white masks*. New York: Grove Press.

Felman, S. (1987). *Jacques Lacan and the adventure of insight*. Cambridge, MA: Harvard University Press.

Felman, S & D. Laub, D. (Eds.). (1992). *Testimony: Crises of witness in literature, psychoanalysis, and history*. New York & London: Routledge.

Field, K., Cohler, B., & Wool, G. (Eds.). (1989). *Learning and education: Psychoanalytic perspectives*. Madison, CT: International Universities Press.

Fine, M. (1991). *Framing dropouts*. Albany, NY: SUNY Press.

Fine, M. (1987). Silencing in the public schools. *Language Arts, 64,* 157–74.

Fine. M., & Weis, L. (2003). *Silenced voices and extraordinary conversations: Re-imagining schools*. New York: Teachers College Press.

Fine, M., Weis, L., Powell, L.C., & Wong, L.M. (Eds.). (1996). *Off white: Readings on race, power, and society*. New York and London: Routledge.

Fink, B. (1997). *A clinical introduction to Lacanian Psychoanalysis*. Cambridge: Harvard University Press.

Fink, B. (1995). *The Lacanian subject*. Princeton: Princeton University Press.

Finnegan, F. (2001). *Do penance or perish: Magdalen asylums in Ireland.* London: Oxford University Press.

Fixico, D. (2003). *The American Indian mind in a linear world.* New York & London: Taylor & Francis.

Foucault, M. (1995). *Discipline and punish: The birth of the prison.* New York: Vintage.

Foucault, M. (1988). *Madness and civilization: A history of insanity in the age of reason.* New York: Vintage.

Fournier, S. & Crey, E. (1997). *Stolen from our embrace: The abduction of First Nations children and the restoration of aboriginal communities.* Vancouver/Toronto: Douglas & McIntyre.

Fraiberg, L. (Ed.). (1987). *Selected writings of Selma Fraiberg.* Columbus: Ohio State University Press.

Fraiberg, S. (1996). *The magic years.* New York: Scribner.

Fraiberg, S., Adelson, E., & Shapiro, V. (1975). Ghosts in the nursery. *Journal of the American Academy of Child Psychiatry, 14,* 387–421.

Frankenberg, R. (1996) "When we are capable of stopping we begin to see": Being white, seeing whiteness. In B. Thompson & S. Tyagi (Eds.), *Names we call home: Autobiography on racial identity.* London & New York: Routledge.

Frankenberg, R. (1993). *White women, race matters: The social construction of whiteness.* Minneapolis: University of Minnesota Press.

Freire, P. (1996), *Letters to Cristina: Reflections on my life and work.* New York :Routledge.

Freire, P. (1972). *Pedagogy of the oppressed.* New York: Continuum.

Freire, P. (1969). *Education for critical consciousness.* New York: Continuum.

Freud, A. (1935/1979). *Psychoanalysis for teachers and parents.* New York: Norton.

Freud, S. (1959). *Group psychology and the analysis of the ego.* New York: Norton.

Freud, S. (1909/1960). Analysis of a phobia in a 5-year-old boy. In the *Standard Edition of the complete psychological works of Sigmund Freud,* vol. X, pp. 1–149. New York: Basic Books.

Freud, S. (1899/1960). Screen memories. In the *Standard Edition of the complete psychological works of Sigmund Freud,* vol. III, pp. 47–69. New York: Basic Books.

Gagné, M. (1998). The role of dependency and colonialism in generating trauma in First Nations citizens. In Y. Danieli (Ed.), *International handbook of multigenerational legacies of trauma.* New York: Plenum Press.

Gallas, K. (1992). When children take the chair: A study of sharing time in a primary classroom. *Language Arts, 69,* 172–182.

Galvin, P. (2002). *The raggy boy trilogy.* Dublin: New Island Books.

Gans, H. (1995). *The war against the poor.* New York: Basic Books.

Gardner, S. (1993). What's a nice working-class girl like you doing in a place like this? In M. Tokarczyk & E. Fay (Eds.), *Working-class women in the academy: Laborers in the knowledge factory.* Amherst, MA: University of Massachusetts Press.

Gee, J. (2004). *Situated language and learning: A critique of traditional schooling.* New York: Routledge.

Gee, J. (1996). *Social linguistics and literacies: Ideology in discourses.* London: Taylor & Francis.

Goffman, E. (1961). *Asylums: Essays on the social situation of mental patients and other inmates.* New York: Anchor.

Goldsmith, O. (1770/2003). The village schoolmaster. In T. Hosic (Ed.), *Gray's Elegy and Goldsmith's The deserted village, The traveler, and other poems.* Honolulu, HI: University Press of the Pacific.

Goodlad, J. (1983). *A place called school.* New York: McGraw Hill.

Gordon, A. (1997). *Ghostly matters: haunting and the sociological imagination.* Minneapolis: University of Minnesota Press.

Gramsci. A. (1971). *Selections from the prison notebooks.* New York: International Publishers

Graves, D. (1983). *Writing: Teachers and children at work.* Portsmouth, NH: Heinemann.

Green, A. (2000). *A dual conception of narcissism: Positive and negative organizations.* Presented at 2002 Symposium, New York City.

Green, A. (1999). *The work of the negative.* New York: Free Association.

Green, A. (1986a). *On private madness.* Madison, CT: International Universities Press.

Green, A. (1986b). *The dead mother.* In (Author), *On private madness.* Madison, CT: International Universities Press.

Greenson, R. (1978). *Explorations in Psychoanalysis.* New York: International Universities Press.

Groening, M. (1987). *School is hell: A cartoon book by Matt Groening.* New York: Pantheon Books.

Grossberg, L., Nelson, C., & Treichler, P. (Eds.). (1992). *Cultural Studies.* New York: Routledge.

Haberman, M. (1991). The pedagogy of poverty versus good teaching. *Phi Delta Kappan, 73,* 290–294.

Hale, J. (1994). *Unbank the fire: Visions for the education of African American Children.* Baltimore, MD: John's Hopkins University Press.

Hall, S. (1996a). New ethnicities. In D. Morley & K. Chen (Eds.), *Stuart Hall: Selected dialogues in cultural studies.* New York and London: Routledge.

Hall, S. (1996b).When was the "post-colonial"? Thinking at the limit. In I. Chambers & L. Curti (Eds.), *The post-colonial question.* New York and London: Routledge.

Hayes, C.W., Bahruth, R., & Kessler, C. (1991). *Literacy con cariño.* Portsmouth, NH: Heinemann.

Heath, S.B. (2006). *Ways with words: Language, life and work in classrooms and communities.* Cambridge: Cambridge University Press.

Heimann, P. (1991). Some aspects of the role of introjection and projection in early development. In P. King & R. Steiner (Eds.), *The Freud-Klein Controversies 1941–45,* pp. 502–530. London: Routledge.

Henriques, J., Holloway, W., Urwin, C., Venn, C. & Walkerdine, V. (1984). *Changing the subject: Psychology, social regulation, and subjectivity.* London: Methuen.

Hillard, A.G. III. (1995). *The maroon within us: Selected essays on African American socialization.* Baltimore, MD: Black Classic Press.

Hinkson, J. (2007). The "Innocence" of the settler imagination. In J. Altman & M. Hinkson (Eds.), *Coercive reconciliation: Stablise, normalize, exit Aboriginal Australia.* North Carlton, Australia: Arena Publications Association.

Hodgson Burnett, F. (2003). *The secret garden.* New York: Signet Classics.

Hoffman, E. (1999). The new nomads. In A. Aciman (Ed.), *Letters of transit.* New York: New Press.

Hoffman, E. (1990). *Lost in translation: A life in a new language.* New York: Penguin Books.

Hollins, E.R. (1996). *Culture in schooling: Revealing the deep meaning.* Mahwah, NJ: Erlbaum.

Holt, J. (1964). *How children fail.* New York: Pittman.

Homer, S. (2005). *Jacques Lacan.* New York & London: Routledge.

hooks, b. (1990). Choosing the margin as a space of radical openness. In (Author), *Yearning: Race, gender and cultural politics.* Boston: South End Press.

Horney, K. (1991). *Neurosis and human growth: The struggle toward self-realization*. New York: Norton.

Horton, M. (1990). *The long haul: An autobiography*. New York: Doubleday.

Horton, M. & Freire, P. (1990). *We make the road by walking: Conversations on education and social change*. Philadelphia: Temple University Press.

Hughes, L. (1987). I, Too. In *Selected poems of Langston Hughes*. New York: Vintage.

Hulan, R. & Eigenbrod, R. (2008). *Aboriginal oral traditions: Theory, practice, ethics*. Halifax: Fernwood Publishers.

Ignatiev, N. (1995). *How the Irish became white*. New York: Routledge.

James, A. & Prout, A. (Eds). (1997). *Constructing and reconstructing childhood: Contemporary issues in the sociological study of childhood* (Second ed.). London: Falmer.

Jay, G. (1987). The subject of pedagogy: Lessons in psychoanalysis and politics. *College English*, 49, 785–800.

Jersild, A. (1955). *When teachers face themselves*. New York: Teachers College Press.

Johnson, R. (2000). *Hands off: The disappearance of touch in the care of children*. New York: Peter Lang.

Kaplan, L. (1996a). Images of absence, voices of silence. In (Author), *No Voice is Ever Wholly Lost: An exploration of the everlasting attachment between parent and child*. New York, Simon & Schuster.

Kaplan, L. (1996b). *No voice is ever wholly lost: An exploration of the everlasting attachment between parent and child*. New York: Simon & Schuster.

Katz, M. (1990). *The undeserving poor: From the war on poverty to the war on welfare*. New York: Pantheon.

Kay, S. (2003). *Žižek: A critical introduction*. Cambridge: Polity Press.

Kearney, R. (1985). Introduction. In (Author), *The Irish mind*. Dublin: Wolfhound Press.

Kehily, M.J. (2004). *An introduction to childhood studies*. Maidenhead: Open University Press.

Kernberg, O. (1998). *Ideology, conflict, and leadership in groups and organizations*. New Haven: Yale University Press.

Kessen, W. (1979). The American child and other cultural inventions. *American Psychologist*, 34, 815–20.

Kinealy, C. (2006). *This great calamity: The Irish Famine 1845–52*. Dublin: Gill & Macmillan.

King, S.H. (1993). The limited presence of African American teachers. *Review of Educational Research*, 63, 115–50.

King, T. (2003). *The truth about stories: A native narrative*. Toronto: House of Anansi Press.

Klein, M. (1984a). *Love, Guilt, and Reparation and Other Works*, vol. 1. In R. Money Kyrle (General Editor), *The writings of Melanie Klein*. New York: Free Press.

Klein, M. (1984b). *The Psychoanalysis of Children*, vol. 2. In R. Money Kyrle (General Editor), *The writings of Melanie Klein*. New York: Free Press.

Klein, M. (1984c). *Envy and Gratitude and Other Works*, vol. 3. In R. Money Kyrle (General Editor), *The writings of Melanie Klein*. New York: Free Press.

Klein, M. (1984d). *Narrative of a Child Analysis*, vol. 4. In R. Money Kyrle (General Editor), *The writings of Melanie Klein*. New York: Free Press.

Klein, M. (1964). Love, Guilt and Reparation. In M. Klein & J. Riviere (Eds.), *Love, hate and reparation*, pp. 57–119. New York: Norton.

Knorr-Cetina, K. (1999). *Epistemic cultures: How the sciences make knowledge*. Cambridge, MA: Harvard University Press.

Kohl, H. (1994). *I won't learn from you and other thoughts on creative maladjustment*. New York: The New Press.

Kohl, H. (1967). *36 Children*. New York: Penguin.

Kohon, G. (Ed.). (1999). *The dead mother: The work of André Green*. New York: Routledge.

Kohut, H. (1977). *The restoration of the self*. Madison, CT: International Universities Press.

Kohut, H. (1971). *The analysis of the self*. Madison, CT: International Universities Press.

Kozol, J. (1967). *Death at an early age*. Boston: Houghton-Mifflin.

Kozol, J. (1991). *Savage inequalities: Children in American schools*. New York: Crown.

Kristeva, J. (2001). *Melanie Klein*. New York: Columbia University Press.

Kristeva, J. (1991). *Strangers to ourselves*. [L.S. Roudiez, Trans.]. New York: Columbia University Press.

Kristeva, J. (1989). *Black sun: Depression and melancholia*. New York: Columbia University Press.

Kristeva, J. (1982). *Powers of horror: Essays on abjection*. New York: Columbia University Press.

Lacan, J. (2007). *Ecrits: First complete edition in English*. [B. Fink, Trans.]. New York: Norton.

Lacan, J. (1998). *The four fundamental concepts of psychoanalysis*. New York: Norton.

Lacan, J. (1977). *Ecrits—a selection*. London: Tavistock.

Lacan, J. (1968). *The language of the self: The function of language in psychoanalysis*. [A. Wilden, Trans.]. Baltimore, MD: Johns Hopkins University Press.

Ladson-Billings, G. (1994). *The dreamkeepers: Successful teachers of African American Children*. San Francisco: Jossey-Bass.

Lane, C. (1998). *The psychoanalysis of race*. New York: Columbia University Press.

Langer, L. (1991). *Holocaust testimonies: The ruins of memory*. New Haven: Yale University Press.

Lanzmann, C. [Director]. (2000). *Shoah*. New Yorker Video.

Lather, P. (1991). *Getting smart: Feminist research and pedagogy with/in the postmodern*. New York: Routledge.

Lather, P. (1986). Research as Praxis. *Harvard Educational Review, 56*, 257–277.

Latour, B., Woolgar, S. & Salk, J. (1986). *Laboratory life: The construction of scientific facts*. Princeton: Princeton University Press.

Laub, D. (1995). Truth and testimony: The process and the struggle. In C. Caruth, *Trauma: Explorations in memory*. Baltimore: Johns Hopkins University Press.

Laub, D. (1992). An event without a witness: Truth, testimony and survival. In S. Felman & D. Laub (Eds.), *Testimony: Crises of witnessing in literature, psychoanalysis, and history*. New York: Routledge.

Lave, J. (1988). *Cognition in practice: Mind, mathematics, and culture in everyday life*. Cambridge: Cambridge University Press.

Lave, J. & Wenger, E. (1991). *Situated learning: Legitimate peripheral participation*. Cambridge: Cambridge University Press.

Lawrence, S.M. & Tatum, B.D. (1997). White educators as allies: Moving from awareness to action. In M. Fine, L. Weis, L.C. Powell, & L.M. Wong (Eds.), *Off white: Readings on race, power, and society*, pp. 333–342. New York: Routledge.

Lear, J. (2006). *Radical hope: Ethics in the face of cultural devastation*. Cambridge, MA: Harvard University Press.

Le Compte, M. (1993). A framework for hearing silence: What does telling stories mean when I are supposed to be doing science? In D. McLaughlin & W. Tierney (Eds.), *Naming silenced lives: Personal narratives and the process of educational change*. New York: Routledge.

Lemke, J. (1990). *Talking science: Language, learning and values*. Norwood, NJ: Ablex.

Lensmire, T. (1994). *Writing workshop as carnival*. Presented at the Annual Meeting of the American Educational Research Association, New Orleans, LA.

Levi, P. (1996). *Survival in Auschwitz*. New York: Simon & Schuster.

Levi, P. (1989). *The drowned and the saved*. New York: Vintage.

Lipka, J. (With G. Mohatt & the Cuilistet Group). (1998). *Transforming the culture of schools: Yupik Eskimo examples*. Hillsdale, NJ: Erlbaum.

Loewen, J. (1995). *Lies my teacher told me*. New York: Simon & Schuster.

Lombardi, K. & Rucker, N. (1998). The Political and the personal: cultural expressions of identification and disidentification. In N. Rucker & K. Lombardi (Eds.), *Subject relations: Unconscious experience and relational psychoanalysis*. New York: Routledge.

Luepnitz, D. (2003). *Schophenhauer's porcupines: Intimacy and its dilemmas*. New York: Basic Books.

Lynch, K. & O'Neill, C. (1994). The colonization of social class in education. *British Journal of Sociology of Education, 15*, 307–324.

MacLeod, J. (1995). *Ain't no makin' it: Aspirations and attainment in a low-income neighborhood*. Boulder, CO: Westview.

Mama, A. (1995). *Beyond the masks: Race, gender and subjectivity*. London: Routledge.

Mannoni, M. (1999). *Separation and creativity: Refinding the lost language of childhood*. New York: Other Press.

Mannoni, M. (1970). *The child, his 'illness' and the others*. London: Karnac.

Mathelin, C. (1999). *The broken piano: Lacanian psychotherapy with children*. New York: Other Press.

McConaghy, C. (2000). *Rethinking indigenous education: Culturalism, colonialism and the politics of knowing*. Flaxton, Queensland: Post Pressed.

McCourt, F. (1996). *Angela's ashes*. New York: HarperCollins.

McIntosh, P. (1988). White privilege: Unpacking the invisible knapsack. Retrieved from http://seamonkey.ed.asu.edu/~mcisaac/emc598ge/Unpacking.html.

McKegney, S. (2007). *Magic weapons: Aboriginal writers remaking community after residential school*. Winnipeg: University of Manitoba Press.

Menchu, R. (1984). *I, Rigoberta Menchu: An Indian woman in Guatemala*. London: Verso.

Miller, A. (1997). *The drama of the gifted child: The search for the true self*. New York: Basic Books.

Miller, A. (1987). *For your own good: The roots of violence in child-rearing*. London: Virago.

Miller, G., Galanter, E. & Pribram, K. (1967). *Plans and the structure of behavior*. New York: Holt.

Milligan, S. (2006). *Life and legacy of Spike Milligan*. [DVD]. Standing Room Only.

Milligan, S. (2003). *Spike*. [Audio CD]. EMI.

Min, A. (1994). *Red azalea*. New York: Berkley Publishing Corp.

Miner, V. (1993). Writing and teaching with class. In M. Tokarczyk & E. Fay (Eds.), *Working-class women in the academy: Laborers in the knowledge factory*. Amherst, MA: University of Massachusetts Press.

Mitchell, J. (1987). *The Selected Melanie Klein*. New York: Free Press.

Modell, A. (1999). The dead mother syndrome and the reconstruction of trauma. In G. Kohon (Ed.). *The dead mother: The work of Andre Green*. New York: Routledge.

Molino, A. (2004). *Culture, subject, psyche: Dialogues in psychoanalysis and anthropology*. Middletown, CT: Wesleyan University Press.

Morley, D. & Chen, K. (Eds). (1996). *Stuart Hall: Selected dialogues in cultural studies*. New York: Routledge.

Morrison, T. (1988). *Beloved*. New York: Plume.

Morrison, T. (1971). *The bluest eye*. New York: Washington Square Publications.

Morss, J. (1995). *Growing critical: Alternatives to developmental psychology*. New York: Routledge.

Mullan, P. [Director] (2004). *Magadelene Sisters*. [DVD]. Miramax Home Entertainment.

NAEYC (1997). *Developmentally appropriate practice in early childhood programs serving children from birth through age 8: A position statement of the National Association for the Education of Young Children*. Washington D.C.: NAEYC.

Nandy, A. (1983). *The intimate enemy*. New Delhi: Oxford.

Nasaw, D. (1981). *Schooled to order: A social history of public schooling in the United States*. New York: Oxford.

Newell, A. & Simon, H. (1972). *Human problem solving*. Englewood Cliffs, N.J.: Prentice Hall.

Nobus, D. (Ed.). (1998). *Key concepts of Lacanian psychoanalysis*. New York: Other Press.

Noyce, P. [Director]. (2003). *Rabbit-proof fence*. [DVD]. Miramax Home Entertainment.

Oakes, J. (1985). *Keeping track: How schools structure inequality*. New Haven: Yale University Press.

O'Beirne, K. (2006). *Kathy's story: The true story of a childhood hell inside Ireland's Magdalen Laundries*. Dublin: Greystone Books.

Ogden, T. (1992). The Dialectically Constituted/Decentered Subject of Psychoanalysis II: The contributions of Klein and Winnicott. *International Journal of Psychoanalysis, 73*, 613–626.

O'Loughlin, M. (In press, a). *Strangers to ourselves: The decolonizing potential of the displacement, loss, and "homelessness" of migrant experiences*. In D. Caracciolo, & A. Mungai (Eds.), *In the spirit of ubuntu: Stories of teaching and research*. Rotterdam: Sense Publishers.

O'Loughlin, M. (In press, b). An analysis of collective trauma among Indigenous Australians and a suggestion for intervention. *Australasian Psychiatry*.

O'Loughlin, M. (2008). Radical hope or death by a thousand cuts: The future for Indigenous Australians. *Arena Journal, 29/30*, 175–201.

O'Loughlin, M. (2007a). On losses that are not easily mourned. In L. Bohm, R. Curtis, & B. Willock (Eds.), *Psychoanalysts' reflections on deaths and endings: Finality, transformations, new beginnings*. New York: Routledge

O'Loughlin, M. (2007b). *Spectral memory and trauma: Speaking with the ghost*. Presented at Biannual Meeting of International Society for Theoretical Psychology, Toronto.

O'Loughlin, M. (2007c). Bearing witness to troubled memory. *Psychoanalytic Review, 94* (2), 191–212.

O'Loughlin, M. (2006). On knowing and desiring children: The significance of the unthought known. In G. Boldt & P. Salvio (Eds.), *Love's return: Psychoanalytic essays on childhood teaching and learning*. New York: Routledge.

O'Loughlin, M. (2002a). Is a socially responsible and critical psychology of difference possible? *Race, Gender & Class Journal, 9* (4), 175–192.

O'Loughlin, M. (2002b). *A decolonizing pedagogy: Introducing undergraduate students to the psychology of hatred and genocide and the nature of historical memory*. Presented at Fourth Annual Race, Gender, & Class Conference, New Orleans.

O'Loughlin, M. (1995a). *Six propositions concerning children, their growth, and the language we use to describe them*. In M.O'Loughlin (Organizer), If not child development, then what?: Exploring the possibilities of dialogic and sociocultural theories for our understanding of the growth and education of children in communities and schools. Presented at *Reconceptualizing Early Childhood Education, Research, Theory, and Practice: Fifth Interdisciplinary Conference*, Santa Rosa, CA.

O'Loughlin, M. (1995b). Daring the imagination: Unlocking voices of dissent and possibility in teaching. *Theory into Practice, 34*, 110–116.

O'Loughlin, M. (1995c). *Defining literacy, defining literacy research: A critical perspective*. Presented at the Annual Meeting of the American Educational Research Association, San Francisco, CA.

O'Loughlin, M. (1993a). *Developing a rationale for emancipatory knowledge construction: Five questions for constructivists*. In F. Peterman (Organizer), Restructuring constructivism: A conversation about constructivism, teacher education, and the classroom ecology. Symposium presented at the *Annual Meeting of the American Educational Research Association*, Atlanta, GA. Also presented at the *Sixty-sixth Annual Meeting of the National Association for Research in Science Teaching*, Atlanta, GA.

O'Loughlin, M. (1993b). Some further questions for Piagetian constructivists: A reply to Fosnot. *Journal of Research in Science Teaching, 30* (9), 1203–1207.

O'Loughlin, M. (1992a). Engaging teachers in emancipatory knowledge construction. *Journal of Teacher Education, 43*, (4), 373–82.

O'Loughlin, M. (1992b). Rethinking science education: Beyond Piagetian constructivism toward a sociocultural model of teaching and learning. *Journal of Research in Science Teaching, 29*, (8), 791–820.

O'Loughlin, M. (1992c). *Appropriate for whom? A critique of the culture and class bias underlying developmentally appropriate practice in early childhood education*. Paper presented at the *Second Conference on Reconceptualizing Early Childhood Education Research, Theory, and Practice: Reclaiming the Progressive Agenda in Early Childhood Education*, Chicago, IL.

O'Loughlin, M. (1991). *Rethinking early childhood education: A sociocultural perspective*. In J. Jipson (Chair), Deconstructing constructivism. Paper presented at the *First Conference on Reconceptualizing Research in Early Childhood Education: Loosening the Ties that Bind*, University of Wisconsin, Madison, WI.

O'Loughlin, M., Bierwiler, B., & Serra, M. (1996). *The possibilities of literacy on an urban school: Report of a field study*. Presented at the Annual Meeting of the American Educational Research Association, New York, NY.

Paley, V. (2008). *Wally's stories*. Cambridge: Harvard University Press.

Paley, V. (2004a). *A child's work: The importance of fantasy play*. Chicago: University of Chicago Press.

Paley, V. (2004b). *Bad guys don't have birthdays: Fantasy play at four*. Chicago: University of Chicago Press.

Paley, V. (1992). *You can't say you can't play*. Chicago: University of Chicago Press.

Paley, V. (1986). *Mollie is three: Growing up in school*. Chicago: University of Chicago Press.

Paley, V. & Coles, R. (1991). *The boy who would be a helicopter*. Cambridge: Harvard University Press.

Phillips, G. (2007). Healing and public policy. In J. Altman & M. Hinkson (Eds.), *Coercive reconciliation: Stablise, normalise, exit Aboriginal Australia*. North Carlton, Australia: Arena Publications Association.

Philips, S.U. (1983). *The Invisible culture: Communication in classroom and community in the Warm Springs Indian reservation*. New York: Longman.

Pilkington, D. (2002). *Rabbit-proof fence*. New York: Hyperion.

Piontelli, A. (1992). *From fetus to child*. New York: Routledge.

Plasa, C. (Ed.). (1999). *Beloved: The Columbia critical reader*. New York: Columbia University Press.

Polakow, V. (2000). *The public assault on America's children*. New York: Teachers College Press.

Polakow, V. (1993). *Lives on the edge: Single mothers and their children in the other America*. Chicago: University of Chicago Press.

Prigogine, I. (1997). *The end of certainty*. New York: Free Press.

Prigogine, I. (1981). *Time and complexity in the physical sciences*. New York: W. H. Freeman.

Quint, S. (1994). *Schooling homeless children*. New York: Teachers College Press.

Radical Teacher: Special Issue on Working-Class Studies (1995). Kendall Square Post Office, Cambridge, MA. Archived at: *www.radicalteacher.org.*

Raftery, M. & O'Sullivan, E. (1999). *Suffer the little children: The inside story of Ireland's industrial schools.* Dublin: New Island Books.

Raphael, B., Swan, P., & Martinek, N. (1998). Intergenerational aspects of trauma for Australian Aboriginal people. In Y. Danieli (Ed.), *International handbook of multigenerational legacies of trauma.* New York: Plenum Press.

Rashkin, E. (1992). *Family secrets and the psychoanalysis of narrative.* Princeton: Princeton University Press.

Read, J., Mosher, L., & Bentall, R. (2004). *Models of madness: Psychological, sociological, and biological approaches to schizophrenia.* New York: Routledge.

Reyes, M. (1997). Chicanas in academe: An endangered species. In S. de Castell & M. Bryson (Eds.), *Radical in<ter>ventions: Identity, politics, and differences in educational praxis.* Albany: SUNY Press.

Rezentes, W. (1996). *Ka lama kukui—Hawaiian psychology: An introduction.* Honolulu: A'ali'i Books.

Rhode, M. & Klauber, T. (Eds.). (2004). *The many faces of Asperger's Syndrome. (Tavistock Clinic Series).* London: Karnac.

Richards, B. (1984). *Capitalism and infancy: Essays on psychoanalysis and politics.* London: Free Association Books.

Riegel, K. (1979). *Foundations of dialectical psychology.* New York: Academic Press.

Riegel, K. (1978). *Psychology mon amour: A countertext.* New York: Houghton Mifflin.

Ritchie, J. (In press). Mā wai he kapu tī? Being, Knowing and Doing *Otherwise.* In M. O'Loughlin & R. Johnson (Eds.), *Exploring childhood subjectivity.* Albany, NY: SUNY Press.

Roediger, D. (2007). *The wages of whiteness: Race and the making of the American working class: Revised and expanded edition.* London: Verso.

Roediger, D. (2006). *Working toward whiteness: How America's immigrants became white: The strange journey form Ellis Island to the suburbs.* New York: Perseus Books.

Roediger, D. (1998). Introduction. In D. Roediger (Ed.), *Black on white: Black writers on what it means to be white.* New York: Schocken.

Rogers, A. (2006). *The unsayable: The hidden language of trauma.* New York: Random House.

Rogoff, B. (2003). *The cultural nature of human development.* New York: Oxford University Press.

Rogoff, B. (1991). *Apprenticeship in thinking: Cognitive development in social context.* New York: Oxford University Press.

Rose, J. (1993). *Negativity in the work of Melanie Klein.* Cambridge, MA: Blackwell.

Rose, J. (1992). *The case of Peter Pan: Or the impossibility of children's fiction.* Philadelphia: Pennsylvania University Press.

Rousmaniere, K., Delhi, K., & De Coninck Smith, N. (1997). *Discipline, moral regulation and schooling.* New York: Garland.

Rustin, M. (1991). *The good society and the inner world: Psychoanalysis, politics, and culture.* London: Verso.

Rustin, M., Rhode, M., Dubinsky, A., & Dubinsky, H. (Eds.). (1997). *Psychotic states in children.* New York: Routledge.

Ryan, J. & Sackrey, C. (1995). *Strangers in paradise.* Washington D.C.: University Press of America.

Salmon, T. W. (1917). *The care and treatment of mental diseases and war neuroses (Shell shock) in the British army.* New York: War Work Committee of the National Committee for Mental Hygiene.

Scorsese, M. [Director]. (2003). *The gangs of New York.* [DVD]. Miramax Home Entertainment.

Searles, H. (1979). *Selected papers on countertransference*. Madison, CT: International Universities Press.

Segal, H. (1975). *Introduction to the Works of Melanie Klein*. London: Heinemann.

Sendak, M. (1988). *Where the wild things are*. New York: HarperCollins.

Sendak, M. (1970). *In the night kitchen*. New York: HarperCollins.

Sennett, R. & Cobb, J. (1993). *The hidden injuries of class*. New York: Norton.

Seshadri-Crooks, K. (2000). *Desiring whiteness: A Lacanian analysis of race*. London & New York: Routledge.

Shapiro, J. (2000). *Beyond the Grave: Review of Voices from S–21 by David Chandler* (Berkeley: University of California Press), *New York Times Book Review*, 30 January.

Siberell, A. (1982). *Whale in the sky*. New York: Dutton.

Smitherman, G. (1986). *Talking and testifying: The language of Black America*. Detroit: Wayne State University Press.

Soyinka, W. (1999). *The burden of memory, the muse of forgiveness*. New York: Oxford.

Spiegelman, A. (2003). *The complete Maus*. New York: Penguin.

Spitzer, L. (1989). *Lives in between: The experience of marginality in a century of emancipation*. New York: Hill & Wang.

Spivak, G. (1988). Can the subaltern speak? In Nelson, C. & Grossberg, L. (Eds.), *Marxism and the interpretation of culture*. Urbana: University of Illinois Press.

Sroufe, L.A. (1995). *Emotional Development: the organization of emotional life in the early years*. New York: Cambridge University Press.

Stainton-Rogers, R. & Stainton-Rogers, W. (1992). *Stories of childhood: Shifting agendas of child concern*. Toronto: University of Toronto Press.

Stannard, D. (1993). *American Holocaust: The conquest of the new world*. Oxford: Oxford University Press.

Steedman, C. (1995). *Strange dislocations: Childhood and the idea of human interiority, 1780–1930*. Cambridge: Harvard University Press.

Stiver, I. (1991). Beyond the Oedipus Complex: mothers and daughters. In A. Kaplan, J. Miller, J. Jordan, J. Surrey, & I. Stiver (Eds.), *Women's growth in connection: Writings from the Stone Center*. New York: Guilford Press.

Sullivan, H.S. (1968). *The interpersonal theory of psychiatry*. New York: Norton

Tamahori, L. [Director]. (2003). *Once were warriors*. New Line Home Video.

Thompson, B. & S. Tyagi. (Eds.). (1996). *Names we call home: Autobiography on racial identity*. London: Routledge.

Tobin, J. (2009). *Preschool in three cultures revisited: China, Japan, and the United States*. Chicago: University of Chicago Press.

Tobin, J. (Ed.). (1997). *Making a place for pleasure in early childhood education*. New Haven: Yale University Press.

Tokarczyk, M. & Fay, E. (1993). *Working class women in the academy: Laborers in the knowledge factory*. Amherst, MA: University of Massachusetts Press.

Trinh, M. (1989). *Woman, native, other*. Bloomington: Indiana University Press.

Tuckwell, G. (2002). *Racial identity: White counselors and therapists*. London: Open University Press.

Tustin, F. (1992). *Autistic states in children*. London: Routledge.

Tustin, F. (1990). *The protective shell in children and adults*. London: Karnac.

Tyrrell, P. (2006). *Founded on fear*. Dublin: Irish Academic Press.

Van Ausdale, D. & Feagin, J. (2001). *The First R: How children learn race and racism*. Lanham, MD: Rowman & Littlefield.

Van Haute, P. (2002). *Against adaptation: Lacan's "subversion" of the subject.* New York: Other Press.

VanLaan, N. (1989). *Rainbow crow: A Lenape tale.* New York: Dragonfly Books

Van Manen, M. (1986). *The tone of teaching.* Portsmouth, NH: Heinemann.

Venn, C. (2002). Refiguring subjectivity after modernity. In V. Walkerdine (Ed.), *Challenging subjects: Critical psychology for a new millennium.* New York: Palgrave.

Vygotsky, L.S. (1986). (A. Kozulin, Ed.). *Thought and language.* Cambridge, MA: M.I.T. Press.

Vygotsky, L.S. (1978). *Mind in society: The development of higher psychological processes.* Cambridge, MA: Harvard University Press.

Walker, R. (2004). *Ka Whawhai Tonu Matou: Struggle without end.* Auckland, New Zealand: Penguin.

Walkerdine, V. (2004). Developmental psychology and the study of childhood. In M. Kehily (Ed.), *An introduction to childhood studies.* Maidenhead: Open University Press.

Walkerdine, V. (Ed.). (2002). *Challenging subjects: Critical psychology for the new millennium.* London: Palgrave.

Walkerdine, V. (1990). *Schoolgirl fictions.* London: Routledge.

Walkerdine, V. (1987). *Surveillance, subjectivity and struggle: Lessons from pedagogic and domestic practices.* Minneapolis: University of Minnesota Press.

Walkerdine, V. (1984). Developmental psychology and the child-centered pedagogy: The insertion of Piaget's theory into early education. In J. Henriques et al. (Eds.), *Changing the subject: Psychology, social regulation and subjectivity.* London: Methuen.

Walsh, A. [Director]. (2003). *Song for a raggy boy.* Tva Films.

Walshe, C. (Ed.). (1996). Education, reform, and social change: *Multicultural voices, struggles, visions.* Mahwah, NJ: Erlbaum.

Wertsch, J. (2006). *Voice of the mind: A sociocultural approach to mediated action.* Cambridge, MA: Harvard University Press.

Wertsch, J. (1998). *Mind as action.* Oxford: Oxford University Press.

Wiesel, E. (1982). *Night.* New York: Bantam.

Wigginton, E. (1972). *The Foxfire book: Hog dressing; Log cabin building; Mountain crafts and foods; Planting by the signs; Snake lore, hunting tales, faith healing; Moonshining; and other affairs of plain living.* New York: Doubleday.

Wilson, W.J. (1987). *The truly disadvantaged: The inner city, the underclass, and public policy.* Chicago: University of Chicago Press.

Winant, H. (1996). Behind blue eyes: Whiteness and contemporary U.S. racial politics. In M. Fine, L. Weis, L. C. Powell, & L. M. Wong (Eds.), *Off white: Readings on race, power, and society,* pp. 40–53. New York: Routledge.

Winnicott, D.W. (2002). *Winnicott on the child.* New York: Perseus.

Winnicott, D.W. (1989). *Playing and reality.* New York: Routledge.

Winnicott, D.W. (1965). *The maturational processes and the facilitating environment.* New York: International Universities Press.

Winnicott, D.W. (1958). *Through paediatrics to psychoanalysis.* London: Hogarth Press.

Wolcott, D. (1992). *The Antilles; Fragments of epic memory.* [The Nobel Lecture]. New York: Farrar, Strauss & Giroux.

Woodham-Smith, C. (1962). *The great hunger.* London: New English Library.

Woodson, C. (1990). *The mis-education of the Negro.* Trenton, NJ: Africa World Press. [Originally published, 1933.]

X, M. (1965). *The autobiography of Malcolm X.* New York: Ballantine.

Youell, B. (2006). *The learning relationship: Psychoanalytic thinking in education.* London: Karnac.

Young, E. (1989). *Lon Po Po: A Red Riding Hood story from China.* New York: Scholastic.

Zinn, H. (2005). *People's history of the United States: 1492 to present.* New York: Harper Perennial.

Žižek, S. (Ed.). (1994). *Mapping ideology.* London: Verso.

Zwigoff, T. [Director]. (2006). *Crumb.* [DVD]. Sony Pictures.

I wish to thank the publishers who have kindly given me permission to reprint the following:

For "The development of subjectivity in young children: Theoretical and pedagogical considerations" which appeared in *Contemporary Issues in Early Childhood Education*, Vol. 2, pp. 49–65, 2001, thanks to Symposium Journals; for "On knowing and desiring children: The significance of the unthought known," which appeared in G. Boldt and P. Salvio (Eds.) (2006), *Psychoanalytic essays on childhood, teaching, and learning,* and for "On losses that are not easily mourned," which was published in L. Bohm, R. Curtis, and B. Willock, (Eds.) (2007), *Psychoanalysts' Reflections on Deaths and Endings: Finality, Transformations, New Beginnings.* thanks to Routledge Publishing and Taylor & Francis Group LLC; for "Helping poor and working-class children make something of themselves: The contradictions and possibilities of teaching for equity and democracy," thanks to *Democracy and Education*, where the article was originally published in Vol. 12, pp. 30–33, 1997; "Seven principles underlying social just and ethnically inclusive teacher preparation," is reprinted with permission from S.H. King and L. Castenell (Eds.), *Racism in Teacher Education*, Copyright 2001 by the American Association of Colleges for Teacher Education (AACTE), Washington, D.C.; "Facing myself: The struggle for authentic pedagogy" was originally published in *Holistic Education Review* (now *Encounter: Education for Meaning and Social Justice*), Volume 9, pp. 48–52, 1996, and is reprinted with permission of the journal: http://great-ideas.org/enc.htm.

NOTES ON CONTRIBUTORS

Deborah Britzman is Distinguished Research Professor at York University and a candidate with the Toronto Institute for Contemporary Psychoanalysis. Her recent book is *The Very Thought Of Education: Psychoanalysis and the Impossible Professions* with SUNY Press.

Richard Johnson was recently appointed as the Ruth S. Ammon Professor of Childhood Education at Adelphi University. His research interests involve the study of visuality and visual cultural studies as they assist with the interrogation of early childhood education trends and issues, as well as the study of risk and risk analysis in early education. Previously he was the Coordinator of a graduate preservice teacher education program at the University of Hawaii where he worked for 18 years.

Michael O'Loughlin is Professor at Derner Institute of Advanced Psychological Studies and in the School of Education at Adelphi University, New York. He is also a training analyst and supervisor in the Postgraduate Programs in Psychoanalysis and Psychotherapy at Adelphi University and he is in private practice as a psychoanalyst and psychotherapist on Long Island, New York. His book, *Rethinking childhood subjectivity,* edited with Richard Johnson, will be published shortly by SUNY Press.

INDEX

RETHINKING CHILDHOOD

JOE L. KINCHELOE & GAILE CANNELLA, *General Editors*

A revolution is occurring regarding the study of childhood. Traditional notions of child development are under attack, as are the methods by which children are studied. At the same time, the nature of childhood itself is changing as children gain access to information once reserved for adults only. Technological innovations, media, and electronic information have narrowed the distinction between adults and children, forcing educators to rethink the world of schooling in this new context.

This series of textbooks and monographs encourages scholarship in all of these areas, eliciting critical investigations in developmental psychology, early childhood education, multicultural education, and cultural studies of childhood.

Proposals and manuscripts may be sent to the general editors:

Joe L. Kincheloe
c/o Peter Lang Publishing, Inc.
29 Broadway, 18th floor
New York, New York 10006

To order other books in this series, please contact our Customer Service Department at:

(800) 770-LANG (within the U.S.)
(212) 647-7706 (outside the U.S.)
(212) 647-7707 FAX

Or browse online by series at:
www.peterlang.com